Cooking for Beginners

Publisher's Note: Raw or semi-cooked eggs should not be consumed by babies, toddlers, pregnant or breastfeeding women, the elderly, or those suffering from a chronic illness.

Publisher & Creative Director: Nick Wells
Senior Project Editor: Catherine Taylor
Art Director: Mike Spender
Layout Design: Mike Spender
Digital Design & Production: Chris Herbert
Proofreader: Julia Rolf

Special thanks to Gina Steer for her continued help and contributions, and to Chris Herbert, William Greaves and Theresa Bebbington.

This is a **FLAME TREE** Book

FLAME TREE PUBLISHING
Crabtree Hall, Crabtree Lane
Fulham, London SW6 6TY
United Kingdom
www.flametreepublishing.com

Flame Tree is part of The Foundry Creative Media Company Limited

First published 2011

ISBN: 978-0-85775-141-6

All images © The Foundry Creative Media Co., except the following. Courtesy of Fotolia: 74 © Monkey Business. Courtesy of Cephas Picture Library and © the following photographers: 69 Dean Skip, 71 James Jackson, 73 Jean-Paul Boyer. Courtesy of Shutterstock and © the following photographers: 14 vgstudio; 15 Pete Saloutos; 16l Kellie L. Folkerts; 16r Mike Flippo; 17bl DRGill; 17tr, 66, 41t Robyn Mackenzie; 18r erkanupan; 18l, 21br mates; 19tl Aga & Miko (arsat); 19r Ljupco Smokovski; 20bl Alistair Cotton; 20tr Paul Cowan; 24bl hsintzu; 24r ZTS; 25 arenacreative; 28 RookCreations; 29 Steve Lovegrove; 31t Sandra Cunningham; 31b Svetlana Lukienko; 32, 49, 22l Monkey Business Images; 33 silabob; 34br Colour; 34tl Natalia Klenova; 35 Birdy68; 36 Justin Paget; 37t 3445128471; 38 & 48t Joe Gough; 41b fotogiunta; 42 Zamula Artem; 43 Andi Berger; 44t Eugene Berman; 44b SergioZ; 46l ason; 46r Elena Elisseeva; 48b Khorkova Olga; 50 Tatuasha; 53 anlogin; 56l Robert Anthony; 59 Eaststeel; 60 RexRover; 62t Girish Menon; 62b Kateryna Dyellalova; 63 Paul Turner; 64 olszphoto; 65b Elena Schweitzer; 67 viki2win; 68 moonbeam; 81t ilker canikligil; 81b Richard Griffin; 85 Newton Page; 87 Terence Mendoza; 88 Ingrid Balabanova; 89b Kruglov_Orda; 89t LockStockBob.

Cooking for Beginners

Quick and Easy, Proven Recipes

**FLAME TREE
PUBLISHING**

Contents

Soups & Appetizers 94

Soups such as rustic Bread & Tomato Soup and Classic Minestrone offer a reassuring and tasty route into *Cooking for Beginners*, while dishes such as Honey & Ginger Shrimp and Potato Pancakes with Smoked Salmon, in turn, present an opportunity to display your growing confidence in the kitchen by creating dishes for an appetizer course.

Fish & Seafood 136

Delicious *and* healthy, fish and seafood offer a tempting choice for the novice chef. With dishes including Tuna Cannelloni and Ratatouille Mackerel, this chapter is bursting with diverse recipes. There's never been an easier—or tastier—way to get your share of omega-3 fatty acids and other necessary nutrients.

Meat...180

Hungry carnivores have a mouthwatering choice of meaty dishes to prepare—from the simple yet elegant Fillet Steaks with Tomato & Garlic Sauce to the homely and traditional Shepherd's Pie, you'll find dealing with meat in its many forms is nothing to fear. Why not try something a little different and yet so easy you'll be making it again and again, such as Pork Cabbage Pockets?

Poultry 222

Chicken is one of those foods that you must make sure is thoroughly cooked before serving, but you will be able to test this in no time, going on to create tempting and juicy recipes, from the one-pot style Aromatic Chicken Curry or the satisfying Chicken Pie with Sweet Potato Topping, to the fun Cheesy Chicken Burgers or the more adventurous Turkey & Pesto Rice Roulades.

Vegetable Dishes 264

We all need to eat plenty of vegetables, but it can be hard to fit enough of them into our diet. This section will reveal a plethora of tasty dishes that can be created from the wide variety of vegetables out there—they are so easy to prepare, from roasting to stir-frying. Try the sweet yet refreshing Vegetables in Coconut Milk with Rice Noodles or the moreish classic, Melanzane Parmigiana.

☙ Starter suggestion: Mixed Satay Sticks, page 115

Desserts & Cakes 314

Let's not forget that once you've mastered your favourite savoury dishes, if you have a little extra time you may want to try your hand at dessert, or at baking a cake for a real treat. Try classic Rice Pudding—the ultimate in nostalgic comfort food—or, if you're in need of a change, Stir-Fried Bananas & Peaches with Rum Butterscotch Sauce would be a great end to a more exotic main course.

◕ *Main course suggestion: Italian Meatballs in Tomato Sauce, page 217*

◕ *Classic suggestion: Rice Pudding, page 318*

◕ *Main course suggestion: Chicken & Asparagus with Tagliatelle, page 241*

Introduction

So you have never cooked—no problem. If you can read, you can cook. Following a recipe is not difficult; cooking is much easier than you might think. In fact, it is people who make cooking hard because they can make it look complicated and daunting. However, as long as you have a little patience and time, you will easily be able to produce a delicious meal for you, your family, and your friends in a relatively short time.

Maybe you have been put off by the many, differing cooking programs that are dished up on our screens night after night. Here, celebrity chefs demonstrate their skills so easily and so very quickly that it is almost impossible to see what they are preparing and cooking. This can make even the most experienced cooks doubt their abilities, let alone a beginner. My advice is *switch off*. Remember that all the TV chefs have a small team of experts behind the scenes to peel and chop, fry and boil, thicken or clear—doing many of the jobs for the chef, while you have just *yourself* … So do not be put off, switch off.

As with all skills, time is required to learn the basic steps and terminology. Once these are mastered, you will start gaining confidence. Having the correct tools for the different tasks ahead is an essential part of learning to cook. This cookbook aims to take you every step of the way, first explaining in clear, simple terms what tools and equipment you will require and exactly what each tool does, from inexpensive items, such as a zester, to more pricey pieces, such as a freestanding food mixer. The information given will clearly show which items are essential and which may not be necessary but would make life in the kitchen much easier.

A comprehensive explanation of cookery terminology, which can often baffle even the most experienced chef, is also provided—there is no point in being able to read a recipe if you do not know the difference between beating and folding, for instance. As with many things in life, new, more modern terms are being introduced all the time and this simply helps to spread confusion and mayhem.

Next comes an invaluable conversion chart for weights, measures, and temperatures,

followed by reams of information on pantry essentials, essential hygiene practices, nutrition, cooking eggs, and the varieties and cooking techniques for rice, pasta, herbs and spices, meat, poultry, seafood, and vegetables.

So, before you do anything else, make sure that you read through all this essential advice and information in order to get off to the best start on your culinary journey. Of course, practice is the only way to develop your skills, so get started—each recipe in this book has very clear and easy-to-follow, step-by-step instructions, often with photography revealing tricky techniques. Remember to read through the whole of a recipe before beginning to make sure that you do not come across any surprises halfway through. And do not forget—you learn from your mistakes as well as from your successes. Good luck!

Tools and Equipment

In this section, I have listed the tools and equipment you will need in order to start cooking. Some of the tools and equipment are absolutely essential and I would recommend that you invest in these first. Other less essential tools and equipment can also be reasonably expensive, so they might be good ideas to suggest as either birthday or Christmas presents.

Essential Tools

Knives Knives are perhaps the most important tools in the kitchen. It is advisable to have a good selection. First, when buying, make sure that any knife sits comfortably in your hand. You will need a small knife (often called a "paring" knife) for all the little jobs, such as seeding a chile and cutting fruits and vegetables into small pieces. At least another three or four additional knives would be good: a large chef's knife, which has a long, wide blade, is ideal for chopping both meat and fish, as well as fresh herbs; a carving knife; a bread knife, with or without a serrated edge; and a medium-size, all-purpose knife for all other jobs. Make sure that the knives are made by a reputable brand and easy to sharpen—a good knife will last a long while, perhaps forever.

Wooden spoons I feel that you can never have too many wooden spoons! Although they will not last forever, looked after and washed properly, they should last for at least one to two years, depending on what you use them for. I would recommend buying one of the sets that are so readily available. These usually come in different lengths—the shorter one is ideal for sauces and the other two for stirring food, such as meat that is being sealed in a pan, as well as for mixing cakes and batters. Although they wash perfectly well, it is a good idea to keep some spoons for sweet dishes and others for savory dishes. Then there are the wooden spatulas, which are perfect for omelets or frying meats, such as chops, because the flat, wider area makes turning food over so much easier.

Kitchen utensils with rack These are usually stainless steel and, although it is not 100 percent necessary to have the rack attached to the wall, it is a good idea, especially if close to the stove. These racks usually contain at least five utensils, all of which play an important part in cooking.

Large spoons These can be a plain spoon ideal for stirring or dishing out casseroles, stews, and vegetables, or a slotted draining spoon—this refers to the gaps in the bowl of the spoon, which let any liquid drain back into the pan, for example, when removing meat after sealing it for a stew or casserole.

Measuring spoons These ensure that the correct amount of ingredients is used. This is especially useful when either following a specific diet (for example, where oil and butter intake needs to be measured) or for use with a thickening agent, such as cornstarch, or with spices, where too much could completely ruin the dish.

Vegetable peeler Using a peeler makes the job easier and will ensure that you get an even look to the peeled fruit or vegetable, such as peeling pears for cooking in wine or peeling potatoes. I prefer the swivel-blade peeler because it removes only a very thin layer, and this will mean that the many nutrients that are just below the skin will be preserved. However, it is a matter of personal choice, so when buying, try imitating the peeling action you use and see which peeler fits most comfortably with your needs.

Grater For grating cheese, carrots, and other root vegetables, fresh ginger, chocolate, citrus zest, and nutmeg—the last two should be done on the finest side of the grater.

Oven thermometer Especially useful if you plan to make cakes and desserts. Many ovens vary in temperature, and pastry and baked goods need to be cooked at the correct temperature in order to achieve good results.

Timer Again, if planning to bake pastries and cakes, time is critical and it is so easy to get distracted. A timer will ensure that you know when it is time to test to see whether the cake or pastry is cooked. Many ovens have timers built in.

Scissors A pair of serrated kitchen scissors are so useful for all the little jobs, such as snipping a few fresh herbs, chopping bacon or dried fruits into small pieces, removing unwanted fat from chicken pieces or steaks, cutting out liners for cake pans … the list is endless.

Garlic press A handy alternative to crushing or mincing garlic with a knife. This removes the need to peel the garlic, because a clove is simply placed in the bowl and a handle is pulled over, then the garlic comes out of the tiny holes. A garlic press can also double up as a cherry pitter.

Extra Tools

Spatula I am not referring to the more ornate, usually silver utensil that is used when serving fish in front of guests, but the plastic or steel utensil that is superb for turning food over and for removing cooked food from hot baking sheets or roasting pans— I like to have at least two. A spatula may be included in your set of utensils plus rack as discussed earlier (third along from the right in the picture).

Ladle Perfect for hot soups, casseroles, stews, and any other hot liquids that need transferring or serving.

Potato masher This is the only tool to use if you wanted to make mashed potatoes the old-fashioned way. It is ideal for mashing all kinds of vegetables, from potatoes to parsnips, carrots, yams, or sweet potatoes.

Kitchen fork This is perfect for helping to steady large pieces of meat and whole chickens or turkeys when removing from the roasting pan after cooking.

Chopper/meat cleaver Good for chopping herbs and vegetables, as well as meat and poultry.

Kebab sticks and skewers Either metal or wooden, kebab sticks are for cooking both savory and sweet kebabs, koftas and satays, and skewering fish or chicken into a "butterfly" shape—this is where the food is split almost in half, then skewered prior to cooking so that it keeps its shape and lies flat. Remember that wooden kebab sticks or bamboo skewers need first to be soaked in cold water for at least 30 minutes and both ends wrapped in kitchen foil to prevent the ends from burning during cooking—and the cook burning her or his fingers.

Of course skewers are also available in metal. Metal skewers can be used for kebabs, but are also perfect for testing whether cakes are cooked in the middle or if poultry is completely cooked through, especially when cooking a whole turkey, because the long skewers will go right through the thickest part straight to the center cavity.

Pastry brushes These have a variety of uses, including brushing pans and dishes lightly with oil prior to cooking, brushing the sides of the grater with a clean dry brush to remove any remaining cheese or fruit zest after grating, and brushing a glaze or warm jelly over a dessert or cake. You could use them for basting, too, but they are not especially designed to cope with the heat of the foods you will be basting and the bristles may curl up; a spoon, special basting brush, or baster pipette would be better for that particular task.

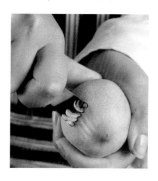

Pastry bags and tips Used mainly for cake decoration, these are for the more adventurous cook. The tips come in a variety of shapes and sizes, letting you create swirls, roses, stars, and many other patterns to decorate cakes, as well as being useful for shaping meringue dishes, such as pavlovas, and even piping mashed potatoes to create a neat topping.

Tongs Good for lifting raw and cooked foods when turning over during cooking or placing on plates or dishes.

Zester This is for removing long, thin strands of the outer colored part of lemon, orange, or lime rind (the zest) to use for decoration purposes.

Whisks Used for whisking or whipping cream, eggs, and sauces in order to create a smooth consistency and incorporate air. Available in different sizes, they are usually formed from interlocking wires formed into a balloon shape.

Basic Equipment

Certain pieces of equipment are essential when cooking. There is no need to go out and spend a fortune, however, I recommend that you buy good-quality pans, ones that will not buckle from the heat after being used a couple of times. Nonstick pans can also make life a lot easier when it comes to washing up. Below is a list of equipment that will start the beginner cook on their way and can easily be added to a little at a time.

Cutting boards Essential for any job that involves cutting. Look for the color-coordinated boards, so that you can use a different color for different types of food to avoid cross-contamination (for example, to keep raw meat, especially chicken, separate from vegetables). Make sure that you wash them thoroughly after use, washing them in the dishwasher if you have one.

Measuring pitchers These are available in different sizes and can be bought as glass pitchers or in plastic. Both do the job of measuring liquids well and both have the measurements marked down the side of the pitcher. For accuracy, make sure the measurements are at eye level when measuring ingredients.

Measuring cups and scales These are essential, especially when baking. Measuring cups come in a set that includes ¼ cup, ⅓ cup, ½ cup, and 1 cup. Unless otherwise stated, always measure the ingredient so it is level with the top edge of the cup—using the back of the knife is a good way of doing this. Some professional cooks prefer to use scales for baking because these are more accurate—only invest in these if you are confident in your baking skills.

Saucepans Perhaps the most expensive investment when first beginning to cook. I would recommend that you buy a set of saucepans, usually there are three to five of differing sizes and these should be adequate to begin with. It would also be a good idea to have a milk pan for making sauces as well as boiling milk, plus a good skillet, preferably with a lid to increase its versatility.

Colander and strainer Used for straining ingredients to remove any lumps, a strainer is usually made of fine-mesh wire and can be used for sifting flour—as can a sifter— while a colander tends to be bigger, with bigger holes or slots, and is used for draining cooked pasta and vegetables. The latter comes in plastic and metal versions.

Baking sheets, pans, and dishes These have many varied uses. Roasting pans are ideal for cooking meats in the oven. Ovenproof baking dishes are essential for baking

Mixing bowls Ideally, you will have at least three—in small, medium, and large. These can be glass or similar, and are essential for many jobs in the kitchen, including soaking, storing, creaming butter and sugar for cakes, pastry making, melting chocolate, whipping cream, and whisking egg whites.

casseroles and other dishes. If you want to also use it on the stove top, make sure it is also flameproof. Dishes such as lasagne can be set on baking sheets so that they are easy to place in the oven, as well as remove; the sheets can also be used for reheating foods. Cookie sheets—baking sheets without a lipped edge—are good for baking such items as cookies, biscuits, and meringues.

Extra Equipment

Food processor A very versatile piece of equipment and one that I would recommend investing in. It will chop vegetables, fruit, nuts, and herbs, and shred vegetables, as well as blend soups and make pastry dough and even cakes (though you run the risk overmixing cakes). Available at different prices.

Blender or liquidizer Very similar to a food processor, this has a pitcher instead of a bowl. It blends and chops, but does not do all the jobs that a food processor will do. You can also get handheld or immersion blenders, useful for pureeing soups and the like.

Food mixer These perform many jobs in the kitchen from whipping cream, whisking egg whites, and creaming butter and sugar for baking cakes, to making dough for bread and rubbing butter into flour for pastry, or where all the ingredients are simply put in the bowl and mixed. Freestanding mixers can be left to mix on their own. Smaller versions are available, but these are handheld. Either way, some form of food mixer will be greatly appreciated if making cakes—hand whisking and beating can be tiring!

Ice-cream maker Useful if you love ice cream and very easy to use, producing creamy delicious ice cream straight from the bowl. Be wary, however—such items run the risk of languishing unused at the back of a cupboard. The same goes for smoothie machines (see below).

Smoothie machine Although a blender or liquidizer will make smoothies, the results are not as smooth as those made in a smoothie machine.

Electric carving knife A luxury item, but useful for carving small joints that do not stand very well and especially good for a whole turkey, because wonderfully thin slices can be achieved.

Trivet A mat, rack, or tripodlike structure, made out of metal, wood, ceramic, fabric, silicone, or cork, and ideal for standing hot casseroles and saucepans on after cooking—in order to prevent your counter or tabletop from being scorched.

Culinary Terms

Over the years the language of cooking has developed and now there are many new words and expressions that perhaps 25 years ago no one would have dreamt of using in connection with cooking. Below are some of the words you are likely to come across and what is meant by them.

Baking Cooking foods in the oven. This usually applies primarily to cakes, breads, pastries, and puddings, but can refer to anything cooked in the dry heat of the oven. "Baking" is often used interchangeably with "roasting," but a distinction can arguably be drawn by saying that roasting implies greater heat and more pronounced browning. Roasting is also the preferred term for meat, poultry, and vegetables, while baking tends to be reserved for fish, seafood, and the items mentioned above.

Basting Brushing or drizzling meat or fish with its own juices, oil, or a prepared sauce, while roasting, broiling, or grilling, to add flavor and prevent the food from drying out.

Beating Using a wooden spoon or handheld mixer to mix together ingredients until smooth, such as when making batter for pancakes.

Blanching Pouring boiling water over fresh green vegetables (or immersing them into boiling water for a short time) in order to preserve the color. They are then typically plunged into cold water to halt the cooking process. This is done when vegetables are either to be frozen or added to a dish toward the end of cooking. It will also speed up their cooking time.

Bruising Slightly crushing an ingredient, usually with the flat side of a chef's knife or cleaver, in order to release its flavor.

Creaming Beating together butter or margarine with sugar until lighter in color and soft and creamy in texture. This applies to making cakes.

Coulis A trendy word for a strained fruit or vegetable sauce that is generally served
with the finished dish.

Drizzling Another trendy word used to signify pouring a little sauce or oil over food, but being careful not to swamp it.

Folding in This applies to stirring another ingredient into an uncooked mixture, such as a meringue or sponge cake mixture. You must be careful to avoid overmixing the mixture, because this will remove the air that has been beaten in, thus preventing a good rise or the required light texture.

Frying Cooking fresh foods in, usually, a skillet or, sometimes, a deep-fat fryer, whether cooking the food to a certain stage or cooking the food completely. Foods are usually fried in a certain amount of fat, such as butter or oil.

Sautéing This simply means frying, usually fairly quickly, and refers mainly to the cooking of meat and vegetables in a skillet when first starting to cook in order to seal in the meat juices and help to preserve their nutrients and flavor.

Steaming A method of cooking food with steam instead of directly in the water. Vegetables are especially good when steamed, as most of the nutrients are preserved and not lost into the water as happens when they are boiled. Food is placed in a container that will let the steam pass through and sits on top of a pan of gently simmering water. The steamer is covered with a lid.

Whipping This is when whipping or heavy cream is beaten until soft peaks are formed in the thickened cream. It can be whipped either by an electric mixer or a balloon whisk.

Whisking Beating a liquid either in a food mixer or using a balloon whisk. To whisk egg whites, whisk until stiff, dry, and holding peaks (this means that the bowl of whisked egg whites can be tipped upside down and the egg white does not move).

Zest What is the difference between "zest" and "rind"? Zest is the outermost colored part of the rind of a citrus fruit, as opposed to the white "pith" underneath, but in a cooking context can refer to the long thin strips of zest made with a "zester" (which are used for decoration only because, if eaten, they will give a bitter taste) or to grated zest (sometimes referred to as "grated rind"), which is made by rubbing the unpeeled but washed or scrubbed fruit up and down the fine side of a grater, creating very fine pieces or shreds. Because these are finer than zest strips, they can be used to flavor dishes.

Useful Conversions

Temperature Conversion

−4°F	−20°C	68°F	20°C
5°F	−15°C	77°F	25°C
14°F	−10°C	86°F	30°C
23°F	−5°C	95°F	35°C
32°F	0°C	104°F	40°C
41°F	5°C	113°F	45°C
50°F	10°C	122°F	50°C
59°F	15°C	212°F	100°C

Oven Temperatures

Keep in mind that, if using a convection oven, you should reduce the stated temperature by around 25°F. Check the manufacturer's instructions for guidance.

225°F	110°C	Gas Mark ¼	Very slow oven
250°F	120/130°C	Gas Mark ½	Very slow oven
275°F	140°C	Gas Mark 1	Slow oven
300°F	150°C	Gas Mark 2	Slow oven
325°F	160/170°C	Gas Mark 3	Moderate oven
350°F	180°C	Gas Mark 4	Moderate oven
375°F	190°C	Gas Mark 5	Moderately hot oven
400°F	200°C	Gas Mark 6	Moderately hot oven
425°F	220°C	Gas Mark 7	Hot oven
450°F	230°C	Gas Mark 8	Hot oven
475°F	240°C	Gas Mark 9	Very hot oven

Dry Weights

U.S. Standard/Metric

¼ oz.	10 g.	2 oz.	50 g.	5½ oz.	165 g.	10 oz.	300 g.
½ oz.	15 g.	2½ oz.	65 g.	6 oz.	175 g.	11 oz.	325 g.
¾ oz.	20 g.	3 oz.	75 g.	6½ oz.	185 g.	12 oz.	350 g.
1 oz.	25 g.	3½ oz.	90 g.	7 oz.	200 g.	13 oz.	375 g.
1½ oz.	40 g.	3½ oz.	100 g.	8 oz.	225 g.	14 oz.	400 g.
		4–4½ oz.	125 g.	9 oz.	250 g.	15 oz.	425 g.
		5 oz.	150 g.	9½ oz.	275 g.	1 lb.	450 g.

Liquid Measures

U.S. Standard, Fluid Ounces, Metric & U.K. Imperial

½ tsp.		2.5 ml.	
1 tsp.		5 ml.	
1 tbsp.	½ fl. oz.	15 ml.	
2 tbsp.	1 fl. oz.	25 ml.	⅛ cup
3 tbsp.	1½ fl. oz.	45 ml.	
4 tbsp.	2 fl. oz.	60 ml.	¼ cup
¼ cup	2 fl. oz.	60 ml.	¼ cup
5 tbsp.	2½ fl. oz.	65 ml.	⅓ cup
⅓ cup	3 fl. oz.	85 ml.	⅓ cup
6 tbsp.	3 fl. oz.	85 ml.	⅓ cup
7 tbsp.	3½ fl. oz.	100 ml.	⅓ cup
8 tbsp.	4 fl. oz.	120 ml.	½ cup
9 tbsp.	4½ fl. oz.	135 ml.	½ cup
⅔ cup	5 fl. oz.	150 ml.	¼ pint
¾ cup	6 fl. oz.	175 ml.	⅓ pint
⅞ cup	7 fl. oz.	210 ml.	⅓ pint
1 cup	8 fl. oz.	240 ml.	⅜ pint
1⅛ cups	9 fl. oz.	265 ml.	½ pint
1¼ cups	10 fl. oz.	300 ml.	½ pint
1½ cups	12 fl. oz.	350 ml.	⅔ pint
1⅔ cups	13 fl. oz.	400 ml.	⅝ pint
1¾ cups	14 fl. oz.	415 ml.	¾ pint
2 cups	16 fl. oz.	475 ml.	⅞ pint
2¼ cups	18 fl. oz.	530 ml.	⅞ pint
2½ cups	20 fl. oz.	600 ml.	1 pint
3⅛ cups	25 fl. oz.	750 ml.	1¼ pints

3¾ cups	30 fl. oz.	900 ml.	1½ pints
4 cups	32 fl. oz.	1 liter	1¾ pints
4⅔ cups	37 fl. oz.	1.1 liters	2 pints
5 cups	40 fl. oz.	1.2 liters	2 pints
5¼ cups	42 fl. oz.	1.25 liters	2¼ pints
5½ cups	44 fl. oz.	1.3 liters	2⅓ pints
6 cups	48 fl. oz.	1.4 liters	2½ pints
6⅓ cups	51 fl. oz.	1.5 liters	2½ pints
6¾ cups	54 fl. oz.	1.6 liters	2¾ pints
7 cups	56 fl. oz.	1.7 liters	3 pints
7⅔ cups	61 fl. oz.	1.8 liters	3⅛ pints
8 cups	64 fl. oz.	1.9 liters	3⅓ pints
8½ cups	68 fl. oz.	2 liters	3½ pints

Note: U.K. cups and pints are larger than U.S. cups.

Pantry Essentials

The first food shopping trip should be focused on setting up a well-stocked pantry. There are a lot of ingredients that you can expect to use again and again, but which you should not have to buy on a frequent basis—you do not use much at a time and they should keep reasonably well. The pantry should also be a source of foods that can make a meal when you have run out of fresh ingredients at the end of the week.

It is worth making a trip to a speciality grocery store to source more "exotic" ingredients. Our society's growing interest in recent years with travel and food from around the world has led us to seek out alternative ingredients with which to experiment and to incorporate into our cooking. As a consequence, even supermarket chains have had to broaden their product range and will often have a speciality range of imported ingredients from around the world.

If your local grocery store carries only a limited choice of products, do not despair. The Internet now offers freedom to food lovers. There are some fantastic food sites (both local and international) where food can be purchased and delivery arranged online.

When thinking about essentials, think of flavor, something that is going to add to a dish without increasing its fat content. It is worth spending a bit more money on these products so that you can make flavorsome dishes that will help to stop the urge to snack on fatty foods.

What to Stock in Your Pantry

There are many different types of pantry ingredients readily available, including myriad varieties of rice and pasta, which can provide much of the carbohydrate required in our daily diets. Store the ingredients in a cool, dark place and remember to rotate them. The ingredients will be safe to use for up to six months.

Herbs and spices These are a must, so it is worth taking a look at the section on pages 62–67 for more information. Often it is preferable to use fresh herbs, but the dried varieties have their merits and dried herbs and spices keep well. Using herbs

when cooking at home should reduce the temptation to buy prepared sauces. Often these types of sauces contain large amounts of salt, sugar, and additives.

Pasta It is good to have a mixture of whole-wheat and plain pasta, as well as a wide variety of flavored pastas. Whether fresh (it can also be frozen) or dried, pasta is a versatile ingredient with which to provide the body with slow-release energy. It comes in many different sizes and shapes, from the tiny tubettini (which can be added to soups to create a more substantial dish), to penne, fusilli, rigatoni, and conchiglie, up to the larger cannelloni and lasagna noodles. (*See also* pages 56–61.)

Noodles Also very useful and can accompany Chinese, Japanese, or Southeast Asian dishes. Noodles are low in fat and can be made with or without egg, in flours ranging from wheat and buckwheat to rice and even mung beans. Rice noodles are especially suitable for people who need a gluten-free diet; like pasta, they provide slow-release energy to the body.

Rice When cooked, rice swells to create a substantial low-fat dish. Long-grain rice, both white and brown, is great for casseroles and for stuffing meat, fish, and vegetables, because it holds its shape and firmness. Long-grain basmati and jasmine rice are two types of aromatic rice especially well suited to make Indian and Thai dishes, because the fine grains absorb the sauce and their delicate creaminess balances the pungency of the spices. Arborio rice is a type of Italian rice with short fat grains traditionally used for making risotto. Short-grain rice can be used in a variety of ways to create an irresistible dessert. (*See also* pages 50–55.)

Couscous Now available in instant form, couscous just needs to be covered with boiling water, then the grains fluffed up with a fork. Couscous is a precooked wheat semolina. Traditional couscous needs to be steamed and is available from health-food stores. This type of couscous contains more nutrients than the instant variety, but needs a far longer cooking time.

Bulgur wheat A cracked wheat that is often used in tabbouleh. Bulgur wheat is a good source of complex carbohydrate.

Barley There are several forms of barley, including pearl barley, which has the outer husk removed. Useful as part of a high-cereal diet, which can help to prevent bowel disorders and diseases.

Beans Vital ingredients for the pantry, beans are easy to store, have a very high nutritional value, and are great when added to soups, casseroles, curries, and hotchpotchs. Beans also act as a thickener, whether flavored or on their own. They come in two forms: either dried (in which case they generally need to be soaked overnight, then cooked before use—it is important to follow the instructions on the back of the package) or canned, which is a convenient time-saver because the preparation of dried beans can take a while. If buying canned beans, try to buy the variety in water with no added salt or sugar. These simply need to be drained and rinsed before being added to a dish.

Kidney, borlotti, cannellini, lima, and flageolet beans, split peas, chickpeas, and lentils all make tasty additions to any dish. Baked beans are a favorite with everyone. When buying canned products, try to make sure they do not contain added sugar or salt.

When boiling previously dried beans, remember that salt should not be added, because this will make the skins tough and inedible.

French green lentils are a small type of lentil. They often have mottled skins and are particularly good for cooking in slow dishes because they hold their shape and firm texture particularly well.

Dried fruit The ready-to-eat varieties are particularly good, because they are plump and juicy, and do not need to be soaked. They are fantastic when pureed into a compote, added to water, and heated to make a pie filling, and when added to stuffing mixtures. They are also good cooked with meats, rice, or couscous.

Flours A useful addition (including cornstarch, which can be used to thicken sauces). It is worth mentioning that whole-wheat flour should not be stored for too long at room temperature, because the fats may turn rancid. While not strictly a flour, cornmeal is a very versatile low-fat ingredient that can be used when making dumplings and gnocchi.

Stock Good-quality stock is a must in low-fat cooking, because it provides a good flavor base for many dishes. Many supermarkets now carry a variety of fresh and organic stocks, which, although they need refrigeration, are probably some of the most time- and effort-saving ingredients available. There is also a fairly large range of dried stock, perhaps the best being bouillon, a high-quality form of stock (available in powder or liquid form) that can be added to any dish whether it be a sauce, casserole, pie, or soup.

Sauce ingredients Many people prefer meals that can be prepared and cooked in 30–45 minutes, so helpful ingredients that jump-start a sauce are great. A good-quality tomato puree or canned plum tomatoes can act as the foundation for any sauce, as can a good-quality green or red pesto. Other handy pantry additions include tapenade, mustard, and anchovies. These have very distinctive tastes and are particularly flavorsome. Roasted red pepper sauce and sun-dried tomato paste, which tends to be sweeter and more intensely flavored than regular tomato puree, are also very useful.

Vinegar This is another worthwhile pantry essential, and with so many uses it is worth splashing out on really good-quality balsamic and wine vinegars.

Yeast extract This is a good pantry ingredient that can pep up sauces, soups, and casseroles. It adds a little substance, particularly to vegetarian dishes.

Oils and other flavors Oil is used for frying, baking, and in salad dressings. There are many to choose from, including canola oil, which is one of the lowest in saturated fats and is ideal for cooking and baking; olive oil, which has a strong flavor that is better for uncooked foods (though a light version is okay for cooking); and peanut oil, often used in Asian cooking. Chinese and Southeast Asian flavors offer a lot of scope where low-fat cooking is concerned. Flavorings such as Thai fish sauce, soy sauce, Thai red and green curry pastes, and Chinese rice wine all provide mouthwatering low-fat flavor. For those who are incredibly short on time, or who rarely shop, it is now possible to purchase a selection of readily prepared freshly minced garlic, ginger, and chile (available in jars or tubes that can be kept in the refrigerator).

Hygiene in the Kitchen

It is important to remember that many foods can carry some form of bacteria. In most cases, the worst it will lead to is a bout of food poisoning or gastroenteritis, although, for certain groups of people, this can be more serious. The risk can be reduced or eliminated by good food hygiene and proper cooking.

Do not buy food that is past its sell, or pull, date and do not consume any food that is past its expiration date. When buying food, use your eyes and nose. If the food looks tired, limp, or a bad color or if it has a rank, acrid, or simply bad smell, do not buy or eat it under any circumstances.

Regularly clean, defrost, and clear out the refrigerator or freezer—it is worth checking the packaging to see exactly how long each product is safe to freeze.

Dish cloths and towels must be washed and changed regularly. Ideally, use disposable cloths, and replace them on a daily basis. More durable cloths should be left to soak in bleach, then washed in the washing machine on a hot cycle.

Always keep your hands, cooking equipment and utensils, and food preparation surfaces clean and never let pets climb onto any work surfaces.

Buying

Avoid massive bulk buying where possible, especially fresh produce, such as meat, poultry, fish, fruit, and vegetables—unless buying for the freezer. Fresh foods lose their nutritional value rapidly, so buying a little at a time minimizes loss of nutrients. It also eliminates a packed refrigerator (which reduces the effectiveness of the refrigeration process). When buying frozen foods, ensure that they are not heavily iced on the outside. Place in the freezer as soon as possible after purchase.

Preparation

Be sure that all work surfaces and utensils are clean and dry. Separate cutting boards should be used for raw and cooked meats, fish, and vegetables. Wash all fruit and vegetables regardless of whether they are going to be eaten raw or lightly cooked. Do not reheat food more than once.

All poultry must be thoroughly thawed before cooking. Let the meat stand in the refrigerator until it is completely thawed. Once defrosted, chicken should be cooked as soon as possible. Again, the only time food can be refrozen is when the food has been thoroughly thawed, then cooked.

All poultry and game (except for duck) must be cooked thoroughly. When cooked, the juices will run clear (pierce with a knife or skewer to test).

Other meats, such as ground meat and pork, should be thoroughly cooked all the way through.

Fish should turn opaque, be firm in texture, and break easily into large flakes.

Storing, Refrigerating, and Freezing

Meat, poultry, fish, seafood, and dairy products should all be refrigerated. The temperature of the refrigerator should be between 34°F and 41°F, while the freezer temperature should not rise above -0.4°F. When refrigerating freshly cooked food, let it stand to cool down completely before refrigerating. Hot food will raise the temperature of the refrigerator and possibly affect or spoil other food stored in it.

Food within the refrigerator and freezer should always be covered. Raw and cooked food should be stored in separate parts of the refrigerator. Cooked food should be kept on the top shelves of the refrigerator, while raw meat, poultry, and fish should be placed on the bottom shelves to avoid drips and cross-contamination.

High-Risk Foods

Certain foods may carry risks to people who are vulnerable, such as the elderly, babies, pregnant women, and those with a chronic illness. Avoid those foods that belong to a higher-risk category.

Eggs

There is a slight chance that some eggs carry the bacteria salmonella. Cook the eggs until both the yolk and the white are firm to eliminate this risk or use pasterized liquid eggs. Sauces, including Hollandaise, mayonnaise, mousses, soufflés, and meringues all use raw or lightly cooked eggs, as do custard-based dishes, ice creams, and sorbets. These are all considered high-risk foods to the vulnerable groups mentioned above.

Meat and Poultry

Certain meats and poultry also carry the potential risk of salmonella and so should be cooked thoroughly until the juices run clear and there is no pinkness left.

Unpasteurized Products

Unpasteurized products, such as milk, cheese (especially soft cheese), pâté, and meat (both raw and cooked), all have the potential risk of listeria and should be avoided.

Seafood

When buying seafood, buy from a reputable source. Fish should have bright clear eyes, shiny skin, and bright pink or red gills. The fish should feel stiff to the touch, with a slight smell of sea air and iodine. The flesh of fish steaks and fillets should be translucent with no signs of discoloration. Avoid any mollusks that are open or do not close when tapped lightly. Univalves, such as cockles, should withdraw into their shells when lightly prodded. Squid and octopus should have firm flesh and a pleasant sea smell.

Be careful when freezing seafood. It is imperative to check whether the fish has been frozen before. If it has been, it should not be frozen again under any circumstances.

Nutrition

A healthy and well-balanced diet is the body's primary energy source. In children, it constitutes the building blocks for future health as well as providing lots of energy. In adults, it encourages self-healing and regeneration within the body. A well-balanced diet will provide the body with all the essential nutrients it needs. This can be achieved by eating a variety of foods, demonstrated in the pyramid shown here.

Fats

Fats fall into two categories: saturated and unsaturated fats. It is very important that a healthy balance is achieved within the diet. Fats are an essential part of the diet and a source of energy, and provide essential fatty acids and fat-soluble vitamins. The right balance of fats should boost the body's immunity to infection and keep muscles, nerves, and arteries in good condition.

Saturated Fats

Saturated fats are of animal origin and are hard when stored at room temperature. They can be found in dairy produce, meat, eggs, margarines, and hard, white cooking fat (lard), as well as in manufactured products, such as pies, cookies, and cakes. A high intake of saturated fat over many years has been proven to increase heart

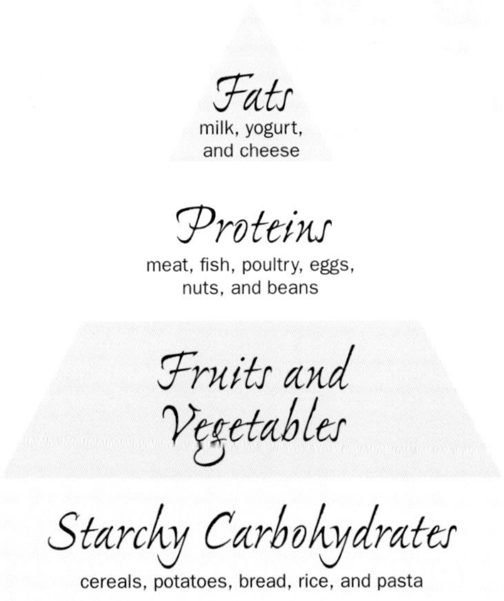

Fats
milk, yogurt, and cheese

Proteins
meat, fish, poultry, eggs, nuts, and beans

Fruits and Vegetables

Starchy Carbohydrates
cereals, potatoes, bread, rice, and pasta

disease and high blood cholesterol levels and often leads to weight gain. The aim of a healthy diet is to keep the fat content low in the foods that we eat. Lowering the amount of saturated fat that we consume is very important, but this does not mean that it is good to consume a lot of other types of fat.

Unsaturated Fats

There are two kinds of unsaturated fats: polyunsaturated fats and monounsaturated fats. Polyunsaturated fats include the following oils: safflower oil, soybean oil, corn oil, and sesame oil. Within the polyunsaturated group are omega oils. The omega-3 oils are of significant interest because they have been found to be particularly beneficial to coronary health and can encourage brain growth and development. Omega-3 oils are mainly derived from oily fish, such as salmon, mackerel, herring, pilchards, and sardines. It is recommended that we should eat these types of fish

at least once a week. However, for those who do not eat fish, liver oil supplements are available in most supermarkets and health food stores. It is suggested that these supplements should be taken on a daily basis.

The most popular oils that are high in monounsaturates are olive oil, sunflower oil, and peanut oil. The Mediterranean diet, which is high in monounsaturated fats, is recommended for heart health. Also, monounsaturated fats are known to help reduce the levels of LDL (the bad) cholesterol.

Proteins

Composed of amino acids (proteins' building bricks), proteins perform a wide variety of essential functions for the body, including supplying energy and building and repairing tissue. Good sources of proteins are eggs, milk, yogurt, cheese, meat, fish, poultry, eggs, nuts, and legumes. (See the second level of the pyramid.) Some of these foods, however, contain saturated fats. To strike a nutritional balance, eat generous amounts of vegetable protein foods, such as beans (including soybeans), lentils, peas, and nuts.

Fruits and Vegetables

Not only are fruit and vegetables the most visually appealing foods, but they are extremely good for us, providing essential vitamins and minerals necessary for growth, repair, and protection in the human body. Fruit and vegetables are low in calories and are responsible for regulating the body's metabolic processes and controlling the composition of its fluids and cells.

Minerals

Calcium Important for healthy bones and teeth, nerve transmission, muscle contraction, blood clotting, and hormone function. Calcium promotes a healthy heart, improves skin, relieves aching muscles and bones, maintains the correct acid-alkaline balance, and reduces menstrual cramps. Good sources are dairy products, bones of small fish, nuts, beans, fortified white flours, breads, and green leafy vegetables.

Chromium Part of the glucose tolerance factor, chromium balances blood sugar levels, helps to normalize hunger and reduce cravings, improves lifespan, helps protect DNA, and is essential for heart function. Good sources are brewer's yeast, whole-wheat bread, rye bread, oysters, potatoes, green bell peppers, butter, and parsnips.

Iodine Important for the manufacture of thyroid hormones and for normal development. Good sources of iodine are seafood, seaweed, milk, and other dairy products.

Iron As a component of hemoglobin, iron carries oxygen around the body. It is vital for normal growth and development. Good sources are liver, corned beef, red meat, fortified breakfast cereals, legumes, green leafy vegetables, egg yolk, and cocoa and cocoa products.

Magnesium Important for efficient functioning of metabolic enzymes and development of the skeleton. Magnesium promotes healthy muscles by helping them to relax and is therefore good for premenstrual syndrome (PMS). It is also important for heart muscles and the nervous system. Good sources are nuts, green vegetables, meat, cereals, milk, and yogurt.

Phosphorus Forms and maintains bones and teeth, builds muscle tissue, helps maintain the body's pH, and aids metabolism and energy production. Phosphorus is present in almost all foods.

Potassium Enables nutrients to move into cells, while waste products move out; promotes healthy nerves and muscles; maintains fluid balance in the body; helps secretion of insulin for blood sugar control to produce constant energy; relaxes muscles; maintains heart functioning and stimulates digestion movement to encourage proper elimination. Good sources are fruit, vegetables, milk, and bread.

Selenium Antioxidant properties help to protect against free radicals and carcinogens. Selenium reduces inflammation, stimulates the immune system to fight infections, promotes a healthy heart, and helps vitamin E's action. It is also required for the male reproductive system and is needed for metabolism. Good sources are tuna, liver, kidney, meat, eggs, cereals, nuts, and dairy products.

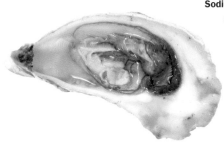

Sodium Important in helping to control body fluid and balance, preventing dehydration. Sodium is involved in muscle and nerve function and helps move nutrients into cells. All foods are good sources, however, processed, pickled, and salted foods are richest in sodium.

Zinc Important for metabolism and the healing of wounds. It also aids ability to cope with stress, promotes a healthy nervous system and brain, especially in the growing fetus, aids bones and teeth formation, and is essential for constant energy. Good sources are liver, meat, beans, whole-grain cereals, nuts, and oysters.

Vitamins

Vitamin A Important for cell growth and development and for the formation of visual pigments in the eyes. Vitamin A comes in two forms: retinol and beta-carotene. Retinol is found in liver, meat and meat products, and whole milk and its products. Beta-carotene is a powerful antioxidant and is found in red, orange, and yellow fruit and vegetables, such as carrots, mangoes, and apricots.

Vitamin B_1 Important in releasing energy from carboydrate-containing foods. Good sources are yeast and yeast products, bread, fortified breakfast cereals, and potatoes.

Vitamin B_2 Important for metabolism of proteins, fats, and carbohydrates to produce energy. Good sources are meat, yeast extracts, fortified breakfast cereals, and milk and its products.

Vitamin B_3 Required for the metabolism of food into energy production. Good sources are milk and milk products, fortified breakfast cereals, legumes, meat, poultry, and eggs.

Vitamin B_5 Important for the metabolism of food and energy production. All foods are good sources but especially fortified breakfast cereals, whole-grain bread, and dairy products.

Vitamin B_6 Important for metabolism of protein and fat. Vitamin B_6 may also be involved with the regulation of sex hormones. Good sources are liver, fish, pork, soybeans, and peanuts.

Vitamin B_{12} Important for the production of red blood cells and DNA. It is vital for growth and the nervous system. Good sources are meat, fish, eggs, poultry, and milk.

Biotin Important for metabolism of fatty acids. Good sources of biotin are liver, kidney, eggs, and nuts. Microorganisms also manufacture it in the digestion system.

Vitamin C Important for healing wounds and the formation of collagen, which keeps skin and bones strong. It is an important antioxidant. Good sources are fruit, such as strawberries and oranges, and vegetables, such as bell peppers and broccoli.

Vitamin D Important for absorption and handling of calcium to help build bone strength. Good sources are oily fish, eggs, whole milk and milk products, margarine, and, of course, sufficient exposure to sunlight, because vitamin D is made in the skin.

Vitamin E Important as an antioxidant vitamin, helping to protect cell membranes from damage. Good sources are vegetable oils, margarines, seeds, nuts, and green vegetables.

Folic acid Also called folate, it is critical during pregnancy for the development of the baby's brain and nerves. It is always essential for brain and nerve function and is needed for utilizing protein and red blood cell formation. Good sources are whole-grain cereals, fortified breakfast cereals, green leafy vegetables, oranges, and liver.

Vitamin K Important for controlling blood clotting. Good sources are cauliflower, Brussels sprouts, lettuce, cabbage, beans, broccoli, peas, asparagus, potatoes, corn oil, tomatoes, and milk.

Carbohydrates

Carbohydrates are an energy source and come in two forms: starch and sugar carbohydrates. Starch carbohydrates are also known as complex carbohydrates and they include all cereals, potatoes, breads, rice, and pasta. (See the fourth level of the pyramid). Eating whole-grain varieties of these foods also provides fiber. Diets high in fiber are believed to be beneficial in helping to prevent bowel cancer and can also keep cholesterol down. High-fiber diets are also good for those concerned about weight gain. Fiber is bulky, so fills the stomach, thereby reducing hunger pangs.

Sugar carbohydrates, which are also known as fast-release carbohydrates (because of the quick fix of energy they give to the body), include sugar and sugar-sweetened products, such as preserves and syrups. Milk provides lactose, which is a milk sugar, and fruit provides fructose, which is a fruit sugar.

Cooking Eggs

Boiled Eggs

Eggs should be boiled in gently simmering water. Remove the egg from the refrigerator at least 30 minutes before cooking. Bring a pan of water to a boil, then, once boiling, reduce the heat to a simmer. Gently lower the egg into the water and cook for 3 minutes for lightly set, or 4 minutes for a slightly firmer set. Remove and lightly tap to stop the egg from continuing to cook. Hard-boiled eggs should be cooked for 10 minutes, then plunged into cold water and left until cold before shelling. Serve lightly boiled eggs with toast or buttered bread cut into strips for dipping.

Fried Eggs

Put a little sunflower oil or butter in a skillet. Break an egg into a cup or small pitcher. Carefully slip into the skillet. Cook, spooning the hot oil or fat over the egg, for 3–4 minutes, until set to personal preference. Remove with a spatula. Serve with freshly cooked bacon or sausages, or on toast.

Poached Eggs

Fill a saucepan halfway with water. Bring to a gentle boil, then reduce the heat to a simmer. Add either a little salt or a few drops of vinegar or lemon juice—this will help the egg to retain its shape. Break the egg into a cup or small pitcher and carefully slip into the simmering water. Lightly oiled round plain pastry cutters can be used to contain the eggs, if preferred. Cover the pan with a lid and cook for 3–4 minutes, until set to personal preference. Once cooked, remove by draining with a slotted spoon or spatula, and serve. Alternatively, special poaching pans are available, if preferred. With these, fill the pan halfway with water and place the tray with the egg containers on top. Put a little butter in the cups and bring to a boil. Swirl the melted butter around and carefully slip in the eggs. Cover with the lid and cook for 3–4 minutes. Serve either on hot buttered toast or on top of sliced ham or freshly cooked spinach

Scrambled Eggs

Melt 1 tablespoon of butter in a small pan. Allowing 2 eggs per person, break the eggs into a small bowl and add

1 tablespoon of milk and seasoning to taste. Whisk until blended with a fork, then pour into the melted butter. Cook over a gentle heat, stirring with a wooden spoon, until set and creamy. Serve on hot buttered toast with smoked salmon or stir in some freshly snipped chives or chopped tomatoes.

Omelets

For a basic omelet, allow 2 eggs per person. Break the eggs into a small bowl, add seasoning to taste, and 1 tablespoon of milk. Whisk with a fork until frothy. Heat 2 teaspoons of olive oil in a skillet and, when hot, pour in the egg mixture. Cook gently, using a wooden spoon to bring the mixture from the edges of the skillet to the center and letting the uncooked egg mixture flow to the edges. When the egg has set, cook without moving for an extra minute before folding the omelet into three and gently turning out onto a warm serving plate. Be careful not to overcook.

Cheese Omelet

Proceed as before, then sprinkle ¼–⅓ cup grated sharp cheddar cheese on top of the lightly set omelet. Cook for an additional 2 minutes, or until the cheese starts to melt. If liked, place under a preheated broiler for 2–3 minutes or until golden. Fold and serve.

Tomato Omelet

Proceed as for a plain omelet. After 2 minutes of cooking time, add 1 chopped tomato on top of the omelet. Cook as above until set.

Fine Herbs Omelet

Stir 1 tablespoon of finely chopped fresh mixed herbs into the beaten eggs before cooking. Proceed as for a plain omelet.

Mushroom Omelet

Wipe and slice 2 oz. button mushrooms. Heat 1 tablespoon of butter in a small pan and cook the mushrooms for 2–3 minutes. Drain and reserve. Cook the omelet as above, adding the mushrooms once it has set.

Rice

Varieties

Rice is the staple food of many countries throughout the world. Every country and culture has its own repertoire of rice recipes—India, for example, has the aromatic biryani, Spain has the saffron-scented paella, and Italy has the creamy risotto. Rice is grown on marshy, flooded land where other cereals cannot thrive and, because it is grown in so many different areas, there is a huge range of rice types.

White rice Probably the most widely used type of rice, white rice (sometimes called polished rice) has been milled so that the husk, bran, and germ are removed. Converted or parboiled white rice has been steamed under pressure before milling. Instant white rice, also known as quick white rice, is white rice that is half or fully cooked after milling, then dried again. It is quick to cook, but has a bland flavor.

Brown rice Where the outer husk is removed, leaving the bran and germ behind. This retains more of the fiber, vitamins, and minerals. It has a nutty, slightly chewy texture and takes longer to cook than white rice.

Basmati rice This slender long-grain rice, which may be white or brown, is grown in the foothills of the Himalayas. After harvesting, it is allowed to mature for a year, giving it a unique aromatic flavor, hence its name, which means "fragrant."

Risotto rice Grown in the north of Italy, this is the only rice that is suitable for making risotto. The grains are plump and stubby, and have the ability to absorb large quantities of liquid without becoming too soft, cooking to a creamy texture with a slight bite. There are two grades of risotto rice: superfino and fino. Arborio rice is the most widely sold variety of the former, but you may also find Carnaroli, Roma, and Baldo in Italian delicatessens. Fino rice, such as Vialone Nano, has a slightly shorter grain, but the flavor is still excellent.

Spanish rice Traditionally used for Spanish paella, Spanish rice is soft and tender when ready. The medium-size grains break down easily, so should be left unstirred during cooking to absorb the flavor of the stock and other ingredients.

Jasmine rice Also known as Thai fragrant rice, this long-grain rice has a delicate, almost perfumed aroma and flavor, and has a soft, sticky texture.

Japanese sushi rice This is similar to glutinous rice in that it has a sticky texture. When mixed with rice vinegar, it is easy to roll up with a filling inside to make sushi.

Short-grain rice This rice's rounded short grains are ideal for desserts. The grains swell and absorb large quantities of milk during cooking, producing a rich, creamy consistency.

Wild rice This is an aquatic grass grown in North America rather than a true variety of rice. The black grains are long and slender, and after harvesting and cleaning they are toasted to remove the chaff and intensify the nutty flavor and slight chewiness. It is often sold as a mixture with long-grain rice.

Rice flour Raw rice can be finely ground to make rice flour, which may be used to thicken sauces (1 tablespoon will thicken 1¼ cups of liquid) or in Asian desserts. It is also used to make rice noodles.

Buying and Storing Rice

Rice will keep for several years if kept in sealed packages. However, it is at its best when fresh. To ensure freshness, always buy rice from reputable stores with a good turnover and buy in small quantities. Once opened, rice should be stored in an airtight container in a cool, dry place to keep out moisture. Most rice (but not risotto rice) benefits from washing before cooking—put into a strainer and rinse under cold running water until the water runs clear. This removes any starch still clinging to the grains.

Cooked rice will keep for up to two days if cooled and stored in a covered bowl in the refrigerator. If eating rice cold, serve within 24 hours—after this time it should be thoroughly reheated.

Cooking Techniques

There are countless ways to cook rice, but much depends on the variety of rice being used, the dish being prepared, and the desired results. Each variety of rice has its own characteristics. Some types of rice cook to light, separate grains, some to a rich, creamy consistency, and some to a consistency where the grains stick together. Different types of rice have different powers of absorption. Long-grain rice will absorb three times its weight in water, whereas 2 tablespoons of short-grain rice can soak up a massive 1¼ cups of liquid.

Cooking Long-Grain Rice

The simplest method of cooking long-grain rice is to add it to plenty of boiling, salted water in a large saucepan. Allow ¼ cup rice per person when cooking as an accompaniment. Rinse under cold running water until clear, then put into rapidly boiling water. Stir once, then, when the water returns to the boil, reduce the heat and simmer uncovered. Allow 10–12 minutes for white rice and 30–40 minutes for brown—check the package for specific timings. The easiest way to test if rice is cooked is to bite a couple of grains—they should be tender but still firm. Drain immediately, then return to the pan with a little butter and herbs, if liked. Fluff up the grains with a fork and serve. To keep the rice warm, put it in a bowl and place over a pan of barely simmering water. Cover the top of the bowl with a dish towel until ready to serve.

Absorption Method

Cooking rice using the absorption method is also simple. Measure out the quantity in a measuring pitcher—you will need ⅔ cup for two people. Rinse the rice, then put into a large saucepan. If liked, cook the rice in a little butter or oil for 1 minute. Pour in two parts of water or stock to one part rice, season with salt, and bring to a boil. Cover, then simmer gently until the liquid is absorbed and the rice is tender. White rice will take 15 minutes to cook, whereas brown rice will take 35 minutes. If there is still a little liquid left when the rice is tender, uncover and cook for 1 minute or until evaporated. Remove from the heat and let stand, covered, for 4–5 minutes, then fluff up the grains with a fork before serving. This method is good for cooking jasmine and Spanish rice.

Oven-Baked Method

The oven-baked method works by absorption, too, but takes longer than cooking on the stove top. For oven-baked rice for two, fry a chopped onion in 1 tablespoon of olive oil in a 1-quart flameproof casserole until soft and golden. Add ½ cup of long-grain rice and cook for 1 minute, then stir in 1¼ cups of stock—add a finely pared strip of lemon zest or a bay leaf, if liked. Cover and bake in a preheated oven at 350°F for 40 minutes, or until the rice is tender and all the stock has been absorbed. Fluff up before serving.

Cooking in the Microwave

Put rinsed long-grain rice in a large, heatproof bowl. Add boiling water or stock, allowing 1¼ cups for ½ cup of rice and 2 cups for 1 cup of rice. Add a pinch salt and a pat of butter, if desired. Cover with pierced plastic wrap and cook on high for 3 minutes. Stir, recover, and cook on medium for 12 minutes for white rice and 25 minutes for brown. Let stand, covered, for 5 minutes before fluffing up and serving.

Cooking in a Pressure Cooker

Follow the quantities given for the absorption method and bring to the boil in the pressure cooker. Stir, cover, and bring to a high 15-lb. pressure. Reduce the heat and cook for 5 minutes for white rice and 8 minutes for brown.

Cooking in a Rice Cooker

Follow the quantities given for the absorption method. Put the rice, salt, and boiling water or stock in the cooker, return to a boil, and cover. When all the liquid has been absorbed, the cooker will turn off automatically.

Health and Nutrition

Rice is low in fat and high in complex carbohydrates, which are absorbed slowly and help to maintain blood sugar levels. It is also a reasonable source of protein and provides many B vitamins and the minerals potassium and phosphorus. It is a gluten-free cereal, making it suitable for celiacs. Brown rice is richer in nutrients and fiber than refined white rice.

Pasta

How to Make Pasta

Homemade pasta has a light, almost silky texture and is different from the fresh pasta that you can buy vacuum-packed in supermarkets. It is also easy to make and little equipment is needed—just a rolling pin and a sharp knife. If you make pasta regularly, it is perhaps worth investing in a pasta machine.

Basic Egg Pasta Dough

1¾ cups Italian type "00" pasta flour or
    all-purpose flour, plus extra for dusting
1 tsp. salt
2 eggs, plus 1 egg yolk
1 tbsp. olive oil
1–3 tsp. cold water

 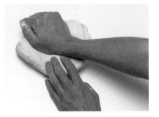

Sift the flour and salt into a mound on a work surface and make a well in the middle, keeping the sides high so that the egg mixture will not trickle out when added. Beat together the eggs, egg yolk, oil, and 1 teaspoon of water. Add to the well, then gradually work in the flour, adding extra water, if needed, to make a soft but not sticky dough. Knead on a lightly floured surface for 5 minutes, or until the dough is smooth and elastic. Wrap in plastic wrap and let stand for 20 minutes at room temperature.

Using a Food Processor

Sift the flour and salt into a food processor fitted with a metal blade. Add the eggs, egg yolk, oil, and water, and blend until mixed and the dough begins to come together, adding extra water, if needed. Knead for 1–2 minutes, then wrap and rest as before.

Rolling Pasta by Hand

Unwrap the pasta dough and cut in half. Work with just a half at a time and keep the other half wrapped in plastic wrap. Place the dough on a lightly floured surface, then flatten and roll out. Always roll away from you. Start from the center, giving the dough a quarter turn after each rolling. Sprinkle a little more flour over the dough if it starts to get sticky. Continue rolling and turning until the dough is as thin as possible, ideally ⅛-inch thick.

Rolling Pasta by Machine

Always refer to the manufacturer's instructions before using. Clamp the machine securely and attach the handle. Set the rollers at their widest setting and sprinkle with flour. Cut the pasta dough into four pieces. Wrap three of them in plastic wrap and reserve. Flatten the unwrapped dough slightly, then feed it through the rollers. Fold the strip of dough in three, rotate, and feed through the rollers a second time. Continue to roll the dough, narrowing the roller setting by one notch every second time and flouring the rollers if the dough starts to get sticky. Fold the dough only the first time it goes through each roller width. If it is hard to handle, cut the strip in half and work with one piece at a time. Fresh pasta should be dried before cutting. Drape over a wooden pole for 5 minutes or place on a dish towel sprinkled with a little flour for 10 minutes.

Shaping up

For shaping freshly made pasta, have several lightly floured dish towels ready.

Farfalle Use a fluted pasta wheel to cut the pasta sheets into rectangles 1 x 2 inches. Pinch the long sides of each rectangle in the middle to make a bow. Spread on a floured dish towel. Let stand for 15 minutes.

Lasagna Trim the pasta noodles until neat and cut into lengths. Spread the noodles on a dish towel sprinkled with flour.

Noodles If using a pasta machine, use the cutter attachment to produce tagliatelle or use a narrower one for spaghetti. To make by hand, sprinkle the rolled-out pasta with flour, then roll up like a jelly roll and cut into thin slices. Unravel immediately after cutting. Let rest over a wooden pole for 5 minutes to dry.

Ravioli Cut the rolled-out sheet of dough in half crosswise. Cover one half. Brush the other sheet of dough with beaten egg. Place 1 teaspoon of filling in even rows, at 1½-inch intervals. Remove the plastic wrap from the reserved pasta sheet and, using a rolling pin, lift over the dough with the filling. Press down between the pockets to push out any air. Cut into squares. Let rest on a floured dish towel for 45 minutes before cooking.

Variations

Flavored pastas are simple and there are many ways to change the flavor and color of pasta.

Chile Add 2 teaspoons crushed dried red chiles to the egg mixture.

Herb Stir 3 tablespoons of chopped fresh herbs into the flour.

Olive Blend 2 tablespoons ripe-olive paste (tapenade) with the egg mixture and omit the water.

Porcini Soak ½ oz. dried porcini mushrooms in boiling water for 20 minutes. Drain and squeeze out as much water as possible, then chop finely. Add to the egg mixture.

Spinach Finely chop scant ½ cup cooked fresh spinach. Add to the egg mixture.

Dried Pasta Varieties

Buckwheat A gluten-free pasta made from buckwheat flour.

Colored and flavored pasta Varieties are endless, the most popular being spinach and tomato. Others include beet, herb, garlic, chile, mushroom, and black octopus ink.

Durum wheat pasta Most readily available and may be made with or without eggs. Look for "durum wheat" or *"pasta di semola di grano duro"* on the package, because pasta made from soft wheat tends to become soggy when cooked.

Whole-wheat pasta Made with whole-wheat flour, this has a higher fiber content than ordinary pasta. Whole-wheat pasta takes longer to cook than the refined version.

Pasta Shapes

Long Pasta

Spaghetti Probably the best known type of pasta, spaghetti derives its name from the word *spago* meaning "string," which describes its round, thin shape perfectly.

Tagliatelle Most common type of ribbon noodle pasta. It is traditionally from Bologna, where it accompanies bolognese sauce (instead of spaghetti). Fettuccine is the Roman version of tagliatelle and is cut slightly thinner.

Short Pasta

There are two types of short pasta: *secca* is factory-made from durum wheat and water and *pasta all'uovo* is made with eggs. There are numerous different shapes and some of the most popular ones are listed below.

Conchiglie Pasta shapes resembling conch shells. Sizes vary from tiny to large. They may be smooth or ridged (conchiglie rigate).

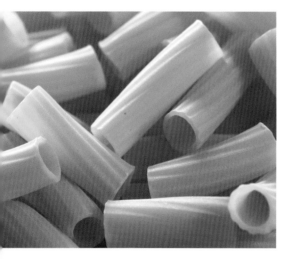

Eliche and fusilli These are twisted into the shape of a screw.

Farfalle Bow- or butterfly-shaped, often with crinkled edges.

Macaroni Known as elbow macaroni or *maccheroni* in Italy. A thin, quick-cook variety is also available.

Penne Slightly larger than macaroni, the ends of these tubes are cut and pointed like quills.

Pipe Curved, hollow pasta and often sold ridged as "pipe rigate."

Rigatoni Substantial, chunky, tubular pasta often used for baking.

Rotelle Thin, wheel-shape pasta, often sold in packages of two or three colors.

Stuffed Pasta

Tortellini The most common variety, consisting of tiny, stuffed pieces of pasta. Larger ones are called tortelloni.

Cappelletti, ravioli, and agnolotti These are sometimes sold dried, but are more often available fresh.

Fresh Pasta

Fresh pasta can be found in grocery stores and speciality stores. It is generally available in the same shapes as dried pasta.

How to Cook Perfect Pasta

Follow a few simple rules to ensure that your pasta is cooked to perfection every time:

1 Choose a large saucepan—there needs to be plenty of room for the pasta to move around so that it does not stick together.

2 Cook the pasta in a large quantity of fast-boiling, well-salted water, ideally 17 cups and 1½–2 tablespoons of salt for every 12 oz.–1 lb. pasta.

3 Put in the pasta all at once, stir, and cover. Return to a rolling boil, then remove the lid. Once it is boiling, reduce the heat to medium-high and cook the pasta for the required time. It should be *al dente,* or tender but still firm to the bite.

4 Drain, reserving a little of the cooking water to stir into the drained pasta. This helps to thin the sauce, if needed, and helps prevent the pasta from sticking together as it cools.

Serving Quantities

As an approximate guide, allow 3–3½ oz. uncooked pasta per person. The amount will depend on whether the pasta is being served for a light or main meal and the type of sauce that it is being served with.

Herbs and Spices

In a culture where fast food, prepared meals, and processed foods are popular, homemade food can sometimes taste bland by comparison, due to the fact that the palate can quickly become accustomed to additives and flavor enhancers. The use of herbs and spices, however, can make all the difference in helping to make delicious homemade dishes.

Herbs are easy to grow and a yard is not necessary, because they can easily thrive on a small patio, in a window box, or even on a windowsill. It is worth the effort to plant a few herbs, because they do not require much attention or nurturing. The reward will be a range of fresh herbs available whenever needed and fresh flavors that cannot be beaten to add to any dish that is being prepared.

While fresh herbs should be picked or bought as close as possible to the time of use, freeze-dried and dried herbs and spices will usually keep for around six months.

The best idea is to buy little and often and to store the herbs in airtight jars in a cool, dark cabinet. Fresh herbs tend to have a milder flavor than dried and equate to around 1 level tablespoon fresh to 1 level teaspoon dried. As a result, quantities used in cooking should be altered accordingly. A variety of herbs and spices and their uses are listed below.

Allspice The dark allspice berries come whole or ground and have a flavor similar to that of cinnamon, cloves, and nutmeg. Allspice can be used with pickles, relishes, cakes, and milk-based desserts, or whole in meat and fish dishes.

Aniseed Comes in whole seeds or ground. It has a strong aroma and flavor and should be used sparingly in baking and salad dressings.

Basil Best fresh but also available in dried form, basil can be used raw or cooked, and works well in many dishes. It is particularly well suited to tomato-based dishes and sauces, salads, and Mediterranean dishes.

Bay leaves Available in fresh or dried form as well as ground. Bay leaves make up part of a bouquet garni and are particularly delicious when added to meat and poultry dishes, soups, stews, vegetable dishes, and stuffing. They also impart a spicy flavor to milk-based desserts and egg custards.

Caraway seeds These have a warm, sweet taste and are often used in breads and cakes, but are also delicious with cabbage dishes and pickles.

Cayenne The powdered form of a red chile pepper said to be native to Cayenne. It is similar in appearance to paprika and can be used sparingly to add a fiery kick to many dishes.

Cardamom Has a distinctive sweet, rich taste. Can be bought whole in the pod, in seed form, or ground. This sweet aromatic spice is delicious in curries, rice, cakes, and cookies, and is great served with rice pudding and fruit. Pods come in green and brown ("black"), the former being more usual.

Chervil Reminiscent of parsley and available in either fresh or dried form, chervil has a faintly sweet, spicy flavor and is particularly good in soups, cheese dishes, stews, and with eggs.

Chile Available whole, fresh, dried and in powdered form. Red chiles tend to be sweeter in taste than their green counterparts. They are particularly associated with Spanish, Mexican, and South and Southeast Asian dishes, but are also delicious with pickles, dips, sauces, and in pizza toppings.

Chives Best used when fresh, but also available in dried form, this member of the onion family is ideal for use when a delicate onion flavor is required. Chives are good with eggs, cheese, fish, and vegetable dishes. They also work well as a garnish for soups, meat, and vegetable dishes.

Cinnamon Comes in the form of reddish brown sticks of bark from an evergreen tree and has a sweet, pungent aroma. Either whole or ground, cinnamon is delicious in cakes and milk-based desserts, particularly with apple, and is used in mulled wine.

Cloves Mainly used whole, although available ground, cloves have a very warm, sweet, pungent aroma and can be used to stud roasted ham and pork, in mulled wine and punch, and when pickling fruit. When ground, they can be used in making mince pies and in Christmas puddings and cookies.

Coriander/cilantro Coriander seeds have an orangey flavor and are available whole or ground. Coriander is particularly delicious (whole or roughly ground) in curries, casseroles, and as a pickling spice. The leaves are known as cilantro and are used both to flavor spicy aromatic dishes and as a garnish.

Cumin Also available ground or as whole seeds, cumin has a strong, slightly bitter flavor. It is one of the main ingredients in curry powder and complements many fish, meat, and rice dishes.

Dill The leaves, referred to as dill weed, are available fresh or dried, and have a mild flavor, while the seeds are slightly bitter. Dill is particularly good with salmon, new potatoes, and in sauces. The seeds are good in pickles and vegetable dishes.

Fennel As whole seeds or ground, fennel has a fragrant, sweet aniseed flavor and is sometimes known as the fish herb because it complements fish dishes so well.

Ginger Comes in many forms, but primarily as a fresh root and in dried ground form, which can be used in baking, curries, pickles, sauces, and Chinese and other Asian cooking.

Lemongrass Available fresh and dried, with a subtle, aromatic, lemony flavor, lemongrass is essential to Thai and other Southeast Asian cooking. It is also delicious when added to soups, poultry, and fish dishes.

Mace The outer husk of nutmeg has a milder nutmeg flavor and can be used in pickles, cheese dishes, stewed fruits, sauces, and hot punch.

Marjoram Often dried, marjoram has a sweet, slightly spicy flavor, which tastes fantastic when added to stuffing, meat, or tomato-based dishes.

Mint Available fresh or dried, mint has a strong, sweet aroma that is delicious in a sauce or jelly to serve with lamb. It is great with fresh peas and new potatoes and can be used to make a mint tea.

Nutmeg The large whole seeds have a warm, sweet taste and complement custards, milk-based desserts, cheese dishes, parsnips, and creamy soups.

Oregano Available fresh or dried; similar to marjoram. The more strongly flavored dried leaves are used extensively in Italian and Greek cooking.

Paprika Often comes in two varieties. One is sweet and mild, and the other has a slight bite to it. Paprika is made from the fruit of the sweet pepper and is good in meat and poultry dishes, and as a garnish. The rule of buying herbs and spices little and often applies particularly to paprika, because, unfortunately, it does not keep particularly well.

Parsley The stems as well as the leaves of parsley can be used to complement most savory dishes, because they contain the most flavor. They can also be used as a garnish.

Poppy seeds These small, gray-black seeds impart a sweet, nutty flavor when added to cookies, vegetable dishes, dressings, and cheese dishes.

Rosemary Delicious fresh or dried, these small, needlelike leaves have a sweet aroma that is particularly good with lamb, stuffing, and vegetable dishes. Also delicious when added to charcoal on the barbecue to give a piquant flavor to both meat and corn on the cob.

Saffron Deep orange in color, saffron is traditionally used in paella, rice, and cakes, but is also delicious with poultry. Saffron is the most expensive of all spices.

Sage These fresh or dried leaves have a pungent, slightly bitter taste that is delicious with pork and poultry, sausages, and stuffing. Stuffed pasta, such as ravioli stuffed with pumpkin, is delicious when tossed in a little butter and fresh sage.

Sesame seeds Sesame seeds have a nutty taste, especially when toasted, and are delicious in baking, on salads, or with Chinese and other East Asian cooking.

Tarragon The fresh or dried leaves of tarragon have a sweet aromatic taste that is particularly good with poultry, seafood, fish, creamy sauces, and stuffing.

Thyme Available fresh or dried, thyme has a pungent flavor and is included in bouquet garni. It complements many meat and poultry dishes and stuffing.

Turmeric Obtained from the root of a lily from Southeast Asia. This root is ground and has a brilliant yellow color. It has a bitter, peppery flavor and is often used in curry powder and mustard, and is delicious in pickles, relishes, and dressings. It can also be used fresh in a similar way to ginger.

Meat

Beef, pork, and lamb are all types of meat readily available from grocery stores, butchers, and farmers' markets. Meat varies in price depending on the cut. The more expensive and tender meats are usually those cuts that received less exercise by the animal. They need a minimal amount of cooking and are suitable for roasting, grilling, frying, and stir-frying. The cheaper cuts need longer, slower cooking and are used in casseroles and for stewing. Meat plays an important part in most people's diet, offering an excellent source of protein, the B vitamins, and iron.

When choosing meat, it is important to buy from a reputable source and to choose the correct cut for the cooking method. Look for meat that is lean without an excess of fat, is a good color, and has no unpleasant odor. If in doubt about the suitability of a cut, ask the butcher, who should be happy to advise.

If buying frozen meat, let it thaw completely before using. This is especially important for both pork and poultry. It is better to thaw meat slowly, lightly covered on the bottom shelf of the refrigerator. Use within 24 hours of thawing, providing it has been kept in the refrigerator. If buying meat to freeze, do not freeze large cuts in a home freezer, because it will not be frozen quickly enough.

Store thawed or fresh meat out of the grocery-store wrappings, on a plate, lightly covered with waxed or parchment paper, then wrapped with plastic wrap, if liked. Do not secure the paper tightly around the meat, because it needs to breathe. Ensure that the raw meat juices do not drip onto cooked foods. The refrigerator needs to be at a temperature of 40°F. Fresh meat, such as joints, chops, and steaks, can be stored for up to 3 days. Ground meats, sausages, and variety meats should be stored for only 1 day.

Different cultures and religions affect the way the meat has been killed and the carcass cut. The following is a description of different cuts of meat. They may be called by different names, depending on where you live.

Beef

When choosing beef, look for meat that is a good color, with creamy yellow fat. There should be small flecks of fat, or marbling, throughout, because this helps the meat to be tender. Avoid meat with excess gristle. Bright red beef means that the animal has been butchered recently, whereas meat that has a dark, almost purple tinge is from meat that has been hung in a traditional manner. The darker the color, especially with roasting cuts, the more tender and succulent the beef will be.

Rib roast ① Suitable for roasting. Sold either on or off the bone, the cut is from between the short loin and chuck of the rib section. Look for meat that is marbled for tenderness and succulence. A standing rib roast will have at least 3 ribs; if the bones are removed and the meat is rolled and tied with string, it's known as a rolled rib roast. The most tender cut from the center of the rib section is the rib-eye roast.

Top round ② Suitable for pot roasting, roasting, or braising. A most lean, tender cut from the hindquarter.

Short loin Suitable for roasting, broiling, frying, or grilling. Sold on or off the bone. A lean and tender cut from the back.

Sirloin Cut into either steaks or roasts, depending if the cut is from near the tender short loin or closer to the tougher round section. Top sirloin is more tender than bottom sirloin. Sirloin steaks include flat bone, round bone, and pinbone.

T-bone steak Suitable for broiling, grilling, or roasting. A tender, succulent cut from the fillet end of the sirloin.

Tenderloin Suitable for broiling, grilling, or frying. A whole fillet is used to make Chateaubriand, some say the best of all cuts, or it can be cut and sold as filet mignon or tournedos steaks. The most tender and succulent cut with virtually no fat.

Sirloin ③ Suitable for broiling, frying, or grilling. Not as tender as top round, but reputed to have more flavor.

Bottom round ④ Suitable for boiling and pot roasts. It is also cut into steaks and cubed.

Minute steaks ⑤ Suitable for frying or grilling. This thin cut of steak is cooked over high heat for 1 minute per side.

Chuck ⑥ A cut of beef from between the shoulder blade and neck, ideal for all braising or stews.

Flank ⑦ Suitable for broiling or grilling after being marinated. A boneless cut from the hindquarter.

Skirt Suitable for stewing or making into ground. A boneless, tough but flavorful cut.

Ground beef Trimmings of beef that have been ground, suitable for burgers, meatloaf, and other dishes. Regular ground beef is the highest in fat; ground chuck still has enough fat to avoid too much shrinkage, so is best for burgers. The leanest is ground round and ground sirloin.

Brisket Suitable for slow or pot roasting. Sold boned and rolled, and can be found salted.

Ox kidney Suitable for using in casseroles and stews. Strong flavor with hard central core that is discarded.

Lamb

Lamb is probably at its best in the spring, when the youngest lamb is available. It is tender to eat, with a delicate flavor, and its flesh is a paler pink than the older lamb, where the flesh is more red. The color of the fat is also a good indication of age: young lamb fat is a very light, creamy color. As the lamb matures, the fat becomes whiter and firmer. Imported lamb also has firmer, whiter fat. Lamb can be fatty, so be careful when choosing a cut. It used to be possible to buy mutton (lamb that is at least one year old), but this now tends to be available only in speciality outlets, halal butchers, and areas with Afro-Caribbean populations. It has a far stronger, almost gamey flavor and the cuts tend to be larger.

Leg ① Suitable for roasting. Often divided into the upper sirloin half, which is more tender (but also has more bone), and the shank half, a leaner cut. An American leg has the bone end cut off, while a French leg has the bone intact, but is exposed by trimming away the meat. Can also be cut into round leg steaks.

Cutlets Suitable for broiling, frying, or grilling. These thin cuts are from either the leg or rib section.

Shoulder ② ⑥ Suitable for pot roasting, braising, or stewing. This large flavorful cut is sold in various ways, for example, as square cut shoulder or boneless rolled shoulder, as well as shoulder chops (also referred to as arm chops) and blade chops, which can be broiled or grilled.

Loin roast ③ Suitable for roasting. Sold on or off the bone. This is one of the more tender cuts of lamb. It can be stuffed and rolled.

Noisette Suitable for broiling, frying, or grilling. A small boneless chop cut from the loin or rib.

Loin chop ④ Suitable for broiling, frying, or grilling. Double loin chops are actually a single cut, but from both sides of the lamb, forming a circle.

Neck ⑤ Suitable for roasting, and slow, moist cooking methods. The flavor makes up for the small amount of meat in this cut.

Breast ⑦ Suitable for pot roast if boned, stuffed, and rolled. Spareribs are from this cut, which is also ground.

Ribs A tender cut suitable for roasting as a rack of lamb—a rib section usually with eight ribs—or for broiling when divided into chops.

Ground Suitable for burgers, pies, meatballs, and stuffings. From various cuts and often fatty.

Liver Suitable for pan-frying or grilling. Milder than ox or pig liver and cheaper than calves' liver.

Kidney Suitable for grilling, pan-frying, or casseroles. Milder than ox or pig kidneys, and usually sold encased in suet, which is discarded.

Pork

Pork should be pale pink in color and slightly marbled with small flecks of fat. There should be a layer of firm white fat with a thin elastic skin (rind), which can be scored before roasting to provide crackling. All cuts of pork are tender, because the pigs are slaughtered at an early age and are reared to be lean instead of fatty. Pork used to be well cooked, if not overcooked, due to the danger of the parasite trichina. This no longer applies, and it is now recommended that the meat is cooked less to keep it moist and tender.

Ham ① Suitable for roasting. The cut from the leg, sold on the bone or boned, as fresh ham or more commonly as processed cured ham. Canned hams may be reformed pieces of ham or a whole cut of boneless meat. These are available uncooked, partially cooked, or completely cooked.

Steaks ② Suitable for broiling, frying, or grilling. A lean cut from the leg or the shoulder. Very tender, but can be dry.

Tenderloin Suitable for roasting, pan-frying, or grilling. A tender cut, often sold already marinated.

Loin ③ Suitable for roasting as a large cut or cut into chops. The most popular cut, supplying the loin, tenderloin, and ribs.

Shoulder ④ Suitable for roasting. Each shoulder is divided into the arm section, or picnic shoulder, and the upper shoulder known as the Boston-style shoulder, or Boston butt.

Spareribs Suitable for grilling, casseroles, and roasting. A fatty but flavorful cut from the lower ribs and breastbone.

Cutlet Suitable for broiling, frying, or grilling. Very lean and tender, and requires very little cooking.

Side ⑤ Suitable for grilling or roasting. From the flank or belly, it can be salted before cooking but is generally used to provide bacon and is perhaps the fattiest cut of all.

Ground pork Suitable for burgers, meatballs, or similar recipes. Often from the cheaper cuts and can be fatty.

Liver Suitable for casseroles or frying. Stronger than lambs' or calves' liver.

Kidney Suitable for casseroles or frying. Often sold as part of a loin chop. Stronger than lambs' kidneys.

Poultry and Game

Poultry relates to turkey, chicken, duck, and geese. Most are sold plucked, drawn, and trussed. Due to extensive farming, chicken in particular offers a good source of inexpensive meat. However, there is a growing movement to return to the more traditional methods of farming. Organically reared chickens offer a far more succulent bird with excellent flavor, although they tend to be more expensive. Both fresh and frozen poultry are available. When buying fresh poultry, look for plump birds with a flexible breastbone, and no unpleasant odor or green tinge.

Frozen poultry should be rock hard with no ice crystals, because this could mean that the bird has thawed and been refrozen. Avoid any produce where the packaging is damaged. When thawing, place in the refrigerator on a large plate and ensure that none of the juices drip onto other

foods. Once the bird has thawed, remove all packaging, the giblets, if any, and reserve separately. Place on a plate and cover. Use within two days and ensure that the meat is thoroughly cooked and the juices run clear. Rest for 10 minutes before carving.

When storing fresh poultry, place on a plate and cover lightly, letting air circulate. Treat as thawed poultry: store for no longer than two days in the refrigerator, storing the giblets separately, and ensure that it is thoroughly cooked. Always use the meat within two days of cooking.

Poultry and game are low in saturated fat and provide a good source of protein as well as selenium, an antioxidant mineral. Remove the skin from poultry before eating if following a low-fat diet.

Poultry

Turkey Whole birds are suitable for roasting and traditionally served at Christmas and Thanksgiving. Various turkey cuts are eaten throughout the year, ranging from breast steaks, diced thigh, and cutlets to small whole breasts, drumsticks, wings, and ground turkey. Specific cuts include:

> **Breast** The whole breast with skin and bone.
> **Hotel-style breast** A whole turkey breast with the wings attached and supplied with giblets.
> **Turkey London broil** Half a turkey breast that is boneless, with or without the skin.
> **Cutlets and scallops** Thin cuts of boneless, skinless turkey breasts.
> **Tenderloins/tenders** Strips of breast meat suitable for stir-frying.

Chicken Suitable for all cooking: roasting, broiling, frying, grilling, stewing, or braising. Also available in many different breeds and varieties, offering a good choice to the consumer. There are many cuts of chicken readily available: breast, wing, and leg quarters, which are still on the bone; drumsticks, thighs, and breasts; boneless and skinless cutlets, diced pieces, and stir-fry strips, as well as ground chicken. There are also several types of chicken:

• **Capon** Suitable for roasting. This is a young castrated cockerel bred for its flavor.

• **Rock Cornish game hen** Suitable for roasting, broiling, or casseroles. These are small, being 4–6 weeks old. They can be butterflied, with the bird split open and held on skewers. One bird serves one person if small (1 lb.), two if large (2 lb.). Use this hen in a recipe for poussin.

• **Broiler/fryer** This is an older chicken at about 2½ months and weighing 3½ lb. As the name implies, best for either frying or broiling.

• **Stewing chicken** This tougher, older bird, at 10–18 months and weighing 3–6 lb., is best for braising or stewing.

Guinea fowl Suitable for roasting or casseroles. It has a slightly gamey flavor. When roasting, use plenty of fat or bacon—it can be dry.

Goose Suitable for roasting and often served as an alternative to turkey. Once dressed for the table, a goose will weigh around 10 lb., but there is not much meat and this will serve six to eight people. It is very fatty, so pierce the skin well and roast on a trivet so that the fat can be discarded or used for other cooking. Goose has a rich flavor, slightly gamey and a little like duck. Goose liver is highly prized and is used for foie gras.

Duck Suitable for roasting, broiling, grilling, and casseroles. Ducklings between six weeks and three months old are usually used for the table; adult ducks are not usually eaten. Duck has an excellent flavor, but it is a fatty bird, so cook on a trivet as for goose. Available fresh or frozen, and on average weighs 4–6 lb. Also available in cuts, as boneless breasts, ideal for broiling or grilling, and leg portions, suitable for casseroles. Long Island and Peking are also popular varieties.

Game

Game describes birds or animals that are hunted, not farmed, although some, such as pheasant, quails, and rabbits, are now being reared domestically. Most game has a stronger flavor than poultry and some is at its best when smelling strong. Game is not as popular as most meat or poultry and is an acquired taste. When buying game, it is important to know its age, because this dictates the method of cooking. Usually sold oven-ready, it is best bought from a reputable source who can guarantee the quality.

Pigeon Suitable for casseroles or stews, although the breast from young pigeons can be fried or broiled. Sometimes classified as poultry. Not widely available.

Pheasant Suitable for roasting or casseroles. Breast, which can be broiled, is also available. Pheasant needs to be well hung to give the best flavor.

Rabbit Suitable for casseroles, stews, and possibly roasting or, if young, frying. Also makes excellent pies and fricassée. Sold whole or in pieces, both with and without the bone, and available both fresh and frozen. Frozen rabbit often comes from China. If a milder flavor is preferred, soak in cold salted water for 2 hours before using.

Hare Suitable for casseroles. The most well-known recipe is jugged hare, where the blood is used to thicken the dish. Has a strong, gamey flavor. If a milder flavor is preferred, soak in cold water for up to 24 hours. Available from reputable game dealers.

Venison Suitable for roasting, broiling, casseroles, or making into sausages. The saddle, haunch, and shoulder are best for roasting, although the loin and fillet can also be used. All cuts benefit from marinating to help tenderize.

Other game Less widely available are partridge, grouse, quail, buffalo, squirrel, and boar, among others.

Fish and Seafood

Preparing and Cooking Seafood

Requiring only minimal cooking, all fish is an excellent choice for speedy and nutritious meals. There are two categories of fish: white and oily (*see* pages 81–85). Seafood can be divided into three categories: shellfish, crustaceans, and mollusks (*see* pages 86–87).

Both types of fish are sold fresh or frozen as small whole fish, fillets, or steaks. Store as soon as possible in the refrigerator. Remove from the wrappings, place on a plate, cover lightly, and store toward the top. Use within 1 day of purchase. If using frozen, thaw slowly in the refrigerator and use within 1 day of thawing.

Seafood should be eaten as fresh as possible. Live seafood gives the best flavor, as long as it is consumed on the day of purchase. If live is not available, buy from a reputable source and eat on the day of purchase, refrigerating until required. Clean all seafood thoroughly and, with mussels and clams, discard any that do not close when tapped lightly before cooking. After cooking, discard any that have not opened.

Cleaning Fish

When cleaning whole fish, first remove the scales. Using a round-blade knife, gently scrape the knife along the fish, starting from the tail and moving toward the head. Rinse frequently. To clean round fish, make a slit along the abdomen from the gills to the tail using a small, sharp knife and scrape out the innards. Rinse thoroughly.

For flat fish, open the cavity under the gills and remove the innards. Rinse. Remove the gills and fins and, if preferred, the tail and head. Rinse thoroughly in cold water and pat dry. Steaks and fillets simply need lightly rinsing in cold water and patting dry.

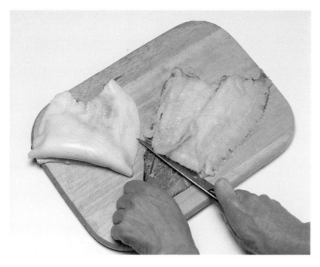

Skinning Fish

For whole flat fish, clean and remove the fins as before. Make a small cut on the dark side of the fish across the tail and slip your thumb between the skin and flesh. Loosen the skin along the side. Holding the fish firmly with one hand, rip off the skin with the other. The white skin can be removed in the same way.

Round fish are usually cooked with the skin on but, if you do want to skin them, start from the head and cut a narrow strip of skin along the backbone. Cut below the head and loosen the skin with the point of the knife. Dip your fingers in salt for a better grip and gently pull the skin down towards the tail. Be careful not to break the flesh.

Filleting Fish

To fillet flat fish, use a sharp knife and make a cut along the line of bones. Insert the knife under the flesh and carefully cut it with long, sweeping strokes. Cut the first fillet from the left-hand side, working from head to tail. Turn the fish around and repeat, this time cutting from tail to head. Turn the fish over and repeat on this side.

For round fish, cut along the center of the back to the bone, then cut along the abdomen. Cleanly remove the flesh with short, sharp strokes from the head downward, pressing the knife against the bones. Turn the fish over and repeat. This is suitable for larger fish, such as salmon.

To fillet herring and mackerel, discard the head, tail, and fins, and clean, reserving any roe, if applicable. Place on a cutting board and gently press along the backbone to open fully and loosen the bone. Turn the fish over, ease the backbone up, and remove, taking as many of the small bones as possible at the same time.

Basic Fish Recipes

Poached Fish

Clean the fish, remove scales, if necessary, and rinse thoroughly. Place in a large skillet with 1 small peeled and sliced onion, 1 small peeled and sliced carrot, 1 bay leaf, 5 black peppercorns, and a few parsley stalks. Pour over sufficient cold water to barely cover, then bring to a boil over medium heat. Reduce the heat to a simmer, cover, and cook gently for 8–10 minutes for fillets or steaks and 10–15 minutes for whole fish.

This method is suitable for fillets and small whole fish. When the fish is cooked, the flesh should yield easily when pierced with a round-bladed knife, and the fish should look opaque.

Broiled Fish

Line a broiler rack with kitchen foil and preheat the broiler to medium-high. Lightly rinse the fish, pat it dry, and place on the foil-lined rack. Season with salt and pepper, and brush lightly with a little oil. Cook under the broiler for 8–10 minutes, until cooked, turning the heat down if the fish is cooking too quickly. Sprinkle with herbs or pour over a little melted butter or herb-flavored olive oil to serve.

This method is suitable for fresh fish fillets (not smoked), sardines, and other small whole fish. Make three slashes across whole fish before broiling.

Grilled Fish

Rinse the fish fillet, pat dry, and, if desired, marinate in a marinade of your choice for 30 minutes. Heat a grill pan until smoking and add the fish, skin-side down. Cook for 5 minutes, pressing the fish down with a spatula. Turn the fish over and continue to cook for another 4–5 minutes, until cooked to personal preference.

Types of Fish and Other Seafood

White Fish

White fish, such as cod, haddock, or flounder, are an excellent source of protein and have a low fat content. They also contain vitamin B_{12} and niacin, plus important minerals, such as phosphorous, iodine, selenium, and potassium.

Bass Saltwater fish. Suitable for broiling or frying. Large bass can be poached whole. Has very white flesh.

Brill Saltwater fish. Suitable for grilling, baking, or poaching, and serving cold. Has firm flesh with a slight yellow tinge.

Cod Saltwater fish. Also available smoked. Suitable for all types of cooking. Perhaps the most popular and versatile of all fish, with white flesh and a very delicate flavor.

Flounder Saltwater fish. The whole fish is suitable for broiilng and pan-frying, while fillets can be steamed, stuffed, and rolled, or used as nuggets. A flat fish that has soft white to whitish gray flesh with a very delicate flavor.

Haddock Saltwater fish. Also available smoked. Suitable for all types of cooking. Has a firm white flesh with a slightly stronger flavor than cod.

Hake Saltwater fish. Suitable for all methods of cooking. Has a firm, close-textured white flesh and is considered to have a better flavor than cod.

Halibut Saltwater fish. Suitable for all methods of cooking except deep-frying. A large flat fish with excellent flavor.

John Dory Saltwater fish. This European fish has a firm white flesh with good flavor. Rarely found in the United States; porgy can be used as a substitute for recipes with John Dory.

Monkfish Saltwater fish. Also called angler fish. Suitable for all methods of cooking, including roasting. A firm white fish with "meaty" texture. A good substitute for lobster. Only the tail is eaten— the central bone is usually discarded and the two fillets are used.

Mullet Saltwater fish. Found in the South Atlantic and Gulf states. Suitable for broiling, frying, or baking. Has a firm white flesh with a mild, nutty flavor. (Note: Not the same as European mullets—use sea bass as a subsitute for the European fish.)

Orange roughy Saltwater fish. Suitable for broiling, baking, poaching, and frying. A New Zealand fish with a mild flavor and firm, white flesh.

Pollock Saltwater fish. Suitable for all types of cooking. A member of the cod family, it has white, firm flesh with a delicate flavor. Available both fresh and frozen, and also smoked.

Sea bream Saltwater fish. Also called porgy. Suitable for broiling, grilling, and frying, can also be stuffed and baked, or poached. Has firm white flesh with a delicate flavor.

Shark Saltwater fish. Suitable for broiling, frying, baking, grilling,and poaching. Smaller fish are sold whole, but fillets and steaks are more commonly available. The low-fat, meatlike flesh is flavorful.

Skate Saltwater fish. Suitable for broiling, frying, or poaching. Only the wings are eaten and the bones are soft and gelatinous. A white fish with a delicate flavor.

Snapper Saltwater fish. Suitable for any cooking method, either whole or cut into fillets and steaks. Of the approximately 250 species of snapper, 15 are found in the United States. Red snapper, named for its red eyes and skin color, is perhaps the best known. Snapper has a firm flesh and little fat with a mild flavor.

Sole Saltwater fish. Suitable for frying or broiling. Has a firm yet delicate white skin with a delicious flavor. Available frozen as Dover sole from Europe and sold in better fish markets. (Note: Flounder is often mislabeled as sole in the United States.)

Tilapia Freshwater fish. Suitable for broiling, baking, poaching, and grilling. A low-fat fish with soft, fine-textured white flesh and mild flavor, raised on farms around the world.

Turbot Saltwater fish. Suitable for broiling or baking. This European fish has a creamy white flesh with a delicious flavor, and is reputed to be the best of all flat fish. It is imported and sold frozen.

Whiting Saltwater fish. Suitable for all methods of cooking. Cooked whole or in fillets, it has a white, delicately flavored flesh.

Oily Fish

Oily fish, such as sardines, mackerel, salmon, and herring, have a higher fat content than white fish, but are an excellent source of the omega-3 polyunsaturated fatty acids, which are important in fighting heart disease, cancer, and arthritis. Oily fish also contains niacin, vitamins B_6 and B_{12}, and vitamin D, and selenium, iodine, potassium, and phosphorus minerals. The flavor is stronger and more robust, enabling stronger flavors, such as chile and garlic to be used. It is recommended that at least one portion of oily fish should be eaten each week.

Herring Saltwater fish. Suitable for frying, broiling, or preserving in vinegars. A small fish with creamy colored flesh and fairly strong flavor; herring contain many bones.

Mackerel Saltwater fish. Suitable for broiling and frying, while whole fish can be stuffed or baked. This fish is known for its distinctive bluish-colored skin with blue/black lines and creamy underside.

Pilchard Saltwater fish. Usually sold canned in either oil or tomato sauce. Similar to herring but smaller.

Salmon Freshwater fish. The whole fish is suitable for poaching or baking to serve hot or cold. Fillets or steaks can be fried, broiled, baked, steamed, or grilled. Farmed salmon has a milder flavor than wild, and the deep pink flesh is not as firm as that of wild salmon. The smaller wild salmon is much paler in color, with a far-superior flavor and texture. There are several North American varieties, most from Alaskan waters. Today, farmed salmon is available all year round—wild salmon is available seasonally. Salmon is also available smoked and in cans.

Sardine Saltwater fish. Suitable for broiling or frying. Sardines are young pilchards, sprats, or herrings.

Sprat Saltwater fish. Suitable for frying or broiling. A small fish similar to herring and available salted or smoked.

Rainbow trout Freshwater fish. Suitable for broiling, frying, poaching, and baking. Can be cooked whole or in fillets. Has a delicate pale pink flesh.

Speckled or brook trout Freshwater fish. Suitable for broiling or frying. The flavorful flesh is considered to be better than that of rainbow trout.

Tuna Saltwater fish. Suitable for all methods of cooking. Does not count as an oily fish when canned. Tuna has a rich flavor and a firm, flaky texture. Due to overfishing concerns, it is advisable to avoid bluefin and ideally yellowfin, too, sticking to skipjack, preferably pole-and-line caught.

Shellfish and Other Seafood

Crustaceans, such as lobsters, have hard shells that they shed and replace during their lifetime. Mollusks are animals that have hinged shells, such as scallops, or single shells, such as whelks. Other seafood for consumption includes cephalopods, such as squid, cuttlefish, and octopus.

Clams Usually eaten raw like oysters, or cooked as for mussels. Clams are divided into two types, those that have a hard shell and those with a soft shell. Many varieties are available, with steamer clams being the most common soft-shell clams from the East Coast and razor clams being common on the West Coast. Littlenecks are the smallest. Clams are sold live, or shucked and

frozen, and they are also available canned.

Cockles Usually eaten cooked in recipes such as paella.

Crab Many varieties are available, including Dungeness crabs, blue crabs, stone crabs, and rock crabs. Crabs are classified as either hard shell or soft shell, at a stage when the shells are discarded to grow a new shell, but before the new shell has hardened. Hard-shell crabs are sold whole, either cooked or live, and as cooked lump meat or flaked; soft-shell crabs are always sold whole and seasonally, from April to September.

Crayfish Also known as crawfish. Resembles a miniature lobster and has a delicate flavor.

Dublin Bay prawns Also called langoustine. They have bodies shaped like lobsters and a sweet, delicate taste.

Mussels Usually sold live and can be steamed, baked, or fried. The tough meat has a slightly sweet, delicious flavor.

Oysters Usually eaten raw on day of purchase, but can be cooked. Must be eaten absolutely fresh.

Periwinkles Can be sold cooked or raw. Usually served cooked and with vinegar.

Shrimp Available all year round, fresh or frozen. There are many species available, with cold-water shrimp being smaller and more flavorful than larger warm-water shrimp. Sizes vary from miniature to colossal. Shrimp turn pink once cooked.

Scallops Available fresh seasonally or frozen all year. Scallops have a bright orange roe, the "coral," which is edible. Serve cooked.

Squid/octopus Available all year round, sold fresh but previously frozen. The chewy meat has a mild, sweet flavor. Squid is popular as calamari. Their black ink is often used in sauces, and is also used to make black pasta.

Whelks Fresh whelks are available in both the spring and fall. The are also sold cooked, preserved with vinegar and canned.

Vegetables and Salads

Vegetables add color, texture, flavor, and valuable nutrients to a meal. They play an important role in the diet, providing necessary vitamins, minerals, and fiber. Vegetables are versatile: They can be served as an accompaniment to other dishes—they go well with meat, poultry, and fish—or they can be used as the basis for the whole meal.

There is a huge range of fresh vegetables on sale today in grocery stores and local markets. Also available is a growing selection of fresh organic produce, plus a wide variety of seasonal pick-your-own vegetables from farms. For enthusiastic gardeners, a vast range of vegetable seeds are available. In addition, the increase of ethnic stores has introduced an extensive choice of exotic vegetables, such as chayote and breadfruit. With improved refrigeration and transport networks, vegetables are now flown around the world, resulting in year-round availability.

Vegetables are classified into different groups: leaf vegetables; roots and tubers; beans, pods, and shoots; bulb vegetables; heat-loving vegetables; brassicas; cucumbers and squashes; sea vegetables; and mushrooms and fungi.

Leaf Vegetables

This includes lettuce and other salad greens, such as chicory, frisée, radicchio, and mâche, as well as arugula, spinach, Swiss chard, and watercress. These are available all year round, as most are now grown under glass. Many leaf vegetables, such as watercress and spinach, are delicious cooked and made into soups.

Roots and Tubers

This group includes beet, carrots, celeriac (also known as celery root), daikon, Jerusalem artichokes, parsnips, potatoes, radish, rutabaga, salsify, scorzonera, sweet potatoes, turnip, and yam. Most are available all year round.

Beans, Pods, and Shoots

This category includes all the beans, such as fava beans, green beans, snow peas, and runner beans, as well as peas and sweetcorn, baby corn, and okra. Shoots include asparagus, bamboo shoots, celery, chicory, fennel, globe artichokes, and palm hearts. The majority are available all year round.

Bulb Vegetables

This is the onion family and includes all the different types of onion, from the common yellow-, red-, or white-skinned globe onion, Italian red onion, and Bermuda onion to shallots, pearl onions, and scallions. This category also includes leeks, chives, and garlic. All are available throughout the year.

Heat-Loving Vegetables

Grown mainly in hot climates, this group includes eggplants, avocados, chiles, bell peppers, and tomatoes. These are available all year round, but are more plentiful in the summer.

Brassicas

This is the cabbage family and includes all the different types of cabbage, broccoli, Brussels sprouts, cauliflower, curly kale, Chinese cabbage, bok choy and collard greens. Some of the cabbages are only seasonal, such as savoy cabbage and red cabbage, while summer cabbages are available only during the summer months.

Cucumbers and Squashes

These vegetables are members of the gourd family and include cucumbers, pumpkins, and other squashes. There are two types of squash: summer squashes, which include zucchini, yellow squash, and pattypan squashes, and winter squashes, such as pumpkins and butternut, acorn, and spaghetti squashes. Zucchini and cucumbers are available all through the year, but pumpkins and other winter squashes are seasonal.

Sea Vegetables

The vegetables from this group may be a little difficult to find in grocery stores. The most readily available are seaweed (usually available dried) and sea kale.

Mushrooms and Fungi

This category includes all the different types of mushroom: the cultivated button mushrooms, cremini mushrooms, large portobello or flat mushrooms, oyster and shiitake mushrooms, as well as wild mushrooms such as porcini, morels, chanterelles, and truffles. Cultivated mushrooms are available throughout the year, but wild ones are around only from late summer. If you collect your own wild mushrooms, make sure that you correctly identify them before picking, because some are very poisonous and can be fatal if eaten. Dried mushrooms are also available, including porcini, morels, and oyster mushrooms. They add a good flavor to a dish, but need to be reconstituted before use.

Buying and Storage

When buying fresh vegetables, always look for ones that are bright and feel firm to the touch, and avoid any that are damaged or bruised. Choose onions and garlic that are hard and not sprouting, and avoid ones that are soft, because they may be damaged. Salad greens and other leaf vegetables should be fresh, bright, and crisp—do not buy any that are wilted, look limp, or have yellow leaves. Vegetables such as peas and beans do not keep for very long, so try to eat them as soon as possible after buying or picking. Most vegetables can be stored in a cool, dry place that is frost-free, such as a pantry or garage. Green vegetables, heat-loving vegetables, and salad greens should be kept in the salad drawer of the refrigerator, while root vegetables, tuber vegetables, and winter squashes should be kept in a cool, dark place. Winter squashes can be kept for several months if stored correctly.

Preparation

Always clean vegetables thoroughly before using. Brush or scrape off any dirt and wash well in cold water. Wash lettuce and other salad greens gently under cold running water and tear instead of cutting the leaves. Dry thoroughly in a salad spinner or on paper towels before use, otherwise the leaves tend to wilt. Spinach should be washed thoroughly to remove all traces of dirt. Cut off and discard any tough stalks and damaged leaves. Wash leaf vegetables and salad greens well, then pull off and discard any tough stalks or outer leaves. Leeks need to be thoroughly cleaned before use to remove any grit and dirt. Most mushrooms just need wiping with a damp cloth. Prepare the vegetables just before cooking, because once peeled they lose nutrients. Do not let them stand in water, because valuable water-soluble vitamins will be lost.

Cooking Techniques

Vegetables can be cooked in a variety of different ways, such as baking, barbecuing, blanching, boiling, braising, deep-frying, broiling, roasting, sautéing, steaming, and stir-frying.

Boiling Always cook vegetables in a minimum amount of water and do not overcook, or valuable nutrients will be lost. It is best to cut vegetables into even pieces and briefly cook them in a small amount of water.

Blanching and parboiling These terms mean lightly cooking raw vegetables for a brief period of time, whether parboiling potatoes before roasting, cooking cabbage before braising or cooking leafy vegetables, such as spinach. Spinach should be cooked for 2–3 minutes until wilted, in only the water clinging to its leaves. Blanching is also used to remove skins easily from tomatoes. Cut a small cross in the bottom of the tomato and place in a heatproof bowl. Cover with boiling water and let stand for a few seconds, then drain and peel off the skin.

Braising This method is a slow way of cooking certain vegetables, notably cabbage and leeks. The vegetable is simmered for a long period of time in a small amount of stock or water.

Steaming This is a great way to cook vegetables such as broccoli, cauliflower, beans, carrots, parsnips, and peas. Fill a large saucepan with about 2 inches water. Cut the vegetables into even pieces, put in a metal steamer basket, and lower into the saucepan, then cover and steam until tender. Alternatively, use a plate standing on a trivet in the pan. Do not let the water boil—it should just simmer. Once tender, refresh under cold running water. Asparagus is traditionally cooked in an asparagus steamer.

Deep-frying This method is suitable for most vegetables except leafy ones. The vegetables can be cut into small pieces, coated in batter, then deep-fried briefly in hot oil.

Stir-frying When stir-frying, all the nutrients are retained due to the short cooking time. Vegetables suitable for stir-frying include bell peppers, zucchini, sugar snaps, beans, baby corn, carrots, bok choy, spinach, tiny broccoli florets, scallions, and mushrooms. Heat a wok until very hot, add 1–2 tablespoons oil and swirl around the wok. Add spices and flavours such as grated fresh ginger, chopped chile, and lemon grass and cook for 1 minute, then add vegetables cut into thin strips, starting with the firmest, such as carrot. Using a large spatula or spoon, stir-fry over a high heat, adding soy sauce or other sauce as required. Cook for 3–4 minutes, ensuring that the vegetables are still crisp.

Broiling For bell peppers, eggplants, and tomatoes, brush them with a little oil first, because they quickly dry out. To remove the skins from bell peppers, cut them in half lengthwise and seed. Place them skin-side up on the broiler rack under a

preheated hot broiler and cook until the skins are blackened and blistered. Remove with tongs and place in a plastic bag, which will retain moisture. Seal and let stand until the peppers are cool enough to handle. Once cool, remove from the bag and carefully peel away the blackened skin.

Roasting Suitable for vegetables such as fennel, zucchini, pumpkin, squash, bell peppers, garlic, eggplants, and tomatoes. Cut the vegetables into even chunks. Heat some oil in a roasting pan in a preheated oven at 400°F. Put the vegetables in the hot oil, baste, and roast in the oven for 30 minutes. Garlic can be split into separate cloves or whole heads can be roasted. It is best not to peel them until cooked.

Health and Nutrition

Vegetables contain many essential nutrients and are especially high in vitamins A, B, and C. They contain important minerals, in particular iron and calcium, and are also low in fat, high in fiber, and have low cholesterol value. Red and orange vegetables, such as bell peppers and carrots, and dark green vegetables, such as broccoli, contain excellent anticancer properties, as well as helping to prevent heart disease. Current healthy eating guidelines suggest that at least five portions of fruit and vegetables should be eaten per day, with vegetables being the more essential.

Soups & Appetizers

Tuna Chowder

SERVES 4

2 tsp. oil
1 onion, peeled and
    finely chopped
2 sticks celery, trimmed
    and finely sliced
1 tbsp. all-purpose flour
2½ cups milk

7 oz. canned tuna in water
11 oz. canned corn, drained
2 tsp. freshly
    chopped thyme
salt and freshly ground
    black pepper

To serve:
pinch cayenne pepper
2 tbsp. freshly
    chopped parsley

Heat the oil in a large, heavy saucepan. Add the onion and celery, and gently cook for about 5 minutes, stirring from time to time until the onion is softened.

Stir in the flour and cook for about 1 minute to thicken.

Take the saucepan off the heat and gradually pour in the milk, stirring throughout.

Add the tuna and its liquid, the drained corn, and the freshly chopped thyme.

Mix gently, then bring to a boil. Cover with a lid and simmer for 5 minutes.

Remove the saucepan from the heat and season to taste with salt and pepper.

Sprinkle the chowder with the cayenne pepper and chopped parsley. Divide among soup bowls and serve immediately.

TASTY TIP

This creamy soup also works well using equivalent amounts of canned crab meat instead of the tuna.

Clear Chicken & Mushroom Soup

SERVES 4

2 large chicken legs, about
   1 lb. total weight
1 tbsp. peanut oil
1 tsp. sesame oil
1 onion, peeled and very
   thinly sliced
1 in. piece ginger, peeled
   and very finely chopped

5 cups clear chicken stock
1 lemongrass stalk, bruised
⅛ cup long-grain rice
1 cup wiped and finely sliced
   button mushrooms
4 scallions, trimmed, cut into
   2-in. pieces, and shredded
1 tbsp. dark soy sauce

4 tbsp. dry sherry
salt and freshly ground
   black pepper

Skin the chicken legs and remove any fat. Cut each in half to make 2 thigh and 2 drumstick portions, and set aside. Heat the peanut and sesame oils in a large saucepan. Add the sliced onion and cook gently for 10 minutes, or until soft but not beginning to brown.

Add the chopped ginger to the saucepan, and cook for about 30 seconds, stirring constantly to prevent it from sticking, then pour in the stock. Add the chicken and the lemongrass, cover, and simmer gently for 15 minutes. Stir in the rice and cook for an additional 15 minutes or until the chicken is cooked.

Remove the chicken from the saucepan and leave until cool enough to handle. Finely shred the flesh, then return to the saucepan with the mushrooms, scallions, soy sauce, and sherry. Simmer for 5 minutes or until the rice and mushrooms are tender. Remove the lemongrass.

Season the soup to taste with salt and pepper. Ladle into warmed serving bowls, making sure each has an equal amount of shredded chicken and vegetables, and serve immediately.

Creamy Caribbean Chicken & Coconut Soup

SERVES 4

6–8 scallions
2 garlic cloves
1 red chile
2 cups shredded or diced
   cooked chicken
2 tbsp. vegetable oil
1 tsp. ground turmeric

1 cup coconut milk
3 cups chicken stock
½ cup small soup pasta or
   small spaghetti pieces
½ lemon, sliced
salt and freshly ground
   black pepper

1–2 tbsp. freshly
   chopped cilantro
fresh cilantro sprigs,
   to garnish

Trim the scallions and slice thinly; peel the garlic and chop finely. Cut off the top from the chile, slit down the side and remove the seeds and membrane, then chop finely and set aside.

Heat a large wok, add the oil and, when hot, add the scallions, garlic, and chile, and stir-fry for 2 minutes or until the scallions have softened. Stir in the turmeric and cook for 1 minute.

Blend the coconut milk with the chicken stock until smooth, then pour into the wok. Add the pasta or spaghetti with the lemon slices, and bring to a boil.

Simmer, half covered, for 10–12 minutes until the pasta is tender; stir occasionally.

Remove the lemon slices from the wok and add the chicken. Season to taste with salt and pepper, and simmer for 2–3 minutes until the chicken is heated through.

Stir in the chopped cilantro and ladle into heated bowls. Garnish with sprigs of fresh cilantro and serve immediately.

HELPFUL HINT

Be careful handling chiles. Either wear rubber gloves or scrub your hands thoroughly, using plenty of soap and water. Avoid touching eyes or any other sensitive areas.

Carrot & Ginger Soup

SERVES 4

4 slices bread,
   crusts removed
1 tsp. yeast extract
2 tsp. olive oil
1 onion, peeled
   and chopped
1 garlic clove, peeled
   and crushed
½ tsp. ground ginger

2½ cups peeled
   and chopped carrots
4 cups vegetable stock
1-in. piece of ginger, peeled
   and finely grated
salt and freshly ground
   black pepper
1 tbsp. lemon juice

To garnish:
chives
lemon zest

Preheat the oven to 350°F. Coarsely chop the bread. Dissolve the yeast extract in 2 tablespoons of warm water, and mix with the bread.

Spread the bread cubes over a lightly greased baking sheet and cook for 20 minutes, turning halfway through. Remove from the oven and set aside.

Heat the oil in a large saucepan. Gently cook the onion and garlic for 3–4 minutes.

Stir in the ground ginger and cook for 1 minute to release the flavor.

Add the chopped carrots, then stir in the stock and the fresh ginger. Simmer gently for 15 minutes.

Remove from the heat and allow to cool slightly. Blend until smooth, then season to taste with salt and pepper. Stir in the lemon juice. Garnish with the chives and lemon zest, and serve immediately.

TASTY TIP

Lightly grill thick slices of ciabatta bread on both sides. While still warm rub the top of the bruschetta with a peeled garlic clove and drizzle with a little olive oil.

Bread & Tomato Soup

SERVES 4

6 medium, very
ripe tomatoes
¼ cup olive oil
1 onion, peeled and
finely chopped
1 tbsp. freshly chopped basil
3 garlic cloves, peeled
and crushed

¼ tsp. hot chili powder
salt and freshly ground
black pepper
2½ cups chicken stock
6 slices stale white bread

To garnish:
¼ small cucumber, cut into
small dice
4 whole basil leaves

Make a small cross in the base of each tomato, then place in a bowl and cover with boiling water. Allow to stand for 2 minutes or until the skins have started to peel away, then drain, remove the skins and seeds, and chop into large pieces.

Heat 3 tablespoons of the olive oil in a saucepan and gently cook the onion until softened. Add the peeled tomatoes, chopped basil, garlic, and chili powder. Season to taste with salt and pepper. Pour in the stock, cover the saucepan, bring to a boil, and simmer gently for 15–20 minutes.

Remove the crusts from the bread and break into small pieces. Remove the tomato mixture from the heat and stir in the bread. Cover and allow to stand for 10 minutes or until the bread has blended with the tomatoes. Season to taste. Serve the soup warm or cold with a swirl of olive oil on the top, garnished with a spoonful of diced cucumber and basil leaves.

TASTY TIP

This soup is best made when fresh tomatoes are in season. If making it at other times of the year, use 18 oz. canned peeled plum tomatoes instead and cook the soup for 5–10 minutes longer.

Roasted Red Pepper, Tomato & Red Onion Soup

SERVES 4

fine spray of oil
2 large red bell peppers,
    seeded and
    coarsely chopped
1 red onion, peeled and
    coarsely chopped

2 medium tomatoes, halved
1 small, crusty French loaf
1 garlic clove, peeled
2½ cups vegetable stock
salt and freshly ground
    black pepper

1 tsp. Worcestershire sauce
4 tbsp. reduced-fat
    sour cream

Preheat the oven to 375˚F. Spray a large roasting pan with the oil, and place the bell peppers and the onion in the base. Cook in the preheated oven for 10 minutes. Add the tomatoes, and cook for an additional 20 minutes or until the bell peppers are soft.

Cut the bread into ½-inch slices. Cut the garlic clove in half and rub the cut edge of the garlic over the bread.

Place all the bread slices on a large baking sheet, and cook in the oven for 10 minutes, turning halfway through, until golden and crisp.

Remove the vegetables from the oven and allow to cool slightly, then blend in a food processor until smooth. Strain the vegetable mixture through a large strainer into a saucepan to remove the seeds and skin. Add the stock, season to taste with salt and pepper, and stir to mix. Heat the soup gently until piping hot.

In a small bowl, beat together the Worcestershire sauce with the sour cream.

Pour the soup into warmed bowls and swirl a spoonful of the sour cream mixture into each bowl. Serve immediately with the garlic toast.

HELPFUL HINT

You really need a food processor or blender for this soup. Add one to your birthday wish list!

Potato, Leek & Rosemary Soup

SERVES 4

4 tbsp. butter
1 lb. leeks, trimmed and
    finely sliced
4 cups peeled and roughly
    chopped potatoes
3¾ cups vegetable stock

4 fresh rosemary sprigs
2 cups whole milk
2 tbsp. freshly
    chopped parsley
2 tbsp. crème fraîche

salt and freshly ground
    black pepper
whole-wheat rolls, to serve

Melt the butter in a large saucepan, add the leeks, and cook gently for 5 minutes, stirring frequently. Remove 1 tablespoon of the cooked leeks and set aside for garnishing.

Add the potatoes, vegetable stock, rosemary sprigs, and milk. Bring to a boil, then reduce the heat, cover, and simmer gently for 20–25 minutes until the vegetables are tender.

Cool for 10 minutes. Discard the rosemary, then pour into a food processor or blender, and blend well to form a smooth-textured soup.

Return the soup to the cleaned saucepan and stir in the chopped parsley and crème fraîche. Season to taste with salt and pepper. If the soup is too thick, stir in a little more milk or water. Reheat gently, without boiling, then ladle into warm soup bowls. Garnish the soup with the set-aside leeks and serve immediately with whole-wheat rolls.

HELPFUL HINT

If you don't have a food processor or blender you could use a potato masher and muscle power to mash the vegetables together as much as possible, to create a more rustic, chunky soup.

Italian Bean Soup

SERVES 4

2 tsp. olive oil
1 leek, washed and chopped
1 garlic clove, peeled
  and crushed
2 tsp. dried oregano

¾ cup trimmed and bite-size
  green bean pieces
14 oz. canned lima beans,
  drained and rinsed
¾ cup small pasta shapes
4 cups vegetable stock

8 cherry tomatoes
salt and freshly ground
  black pepper
3 tbsp. freshly torn basil

Heat the oil in a large saucepan. Add the leek, garlic, and oregano, and cook for 5 minutes, stirring occasionally.

Stir in the green beans and the lima beans. Sprinkle in the pasta and pour in the stock.

Bring the stock mixture to a boil, then reduce the heat to a simmer.

Cook for 12–15 minutes until the vegetables are tender and the pasta is tender but still firm to the bite. Stir occasionally.

In a heavy skillet, fry the tomatoes over a high heat until they soften and the skins begin to blacken.

Gently crush the tomatoes in the skillet with the back of a spoon, and add to the soup.

Season to taste with salt and pepper. Stir in the shredded basil and serve immediately.

HELPFUL HINT

In general, if you decide to use dried herbs when fresh are required, remember that they are much more pungent: 1 teaspoon dried herbs equals roughly 1 tablespoon fresh herbs.

Classic Minestrone

2 tbsp. butter
3 tbsp. olive oil
3 slices bacon
1 large onion, peeled
1 garlic clove, peeled
1 celery stalk, trimmed
2 carrots, peeled

14 oz. canned
    chopped tomatoes
5 cups chicken stock
1½ cups finely shredded
    green cabbage
½ cup trimmed and halved
    green beans
3 tbsp. frozen peas

¾ cup short spaghetti pieces
salt and freshly ground
    black pepper
Parmesan cheese, to garnish
crusty bread, to serve

Heat the butter and olive oil together in a large saucepan. Chop the bacon and add to the saucepan. Cook for 3–4 minutes, then remove with a slotted spoon and set aside.

Finely chop the onion, garlic, celery, and carrots, and add to the saucepan, one ingredient at a time, stirring well after each addition. Cover and cook gently for 8–10 minutes until the vegetables are softened.

Add the chopped tomatoes, with their juice and the stock, bring to a boil, then cover the saucepan with a lid, reduce the heat, and simmer gently for about 20 minutes.

Stir in the cabbage, beans, peas, and spaghetti. Cover and simmer for an additional 20 minutes or until all the ingredients are tender. Season to taste with salt and pepper.

Return the cooked bacon to the saucepan and bring the soup to a boil. Serve the soup immediately with Parmesan cheese shavings sprinkled on the top and plenty of crusty bread.

TASTY TIP

There are many variations of minestrone. You can add drained canned cannellini beans either in place of or as well as the spaghetti, or use small soup pasta shells.

Potato Pancakes with Smoked Salmon

SERVES 4

2⅔ cups diced floury
   potatoes
salt and freshly ground
   black pepper
1 extra-large egg
1 extra-large egg yolk
2 tbsp. butter

¼ cup all-purpose flour
⅔ cup heavy cream
2 tbsp. freshly
   chopped parsley
5 tbsp. crème fraîche
1 tbsp. horseradish sauce

½ lb. smoked
   salmon, sliced
lettuce leaves, to serve

To garnish:
lemon slices
cut chives

Cook the potatoes in a saucepan of lightly salted, boiling water for 15–20 minutes until tender. Drain thoroughly, then mash until free of lumps. Beat in the whole egg and egg yolk, along with the butter. Beat until smooth and creamy. Slowly beat in the flour and cream, then season to taste with salt and pepper. Stir in the chopped parsley.

Beat the crème fraîche and horseradish sauce together in a small bowl, cover with plastic wrap, and set aside until needed.

Heat a lightly greased, heavy skillet over a medium-high heat. Place a few spoonfuls of the potato mixture in the hot pan, and cook for 4–5 minutes or until cooked and golden, turning halfway through cooking time. Remove from the pan, drain on paper towels, and keep warm. Repeat with the remaining mixture.

Arrange the pancakes on individual serving plates. Place the smoked salmon on the pancakes, and spoon over a little of the horseradish sauce. Serve with salad and the remaining horseradish sauce, and garnish with lemon slices and chives.

HELPFUL HINT

Commercially made sauces vary in hotness, so it is best to add a little at a time to the cream and taste until you have the desired flavor.

Pea & Shrimp Risotto

SERVES 6

1 lb. whole shrimp
½ cup (1 stick) butter
1 red onion, peeled
   and chopped
4 garlic cloves, peeled and
   finely chopped

1 cup risotto rice
⅔ cup dry white wine
5 cups vegetable or
   fish stock
3 cups frozen peas
4 tbsp. freshly chopped mint

salt and freshly ground
   black pepper

Peel the shrimp and set aside the heads and shells. Remove the black vein from the back of each shrimp, then wash and dry on absorbent paper towels. Melt half the butter in a large skillet, add the shrimp heads and shells, and cook, stirring occasionally, for 3–4 minutes until golden. Strain the butter, discard the heads and shells, and return the butter to the skillet.

Add an additional ¼ stick of butter to the skillet, and cook the onion and garlic for 5 minutes until softened but not browned. Add the rice and stir the grains in the butter for 1 minute until they are coated thoroughly. Add the white wine and boil rapidly until the wine is reduced by half.

Bring the stock to a gentle simmer, and add to the rice, a ladleful at a time. Stir constantly, adding the stock as it is absorbed until the rice is creamy but still has a bite in the center.

Melt the remaining butter and stir-fry the shrimp for 3–4 minutes. Stir into the rice, along with the pan juices and the peas. Add the chopped mint and season to taste with salt and pepper. Cover the skillet and let the shrimp infuse for 5 minutes before serving.

FOOD FACT

Frying the shrimp shells and heads before cooking the dish adds a great deal of flavor to the rice.

Crispy Shrimp with Chinese Dipping Sauce

SERVES 4

1 lb. medium-size
  shrimp, peeled
¼ tsp. salt
6 tbsp. peanut oil
2 garlic cloves, peeled and
  finely chopped

1-in. piece fresh ginger,
  peeled and finely chopped
1 green chile, seeded and
  finely chopped
4 stems fresh cilantro,
  leaves and stems
  roughly chopped

**For the Chinese
  dipping sauce**
3 tbsp. dark soy sauce
3 tbsp. rice wine vinegar
1 tbsp. superfine sugar
2 tbsp. chili oil
2 scallions, finely shredded

Using a sharp knife, remove the black veins along the back of the shrimp. Sprinkle the shrimp with the salt, and let stand for 15 minutes. Pat dry on paper towels.

Heat a wok or large skillet, add the peanut oil, and, when hot, add the shrimp and stir-fry in 2 batches for about 1 minute or until they turn pink, and are almost cooked. Using a slotted spoon, remove the shrimp, and set aside in a warm oven.

Drain the oil from the wok, leaving 1 tablespoon. Add the garlic, ginger, and chile, and cook for about 30 seconds. Add the cilantro, return the shrimp, and stir-fry for 1–2 minutes until the shrimp are cooked through and the garlic is golden. Turn into a warmed serving dish.

For the dipping sauce, beat together the soy sauce, rice vinegar, sugar, and chili oil in a small bowl with a fork. Stir in the scallions. Serve immediately with the hot shrimp.

TASTY TIP
You must cook shrimp thoroughly, but it is equally important not to overcook them or they will be tough and chewy. Stir-fry them until pink and opaque, constantly moving them around the pan.

Honey & Ginger Shrimp

SERVES 4

1 carrot
¾ cup bamboo shoots
4 scallions
1 tbsp. honey
1 tbsp. ketchup
1 tsp. soy sauce
1-in. piece fresh ginger,
   peeled and finely grated

1 garlic clove, peeled
   and crushed
1 tbsp. lime juice
6 oz. peeled shrimp,
   defrosted if frozen
2 heads romaine lettuce
2 tbsp. freshly
   chopped cilantro

salt and freshly ground
   black pepper

To garnish:
sprigs of fresh cilantro
lime slices

Cut the carrot into matchstick-size pieces, coarsely chop the bamboo shoots, and finely slice the scallions.

Combine the bamboo shoots with the carrot matchsticks and scallions.

In a wok or large skillet, gently heat the honey, ketchup, soy sauce, ginger, garlic, and lime juice with 3 tablespoons of water. Bring to a boil.

Add the carrot mixture and stir-fry for 2–3 minutes until the vegetables are hot.

Add the shrimp and continue to stir-fry for 2 minutes.

Remove the wok or skillet from the heat, and set aside until cooled slightly.

Divide the romaine lettuce into leaves, and rinse lightly under cold running water.

Stir the chopped cilantro into the shrimp mixture, and season to taste with salt and pepper. Spoon into the lettuce leaves, and serve immediately, garnished with sprigs of fresh cilantro and lime slices.

Thai Fish Cakes

SERVES 4

1 red chile, seeded
  and coarsely chopped
4 tbsp. coarsely chopped
  fresh cilantro
1 garlic clove, peeled
  and crushed

2 scallions, trimmed
  and coarsely chopped
1 lemongrass, outer
  leaves discarded and
  coarsely chopped
3 oz. shrimp, defrosted
  if frozen

10 oz. cod fillet, skinned, pin
  bones removed,
  and cubed
salt and freshly ground
  black pepper
sweet chili dipping sauce,
  to serve

Preheat the oven to 375˚F. Place the chile, cilantro, garlic, scallions, and lemongrass in a food processor, and blend together.

Pat the shrimp and cod dry with paper towels. Add to the food processor and blend until the mixture is coarsely chopped. Season with salt and pepper, and blend to mix.

Dampen your hands, then shape heaping tablespoons of the mixture into 12 little patties.

Place the patties on a lightly greased baking sheet, and cook in the preheated oven for 12–15 minutes or until piping hot and cooked through. Turn the patties over halfway through the cooking time.

Serve the fish cakes immediately with the sweet chili sauce for dipping.

Mixed Satay Sticks

12 jumbo shrimp
¾ lb. beef steak
1 tbsp. lemon juice
1 garlic clove, peeled
    and crushed
salt
2 tsp. dark brown sugar
1 tsp. ground cumin

1 tsp. ground coriander
¼ tsp. ground turmeric
1 tbsp. peanut oil
fresh cilantro, to garnish

For the spicy peanut sauce:
1 shallot, peeled and very
    finely chopped

1 tsp. raw sugar
¼ cup chopped
    creamed coconut
pinch chili powder
1 tbsp. dark soy sauce
½ cup crunchy
    peanut butter

Soak eight bamboo skewers in cold water for at least 30 minutes. Peel the shrimp, leaving the tails on. Using a sharp knife, remove the black vein along the back of the shrimp. Cut the beef into ½-in.-wide strips. Place the shrimp and beef in separate bowls, and sprinkle each with ½ tablespoon of the lemon juice.

Mix together the garlic, sugar, cumin, coriander, turmeric, peanut oil, and a pinch of salt to make a paste. Lightly brush over the shrimp and beef. Cover, and place in the refrigerator to marinate for at least 30 minutes—longer if possible.

Meanwhile, make the sauce. Pour ½ cup of water into a small saucepan, add the shallot and sugar, and heat gently until the sugar has dissolved. Stir in the creamed coconut and chili powder. When melted, remove from the heat and stir in the soy sauce and peanut butter. Let cool slightly, then spoon into a serving dish. Thread 3 shrimp onto each of four skewers, and divide the sliced beef between the remaining skewers.

Cook the skewers under the preheated broiler for 4–5 minutes, turning occasionally. The shrimp should be opaque and pink, and the beef browned on the outside, but still pink in the center. Transfer to warmed individual serving plates, garnish with a few fresh cilantro leaves, and serve immediately with the warm peanut sauce.

Mu Shu Pork

SERVES 4

6 oz. pork fillet
2 tsp. Chinese rice wine or
   dry sherry
2 tbsp. light soy sauce
1 tsp. cornstarch
1 oz. dried tiger lily buds,
   soaked and drained
2 tbsp. peanut oil

3 large eggs,
   lightly beaten
1 tsp. freshly grated ginger
3 scallions, trimmed and
   thinly sliced
⅔ cup fine strips
   bamboo shoots

salt and freshly ground
   black pepper
8 mandarin
   pancakes, steamed
hoisin sauce
cilantro sprigs, to garnish

Cut the pork across the grain into ½-in. slices, then cut into thin strips. Place in a bowl with the Chinese rice wine or sherry, soy sauce, and cornstarch. Mix well and set aside. Trim off the tough ends of the dried tiger lily buds, then cut in half and set aside.

Heat a wok or skillet, and add 1 tablespoon of the peanut oil. When hot, add the eggs, and cook for 1 minute, stirring constantly until scrambled. Remove and set aside. Wipe the wok clean with paper towels.

Return the wok to the heat, add the remaining oil, and, when hot, transfer the pork strips from the marinade mixture to the wok, shaking off as much marinade as possible. Stir-fry for 30 seconds, then add the ginger, scallions, and bamboo shoots, and pour in the marinade. Stir-fry for 2–3 minutes.

HELPFUL HINT

About 2 in. long, tiger lily buds are strongly fragrant and should be brightly golden. Store in a cool, dark place. Omit them if you prefer and increase the quantity of pork to ½ lb.

Return the scrambled eggs to the wok, season to taste with salt and pepper, and stir for a few seconds until mixed well and heated through. Divide the mixture between the pancakes, drizzle each with 1 teaspoon of hoisin sauce, and roll up. Garnish and serve immediately.

Sticky Braised Spareribs

SERVES 4

2 lb. spareribs, cut crosswise
   into 3-in. pieces
½ cup orange juice
¼ cup dry white wine
3 tbsp. black bean sauce
3 tbsp. ketchup
2 tbsp. honey

3–4 scallions, trimmed
   and chopped
2 garlic cloves, peeled
   and crushed
1 tbsp. grated orange zest
salt and freshly ground
   black pepper

To garnish:
scallion tassels
lemon wedges

Put the spareribs in the wok and add enough cold water to cover. Bring to a boil over a medium-high heat, skimming any scum that rises to the surface. Cover and simmer for 30 minutes, then drain and rinse the ribs.

Rinse and dry the wok, and return the ribs to it. In a bowl, blend the orange juice with the white wine, black bean sauce, ketchup, and honey until smooth.

Stir in the scallions, crushed garlic cloves, and the grated orange zest. Stir well until mixed thoroughly.

Pour the mixture over the spareribs in the wok and stir gently until the ribs are lightly coated. Place over a moderate heat and bring to a boil.

HELPFUL HINT

It's probably best to get your butcher to cut the ribs into pieces for you, as they are quite bony.

Cover, then simmer, stirring occasionally for 1 hour or until the ribs are tender and the sauce is thickened and sticky. (If the sauce reduces too quickly or begins to stick, add water, 1 tablespoon at a time, until the ribs are tender.) Adjust the seasoning to taste, then transfer the ribs to a serving plate and garnish with the scallion tassels and lemon wedges. Serve immediately.

Penne with Artichokes, Bacon & Mushrooms

SERVES 6

2 tbsp. olive oil
¾ cup chopped smoked
  bacon or pancetta
1 small onion, peeled and
  finely sliced
1½ cups sliced
  cremini mushrooms

2 garlic cloves, peeled and
  finely chopped
14 oz. canned artichoke
  hearts, drained and halved,
  or quartered if large
7 tbsp. dry white wine
7 tbsp. chicken stock
3 tbsp. heavy cream

½ cup freshly grated
  Parmesan cheese, plus
  extra to serve
salt and freshly ground
  black pepper
4 cups penne
shredded basil leaves,
  to garnish

Heat the olive oil in a skillet and add the pancetta or bacon and the onion. Cook over a medium heat for 8–10 minutes or until the bacon is crisp and the onion is just golden. Add the mushrooms and garlic and cook for an additional 5 minutes or until softened.

Add the artichoke hearts to the mushroom mixture and cook for 3–4 minutes. Pour in the wine and bring to a boil, then simmer rapidly until the liquid is reduced and syrupy.

Pour in the chicken stock and bring to a boil, then simmer rapidly for about 5 minutes or until slightly reduced. Reduce the heat slightly, then slowly stir in the heavy cream and Parmesan cheese. Season the sauce to taste with salt and pepper.

Meanwhile, bring a large pan of lightly salted water to a rolling boil. Add the pasta and cook according to the package directions or until tender but still firm to the bite.

Drain the pasta thoroughly and transfer to a large warmed serving dish. Pour over the sauce and toss together. Garnish with shredded basil and serve with extra Parmesan cheese.

Gnocchetti with Broccoli & Bacon Sauce

SERVES 6

1 lb. broccoli florets
4 tbsp. olive oil
½ cup finely chopped
    pancetta or smoked bacon
1 small onion, peeled and
    finely chopped

3 garlic cloves, peeled
    and sliced
¾ cup milk
4 cups gnocchetti (little
    elongated ribbed shells)

½ cup freshly grated
    Parmesan cheese, plus
    extra to serve
salt and freshly ground
    black pepper

Bring a large pan of salted water to a boil. Add the broccoli florets and cook for about 8–10 minutes or until very soft. Drain thoroughly and leave to cool slightly; then chop finely and set aside.

Heat the olive oil in a heavy pan. Add the pancetta or bacon and cook over a medium heat for 5 minutes or until golden and crisp. Add the onion and cook for an additional 5 minutes or until soft and lightly golden. Add the garlic and cook for 1 minute.

Transfer the chopped broccoli to the bacon or pancetta mixture and pour in the milk. Bring slowly to a boil and simmer rapidly for about 15 minutes until reduced to a creamy texture.

Meanwhile, bring a large pan of lightly salted water to a rolling boil. Add the pasta and cook according to the package directions or until tender but still firm to the bite.

Drain the pasta thoroughly, setting aside a little of the cooking water. Add the pasta and the Parmesan cheese to the broccoli mixture. Toss, adding enough of the cooking water to make a creamy sauce. Season to taste with salt and pepper. Serve immediately with extra Parmesan cheese.

Hoisin Chicken Pancakes

SERVES 4

3 tbsp. hoisin sauce
1 garlic clove, peeled
    and crushed
1-in. piece ginger, peeled
    and finely grated
1 tbsp. soy sauce
1 tsp. sesame oil

salt and freshly ground
    black pepper
4 skinless chicken thighs
½ cucumber,
    peeled (optional)
12 store-bought
    Chinese pancakes

6 scallions, trimmed
    and cut lengthwise
sweet chili dipping sauce,
    to serve

Preheat the oven to 375°F. In a nonmetallic bowl, mix the hoisin sauce with the garlic, ginger, soy sauce, sesame oil, and seasoning.

Add the chicken thighs and coat in the mixture. Cover loosely with plastic wrap, and leave in the refrigerator to marinate for 3–4 hours, turning the chicken occasionally.

Remove the chicken from the marinade and place in a roasting pan. Set the marinade aside. Cook in the preheated oven for 30 minutes, basting occasionally with the marinade.

Cut the cucumber in half lengthwise, and remove the seeds by running a teaspoon down the center to scoop them out. Cut into thin pieces.

Place the pancakes in a steamer to warm, according to package instructions. Thinly slice the hot chicken, and arrange on a plate with the shredded scallions, cucumber, and pancakes.

Place a spoonful of the chicken in the center of each warmed pancake, and top with pieces of cucumber, scallion, and some of the dipping sauce. Roll up and serve immediately.

Cantonese Chicken Wings

SERVES 4

3 tbsp. hoisin sauce
2 tbsp. dark soy sauce
1 tbsp. sesame oil
1 garlic clove, peeled
   and crushed
1-in. piece ginger, peeled
   and finely grated

1 tbsp. Chinese rice wine or
   dry sherry
2 tsp. chili bean sauce
2 tsp. red or white
   wine vinegar
2 tbsp. light brown sugar
2 lb. large chicken wings

½ cup chopped
   cashew nuts
2 scallions, trimmed and
   finely chopped

Preheat the oven to 425°F. Place the hoisin sauce, soy sauce, sesame oil, garlic, ginger, Chinese rice wine or sherry, chili bean sauce, vinegar, and sugar in a small saucepan with 6 tablespoons of water. Bring to a boil, stirring occasionally, then simmer for about 30 seconds. Remove the glaze from the heat.

Place the chicken wings in a roasting pan in a single layer. Pour the glaze on top, and stir until the wings are coated thoroughly.

Cover the pan loosely with aluminum foil, place in the preheated oven, and roast for 25 minutes. Remove the foil, baste the wings, and cook for an additional 5 minutes.

Reduce the oven temperature to 375°F. Turn the wings over, and sprinkle with the chopped cashew nuts and scallions. Return to the oven and cook for 5 minutes or until the nuts are lightly browned, the glaze is sticky, and the wings are tender. Remove from the oven and let stand for 5 minutes before arranging on a warmed platter. Serve immediately with plenty of napkins.

HELPFUL HINT

Though popular in China and Thailand, the wings are often discarded when cutting chickens into portions. So give your butcher advance notice and he will probably sell them to you very cheaply.

Soy–Glazed Chicken Thighs

SERVES 6-8

2 tbsp. vegetable oil
2 lb. chicken thighs
3–4 garlic cloves, peeled
   and crushed
½ cup soy sauce

1½-in. piece fresh ginger,
   peeled and finely chopped
   or grated
2–3 tbsp. Chinese rice wine
   or dry sherry
2 tbsp. honey

1 tbsp. brown sugar
2–3 dashes hot chili sauce,
   or to taste
freshly chopped parsley,
   to garnish

Heat a large wok and, when hot, add the oil. Stir-fry the chicken thighs for 5 minutes or until golden. Remove and drain on absorbent paper towels. You may need to do this in 2–3 batches.

Pour off the oil and fat and, using absorbent paper towels, carefully wipe out the wok. Add the garlic, along with the soy sauce, ginger, Chinese rice wine or sherry, and honey to the wok and stir well. Sprinkle in the brown sugar with the hot chili sauce to taste, then place over the heat and bring to a boil.

Reduce the heat to a gentle simmer, then carefully add the chicken thighs. Cover the wok and simmer gently over a very low heat for 30 minutes or until they are tender and the sauce is reduced and thickened, and glazes the chicken thighs.

Stir or spoon the sauce occasionally over the chicken thighs and add a little water if the sauce is starting to become too thick. Arrange in a shallow serving dish, garnish with freshly chopped parsley, and serve immediately.

Mozzarella Frittata
with Tomato & Basil Salad

SERVES 6

For the salad:
6 ripe but firm tomatoes
2 tbsp. fresh basil leaves
2 tbsp. olive oil
1 tbsp. fresh lemon juice

1 tsp. superfine sugar
freshly ground black pepper

For the frittata:
7 medium eggs, beaten
salt

2¾ cups mozzarella cheese
2 scallions, trimmed and
finely chopped
2 tbsp. olive oil
warm, crusty bread, to serve

To make the tomato and basil salad, slice the tomatoes very thinly, tear the basil leaves, and sprinkle the basil over the tomatoes. Make the dressing by beating the olive oil, lemon juice, and sugar together. Season with pepper before drizzling the dressing over the salad.

To make the frittata, place the eggs in a large bowl with plenty of salt and beat. Shred the mozzarella and stir into the egg with the finely chopped scallions.

Heat the oil in a nonstick skillet and pour in the egg mixture, stirring with a wooden spoon to spread the ingredients evenly over the skillet. Cook for 5–8 minutes until the frittata is golden brown and firm on the underside.

Place the whole skillet under the broiler, and cook for about 4–5 minutes until the top is golden brown. Slide the frittata onto a serving plate, cut into six large wedges, and serve immediately with the tomato and basil salad and plenty of warm, crusty bread.

HELPFUL HINT

After grating the mozzarella cheese, firmly press between layers of absorbent paper towels to remove any excess water that might leak out during cooking.

Zucchini & Tarragon Tortilla

SERVES 4

1½ lb. potatoes
3 tbsp. olive oil
1 onion, peeled and
   thinly sliced

salt and freshly ground
   black pepper
1 zucchini, trimmed and
   thinly sliced

6 large eggs
2 tbsp. freshly
   chopped tarragon
tomato wedges, to serve

Peel the potatoes and slice thinly. Dry the slices in a clean dish towel to get them as dry as possible. Heat the oil in a large heavy skillet, add the onion, and cook for 3 minutes. Add the potatoes along with a little salt and pepper, then stir the potatoes and onion lightly to coat in the oil.

Reduce the heat to the lowest possible setting, cover, and cook gently for 5 minutes. Turn the potatoes and onion over and continue to cook for an additional 5 minutes. Give the pan a shake every now and again to ensure that the potatoes do not stick to the base or burn. Add the zucchini, then cover and cook for 10 more minutes.

Beat the eggs and tarragon together, and season to taste with salt and pepper. Pour the egg mixture over the vegetables and return to the heat. Cook on a low heat for up to 20–25 minutes until there is no liquid egg left on the surface of the tortilla.

Turn the tortilla over by inverting the pan onto the lid or a large flat plate. Slide the tortilla back into the pan. Return the pan to the heat and cook for a final 3–5 minutes until the underside is golden brown. If preferred, place the tortilla under a preheated broiler for 4 minutes or until set and golden brown on top. Cut into small squares, and serve hot or cold with tomato wedges.

HELPFUL HINT

Use even-size waxy potatoes, which won't break up during cooking—Yellow Finn, new, red-skinned potato, white round, and purple are all good choices of potato.

127

Potato Skins

SERVES 4

4 large baking potatoes
2 tbsp. olive oil
2 tsp. paprika
¾ cup roughly chopped
   pancetta or bacon

6 tbsp. heavy cream
⅓ cup diced blue cheese,
   such as Gorgonzola
1 tbsp. freshly
   chopped parsley

To serve:
mayonnaise
sweet chili dipping sauce
tossed green salad

Preheat the oven to 400°F. Scrub the potatoes, then prick a few times with a fork or skewer and place directly on the top shelf of the oven. Bake in the preheated oven for at least 1 hour until tender. The potatoes are cooked when they yield gently to the pressure of your hand.

Set the potatoes aside until cool enough to handle, then cut in half and scoop the flesh into a bowl and set aside. Preheat the broiler, and line the pan with aluminum foil.

Mix together the oil and paprika, and use half to brush the outside of the potato skins. Place on the foil-lined pan under the preheated broiler, and cook for 5 minutes or until crisp, turning as necessary.

Heat the remaining paprika-flavored oil and gently fry the pancetta until crisp. Add to the potato flesh along with the cream, blue cheese, and parsley. Halve the potato skins, and fill with the blue-cheese filling. Return to the oven for an additional 15 minutes to heat through. Sprinkle with a little more paprika, and serve immediately with mayonnaise, sweet chili sauce, and a green salad.

Beet Risotto

6 tbsp. extra-virgin olive oil
1 onion, peeled and
  finely chopped
2 garlic cloves, peeled and
  finely chopped
2 tsp. freshly
  chopped thyme
1 tsp. grated lemon zest

2 cups Arborio rice
⅔ cup dry white wine
3¾ cups vegetable
  stock, heated
2 tbsp. heavy cream
1½ cups peeled and finely
  chopped cooked beet

2 tbsp. freshly
  chopped parsley
¾ cup freshly grated
  Parmesan cheese
salt and freshly ground
  black pepper
fresh thyme sprigs,
  to garnish

Heat half the oil in a large heavy skillet. Add the onion, garlic, thyme, and lemon zest. Cook for 5 minutes, stirring frequently, until the onion is soft and transparent, but not browned. Add the rice and stir until it is well coated in the oil.

Add the wine, then bring to a boil and boil rapidly until the wine has almost evaporated. Reduce the heat.

Keeping the pan over a low heat, add a ladleful of the hot stock to the rice, and cook, stirring constantly, until the stock is absorbed. Continue gradually adding the stock in this way until the rice is tender; this should take about 20 minutes. You may not need all the stock.

Stir in the cream, chopped beet, parsley, and half the grated Parmesan cheese. Season to taste with salt and pepper. Garnish with sprigs of fresh thyme, and serve immediately, with the remaining grated Parmesan cheese.

HELPFUL HINT

If you buy ready-cooked beet, choose small ones, which are sweeter. Make sure that they are not doused in vinegar, as this would spoil the flavor of the dish.

Corn Fritters

SERVES 4

4 tbsp. peanut oil
1 small onion, peeled and
   finely chopped
1 red chile, seeded and
   finely chopped
1 garlic clove, peeled
   and crushed

1 tsp. ground coriander
11 oz. corn
6 scallions, trimmed and
   finely sliced
1 large egg,
   lightly beaten

salt and freshly ground
   black pepper
3 tbsp. all-purpose flour
1 tsp. baking powder
scallion curls, to garnish
Thai-style chutney, to serve

Heat 1 tablespoon of the peanut oil in a skillet, add the onion, and cook gently for 7–8 minutes or until beginning to soften. Add the chile, garlic, and ground coriander, and cook for 1 minute, stirring continuously. Remove from the heat.

Drain the corn and tip into a mixing bowl. Lightly crush with a potato masher to break down the corn a little. Add the cooked onion mixture to the bowl with the scallions and beaten egg. Season to taste with salt and pepper, then stir to mix together. Sift the flour and baking powder over the mixture and stir in.

Heat 2 tablespoons of the peanut oil in a large skillet. Drop 4 or 5 heaping teaspoonfuls of the corn mixture into the pan, and using a fish slice or spatula, flatten each to make a ½-in.-thick fritter.

Fry the fritters for 3 minutes or until golden brown on the underside, turn over, and fry for an additional 3 minutes or until cooked through and crisp.

Remove the fritters from the pan and drain on paper towels. Keep warm while cooking the remaining fritters, adding a little more oil if needed. Garnish the fritters with scallion curls, and serve immediately with a Thai-style chutney.

HELPFUL HINT

To make a scallion curl, trim off the root and some green top to leave 4 inches. Make several 1¼ inch cuts down from the top. Soak in iced water for 20 minutes until curled.

Spaghettini with Peas, Scallions & Mint

SERVES 6

pinch saffron strands
1½ lb. fresh peas or 3 cups
   thawed frozen petit pois
6 tbsp. unsalted
   butter, softened

6 scallions, trimmed and
   finely sliced
salt and freshly ground
   black pepper
1 garlic clove, peeled and
   finely chopped

2 tbsp. freshly chopped mint
1 tbsp. freshly cut chives
1 lb. spaghettini
freshly grated
   Parmesan cheese,
   to serve

Soak the saffron in 2 tablespoons hot water while you prepare the sauce. Shell the peas if using fresh ones.

Melt ½ stick of the butter in a medium skillet. Add the scallions and a little salt, and cook over a low heat for 2–3 minutes or until the scallions are softened. Add the garlic, then the peas and 7 tablespoons water. Bring to a boil and cook for 5–6 minutes or until the peas are just tender. Stir in the mint and chives and keep warm.

Blend the remaining butter and the saffron water in a large, warmed serving bowl and set aside.

Meanwhile, bring a large pan of lightly salted water to a rolling boil and add the spaghettini. Cook according to the package directions until tender but still firm to the bite.

Drain thoroughly, reserving 2–3 tablespoons of the pasta cooking water. Spoon into a warmed serving bowl. Add the pea sauce and toss together gently. Season to taste with salt and pepper. Serve immediately with extra black pepper and grated Parmesan cheese.

Tagliatelle with Brown Butter, Asparagus & Parmesan

SERVES 6

1 lb. 10 oz. fresh, or 1 lb. dried, tagliatelle, such as the white and green variety
12 oz. asparagus, trimmed and cut into short lengths
6 tbsp. unsalted butter

1 garlic clove, peeled and sliced
¼ cup coarsely chopped, slivered or whole hazelnuts
1 tbsp. freshly chopped parsley

1 tbsp. freshly snipped chives
salt and freshly ground black pepper
½ cup freshly grated Parmesan cheese, to serve

If making fresh pasta, prepare the dough according to the recipe on page 56. Cut into tagliatelle, wind into nests, and set aside on a floured dish towel until ready to cook.

Bring a pan of lightly salted water to a boil. Add the asparagus and cook for 1 minute. Drain immediately, rinse under cold running water, and drain again. Pat dry and set aside.

Melt the butter in a large skillet, then add the garlic and hazelnuts, and cook over a medium heat until the butter turns golden. Immediately remove from the heat and add the parsley, chives, and asparagus. Leave for 2–3 minutes, until the asparagus is heated through.

Meanwhile, bring a large pan of lightly salted water to a rolling boil, then add the pasta nests. Cook until tender but still firm to the bite: 2–3 minutes for fresh pasta and according to the package directions for dried pasta. Drain the pasta thoroughly and return to the pan. Add the asparagus mixture and toss together. Season to taste with salt and pepper and spoon into a warmed serving dish. Serve immediately with grated Parmesan cheese.

HELPFUL HINT

If you buy loose asparagus, rather than pre-packed, choose stems of similar thickness so that they will all cook in the same time.

Peperonata
(Braised Mixed Peppers)

SERVES 4

2 green bell peppers
1 red bell pepper
1 yellow bell pepper
1 orange bell pepper
1 onion, peeled
2 garlic cloves, peeled

2 tbsp. olive oil
4 very ripe tomatoes
1 tbsp. freshly
   chopped oregano
salt and freshly ground
   black pepper

⅔ cup light chicken or
   vegetable stock
fresh oregano sprigs,
   to garnish
focaccia, to serve

Remove the seeds from the bell peppers and cut into thin strips. Slice the onion into rings and chop the garlic cloves finely.

Heat the oil in a skillet and cook the peppers, onions, and garlic for 5–10 minutes or until soft and lightly browned. Stir continuously.

Make a cross on the top of the tomatoes, then place in a bowl and cover with boiling water. Allow to stand for about 2 minutes. Drain, then remove the skins and seeds, and chop the tomato flesh into cubes.

Add the tomatoes and oregano to the bell peppers and onion, and season to taste with salt and pepper. Cover the skillet and bring to a boil. Simmer gently for about 30 minutes until tender, adding the chicken or vegetable stock halfway through the cooking time.

Garnish with sprigs of oregano and serve hot with plenty of freshly cooked focaccia bread.

Bruschetta with Pecorino, Garlic & Tomatoes

SERVES 4

6 ripe but firm tomatoes
1 cup finely grated
 pecorino cheese
1 tbsp. oregano leaves
salt and freshly ground
 black pepper

3 tbsp. olive oil
3 garlic cloves, peeled
8 slices flat Italian bread,
 such as focaccia
8 thin slices
 mozzarella cheese

marinated ripe olives,
 to serve

Preheat the broiler and line the broiler rack with foil just before cooking. Make a small cross in the top of the tomatoes, then place in a small bowl and cover with boiling water. Allow to stand for 2 minutes, then drain and remove the skins. Cut into quarters, remove the seeds, and dice the flesh.

Mix the tomato flesh with the pecorino cheese and 2 teaspoons of the fresh oregano. Season to taste with salt and pepper. Add 1 tablespoon of the olive oil and mix thoroughly.

Crush the garlic and spread evenly over the slices of bread. Heat 2 tablespoons of the olive oil in a large skillet, and sauté the bread slices until they are crisp and golden.

Place the fried bread on a greased baking sheet and spoon on the tomato and cheese topping. Place some mozzarella on the top and place under the preheated broiler for 3–4 minutes until golden and bubbling. Garnish with the remaining oregano, then arrange the bruschettas on a serving plate and serve with the olives.

Fish & Seafood

Stir–Fried Salmon with Peas

SERVES 4

1 lb. salmon fillet
salt
6 slices bacon
1 tbsp. vegetable oil
¼ cup chicken or fish stock
2 tbsp. dark soy sauce

2 tbsp. Chinese rice wine or
    dry sherry
1 tsp. sugar
heaping ½ cup thawed
    frozen peas
1–2 tbsp. freshly
    shredded mint

1 tsp. cornstarch
fresh mint sprigs,
    to garnish
freshly cooked noodles,
    to serve

Wipe and skin the salmon fillet, and remove any pin bones. Slice into 1-in. strips, place on a plate, and sprinkle with salt. Leave for 20 minutes, then pat dry with paper towels and set aside.

Remove any cartilage from the bacon, dice, and set aside.

Heat a wok or large skillet over a high heat, then add the oil, and, when hot, add the bacon and stir-fry for 3 minutes or until crisp and golden. Push to one side and add the strips of salmon. Stir-fry gently for 2 minutes or until the flesh is opaque.

Pour the chicken or fish stock, soy sauce, and Chinese rice wine or sherry into the wok, then stir in the sugar, peas, and freshly shredded mint.

HELPFUL HINT

Dark soy sauce is used in this recipe because it is slightly less salty than the light version. To reduce the salt content further, cook the noodles in plain boiling water with no added salt.

Blend the cornstarch with 1 tablespoon of water to form a smooth paste, and stir into the sauce. Bring to a boil, reduce the heat, and simmer for 1 minute or until slightly thickened and smooth. Garnish and serve immediately with noodles.

Salmon Fish Cakes

SERVES 4

1 lb. salmon fillet, skinned
salt and freshly ground
    black pepper
2⅔ cups peeled and coarsely
    diced potatoes
2 tbsp. butter
1 tbsp. milk
2 medium tomatoes, skinned,
    seeded, and chopped

2 tbsp. freshly
    chopped parsley
1½ cups whole-wheat
    bread crumbs
¼ cup shredded
    cheddar cheese
2 tbsp. all-purpose flour
2 large eggs, beaten
3–4 tbsp. vegetable oil

To serve:
raita
fresh mint sprigs

Place the salmon in a shallow skillet, and cover with water. Season to taste with salt and pepper, and simmer for 8–10 minutes until the fish is cooked. Drain and flake into a bowl.

Boil the potatoes in lightly salted water until soft, then drain. Mash with the butter and milk until smooth. Add the potato to the bowl of fish and stir in the tomatoes and half the parsley. Adjust the seasoning to taste. Chill the mixture in the refrigerator for at least 2 hours to firm up.

Mix the bread crumbs with the cheese and the remaining parsley. When the fish mixture is firm, form into eight patties. First, lightly coat the patties in the flour, then dip into the beaten egg, allowing any excess to drip back into the bowl. Finally, press the patties into the bread-crumb mixture until well coated.

Heat a little of the oil in a skillet, and fry the patties in batches for 2–3 minutes on each side until golden and crisp, adding more oil if necessary. Serve with raita, garnished with mint sprigs.

HELPFUL HINT

To remove the skins from the tomatoes, pierce each with the tip of a sharp knife, then plunge into boiling water and leave for up to 1 minute. After a cold-water rinsing, the skins should peel off easily.

Salmon with Herbed Potatoes

SERVES 4

1 lb. baby new potatoes
salt and freshly ground
   black pepper
4 salmon steaks, each
   about 6 oz.

1 carrot, peeled and cut into
   fine strips
12 asparagus
   spears, trimmed
1 cup trimmed snow peas

finely grated zest and juice
   of 1 lemon
2 tbsp. butter
4 large fresh parsley sprigs

Preheat the oven to 375°F. Parboil the potatoes in lightly salted, boiling water for 5–8 minutes until they are barely tender. Drain and set aside.

Cut out four pieces of baking parchment, measuring 8 in. square, and place on the work surface. Arrange the parboiled potatoes on top. Wipe the salmon steaks and place on top of the potatoes.

Place the carrot strips in a bowl with the asparagus spears, snow peas, and grated lemon zest and juice. Season to taste with salt and pepper. Toss lightly together.

Divide the vegetables evenly between the salmon. Dot the top of each pocket with butter and add a sprig of parsley.

To wrap a pocket, lift up two opposite sides of the paper and fold the edges together. Twist the paper at the other two ends to seal the pocket well. Repeat with the remaining pockets.

Place the pockets on a baking sheet and bake for 15 minutes. Place an unopened pocket on each plate, and open before eating.

Pan-Fried Salmon with Herb Risotto

SERVES 4

4 salmon fillets
3–4 tbsp. all-purpose flour
1 tsp. dried mustard powder
salt and freshly ground
    black pepper
2 tbsp. olive oil
3 shallots, peeled
    and chopped

1 cup risotto rice
⅔ cup dry white wine
5¼ cups vegetable or
    fish stock
4 tbsp. butter
2 tbsp. freshly cut chives
2 tbsp. freshly chopped dill

2 tbsp. freshly chopped
    Italian flat-leaf parsley
pat of butter

To garnish:
lemon slices
fresh dill sprigs
tomato salad, to serve

Wipe the salmon fillets with a clean, damp cloth. Mix together the flour, mustard powder, and seasoning on a large plate, and use to coat the salmon fillets. Set aside.

Heat half the olive oil in a large skillet, and cook the shallots for 5 minutes until softened but not browned. Add the rice and stir for 1 minute, then slowly add the wine, bring to a boil and boil rapidly until reduced by half.

Bring the stock to a gentle simmer, then add to the rice, a ladleful at a time. Cook, stirring frequently, adding the stock as needed until the rice is cooked yet firm. Stir in the butter, freshly chopped herbs, and season to taste with salt and pepper.

Heat the remaining olive oil and the pat of butter in a large griddle pan, add the salmon fillets, and cook for 2–3 minutes on each side until done. Arrange the herb risotto on warm serving plates and top with the salmon. Garnish with slices of lemon and sprigs of dill, and serve immediately with a tomato salad.

HELPFUL HINT

Stirring butter into the risotto at the end is an important step – in Italian it is called *mantecare*. This final addition gives the risotto its fine texture and a beautiful shine. Serve as soon as it is cooked.

Salmon Noisettes with Fruit Sauce

SERVES 4

4 salmon steaks	1 tbsp. honey	2½ cups mixed salad
2 tbsp. grated lemon zest	1 tbsp. mustard	leaves, washed
¼ cup lemon juice	coarse sea salt and freshly	1 bunch watercress, washed
2 tsp. grated lime zest	ground black pepper	and thick stalks removed
1 tbsp. lime juice	1 tbsp. peanut oil	2¼ cups halved baby
3 tbsp. olive oil		plum tomatoes

Using a sharp knife, cut the bone away from each salmon steak to create two salmon fillets. Repeat with the remaining salmon steaks. Shape the salmon fillets into noisettes and secure with kitchen string.

Mix together the citrus zests and juices, olive oil, honey, mustard, salt, and pepper in a shallow dish. Add the salmon fillets, and turn to coat. Cover, and allow to marinate in the refrigerator for about 4 hours, turning them occasionally in the marinade.

Heat the wok, then add the peanut oil and heat until hot. Lift out the salmon noisettes, setting the marinade aside. Add the salmon to the wok and cook for 6–10 minutes, turning once during cooking, until cooked and the fish is just flaking. Pour the marinade into the wok and heat through gently.

Mix together the salad leaves, watercress, and tomatoes, and arrange on serving plates. Top with the salmon noisettes and drizzle with any remaining warm marinade. Serve immediately.

Seared Salmon & Lemon Linguine

SERVES 4

4 small skinless salmon
   fillets, each about 3 oz.
2 tsp. sunflower oil
½ tsp. mixed or black
   peppercorns, crushed
14 oz. linguine
1 tbsp. unsalted butter

1 bunch scallions, trimmed
   and shredded
1¼ cups sour cream
zest of 1 lemon, finely grated
½ cup freshly grated
   Parmesan cheese
1 tbsp. lemon juice

To garnish:
dill sprigs
lemon slices

Brush the salmon fillets with the sunflower oil, sprinkle with crushed peppercorns, and press on firmly. Set aside.

Bring a large pan of lightly salted water to a rolling boil. Add the linguine and cook according to the package directions or until tender but still firm to the bite.

Meanwhile, melt the butter in a pan and cook the shredded scallions gently for 2–3 minutes until soft. Stir in the sour cream and the lemon zest, and remove from the heat.

Preheat a griddle or heavy skillet until very hot. Add the salmon and sear for 1½–2 minutes on each side. Remove from the pan and leave to cool slightly.

Bring the sour cream sauce to a boil, and stir in the Parmesan cheese and lemon juice. Drain the pasta thoroughly and return to the pan. Pour over the sauce and toss gently to coat.

Spoon the pasta onto warmed serving plates and top with the salmon fillets. Serve immediately with sprigs of dill and lemon slices.

Farfalle with Smoked Trout in a Dill & Vodka Sauce

SERVES 4

3½ cups farfalle
5 oz. smoked trout
2 tsp. lemon juice
about ¾ cup heavy cream

2 tsp. whole-grain mustard
2 tbsp. freshly chopped dill
4 tbsp. vodka

salt and freshly ground
black pepper
dill sprigs, to garnish

Bring a large pan of lightly salted water to a rolling boil. Add the pasta and cook according to the package directions or until tender but still firm to the bite.

Meanwhile, cut the smoked trout into thin slivers, using scissors. Sprinkle lightly with the lemon juice and set aside.

Place the cream, mustard, chopped dill, and vodka in a small pan. Season lightly with salt and pepper. Bring the contents of the pan to a boil and simmer gently for 2-3 minutes or until slightly thickened.

Drain the cooked pasta thoroughly, then return to the pan. Add the smoked trout to the dill and vodka sauce, then pour over the pasta. Toss gently until the pasta is coated and the trout evenly mixed.

Spoon into a warmed serving dish or onto individual plates. Garnish with sprigs of dill and serve immediately.

Ratatouille Mackerel

1 red bell pepper
1 red onion, peeled
1 tbsp. olive oil
1 garlic clove, peeled and
   thinly sliced
2 zucchini, trimmed
   and sliced

14 oz. canned
   chopped tomatoes
sea salt and freshly ground
   black pepper
4 10-oz. small mackerel,
   cleaned and
   heads removed

1 spray olive oil
lemon juice, for drizzling
12 fresh basil leaves
couscous or rice mixed with
   chopped parsley, to serve

Preheat the oven to 375˚F. Cut the top off the red bell pepper, remove the seeds and membrane, then cut into chunks. Cut the red onion into thick wedges.

Heat the oil in a large saucepan, and cook the onion and garlic for 5 minutes or until beginning to soften.

Add the bell pepper chunks and zucchini slices, and cook for an additional 5 minutes.

Pour in the chopped tomatoes with their juice, and cook for an additional 5 minutes. Season to taste with salt and pepper, and pour into an ovenproof dish.

Season the fish with salt and pepper and arrange on top of the vegetables. Spray with a little olive oil and lemon juice. Cover and cook in the preheated oven for 20 minutes.

Remove the cover, add the basil leaves, and return to the oven for an additional 5 minutes. Serve immediately with couscous or rice mixed with parsley.

FOOD FACT

Ratatouille is a very versatile dish to which many other vegetables can be added. For that extra kick, why not add a little chopped chile.

Smoked Mackerel & Pasta Frittata

SERVES 4

¼ cup tricolor pasta spirals or shells
8 oz. smoked mackerel (or salmon)
6 large eggs
3 tbsp. milk
2 tsp. whole-grain mustard

2 tbsp. freshly chopped parsley
salt and freshly ground black pepper
2 tbsp. unsalted butter
6 scallions, trimmed and diagonally sliced

2 oz. frozen peas, thawed
¾ cup shredded sharp cheddar cheese

To serve:
green salad
warm crusty bread

Preheat the broiler to high just before cooking. Bring a pan of lightly salted water to a rolling boil. Add the pasta and cook according to the package directions or until tender but still firm to the bite. Drain thoroughly and set aside.

Remove the skin from the mackerel and break the fish into large flakes, discarding any bones, and set aside.

Place the eggs, milk, mustard, and parsley in a bowl and whisk together. Season with salt and plenty of freshly ground black pepper, and set aside.

Melt the butter in a large heavy skillet. Cook the scallions gently for 3–4 minutes, until soft. Pour in the egg mixture, then add the drained pasta, peas, and half of the mackerel.

Gently stir the mixture in the pan for 1–2 minutes until beginning to set. Stop stirring and cook for about 1 minute until the underneath is golden brown.

Spread the remaining mackerel over the frittata, followed by the shredded cheese. Place under the preheated broiler for about 1½ minutes until golden brown and set. Cut into wedges and serve immediately with salad and crusty bread.

Tuna & Mushroom Ragout

SERVES 4

1⅓ cups mixed basmati and wild rice
4 tbsp. butter
1 tbsp. olive oil
1 large onion, peeled and finely chopped
1 garlic clove, peeled and crushed
¾ lb. baby button mushrooms, halved

2 tbsp. all-purpose flour
14 oz. canned chopped tomatoes
1 tbsp. freshly chopped parsley
dash Worcestershire sauce
14 oz. canned tuna in oil, drained
salt and freshly ground black pepper

4 tbsp. grated Parmesan cheese
1 tbsp. freshly shredded basil

To serve:
green salad
garlic bread

Cook the basmati and wild rice in a saucepan of boiling salted water for 20 minutes, then drain and return to the pan. Stir in half of the butter, cover the pan, and let stand for 2 minutes until the butter has melted.

Heat the oil and the remaining butter in a skillet, and cook the onion for 1–2 minutes until soft. Add the garlic and mushrooms, and continue to cook for an additional 3 minutes.

Stir in the flour and cook for 1 minute, then add the tomatoes and bring the sauce to a boil. Add the parsley, Worcestershire sauce, and tuna, and simmer gently for 3 minutes. Season to taste with salt and freshly ground pepper.

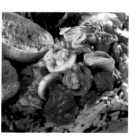

Stir the rice well, then spoon onto four serving plates, and top with the tuna and mushroom mixture. Sprinkle with a spoonful of grated Parmesan cheese and some shredded basil, and serve immediately with a green salad and chunks of garlic bread.

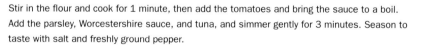

Seared Tuna with Pernod & Thyme

SERVES 4

4 tuna or swordfish steaks
salt and freshly ground
   black pepper
3 tbsp. Pernod
1 tbsp. olive oil

3 tsp. each lime zest
   and juice
2 tsp. fresh thyme leaves
4 sun-dried tomatoes

To serve:
freshly cooked mixed rice
tossed green salad

Wipe the fish steaks with a damp cloth or dampened paper towels.

Season both sides of the fish with salt and pepper, then place in a shallow bowl and set aside.

Mix together the Pernod, olive oil, lime zest, and juice with the fresh thyme leaves.

Finely chop the sun-dried tomatoes, and add to the Pernod mixture.

Pour the Pernod mixture over the fish and chill in the refrigerator for about 2 hours, occasionally spooning the marinade over the fish.

Heat a griddle or heavy skillet. Drain the fish, setting aside the marinade. Cook the fish for 3–4 minutes on each side for a steak that is still slightly pink in the center. Alternatively, cook the fish for 1–2 minutes longer on each side if you prefer your fish cooked through.

Place the remaining marinade in a small saucepan, and bring to a boil. Pour the marinade over the fish, and serve immediately with the mixed rice and salad.

Tuna Cannelloni

SERVES 4

1 tbsp. olive oil
6 scallions, trimmed and
    finely sliced
1 red bell pepper, seeded
    and finely chopped
7 oz. canned tuna in water
9-oz. tub ricotta cheese

1 tbsp. lemon zest
2 tbsp. lemon juice
1 tbsp. freshly cut chives
salt and freshly ground
    black pepper
8 dried cannelloni tubes
1 large egg, beaten

¼ cup cottage cheese
½ cup plain yogurt
pinch freshly grated nutmeg
¼ cup shredded
    mozzarella cheese
tossed green salad, to serve

Preheat the oven to 375°F. Heat the olive oil in a skillet, and cook the scallions and bell pepper until soft. Remove from the skillet with a slotted spoon and place in a large bowl.

Drain the tuna, and mix with the scallions and bell pepper. Beat the ricotta cheese with the lemon zest, lemon juice, and chives, and season to taste with salt and pepper until soft and blended. Add to the tuna and mix together. If the mixture is still a little stiff, add some extra lemon juice.

With a teaspoon, carefully spoon the mixture into the cannelloni tubes, then lay the filled tubes in a lightly greased, shallow, ovenproof dish. Beat the egg, cottage cheese, yogurt, and nutmeg together, and pour over the cannelloni. Sprinkle over the shredded mozzarella cheese, and cook in the preheated oven for 15–20 minutes or until the topping is golden brown and bubbling. Serve immediately with a tossed green salad.

HELPFUL HINT

Don't be tempted to partly cook the cannelloni tubes before stuffing them; this makes them too slippery to handle. They will cook thoroughly in the sauce while they are baking.

Tuna Fish Burgers

2⅔ cups peeled and coarsely diced potatoes
4 tbsp. butter
2 tbsp. milk
14 oz. canned tuna in oil
1 scallion, trimmed and finely chopped
1 tbsp. freshly

chopped parsley
2 large eggs, beaten
salt and freshly ground black pepper
2 tbsp. seasoned all-purpose flour
2 cups fresh white bread crumbs

4 tbsp. vegetable oil
4 hamburger buns

To serve:
french fries
mixed salad greens
tomato chutney

Place the potatoes in a large saucepan, cover with boiling water, and simmer until soft. Drain, then mash with 3 tablespoons of the butter and the milk. Turn into a large bowl. Drain the tuna, discarding the oil, and flake into the bowl of potatoes. Stir well to mix.

Add the scallion and parsley, and season to taste with salt and pepper. Add 1 tablespoon of the beaten egg to bind the mixture together. Chill in the refrigerator for at least 1 hour.

Shape the chilled mixture with your hands into four large patties. First, coat the patties with seasoned flour, then brush them with the remaining beaten egg, allowing any excess to drip back into the bowl. Finally, coat them evenly in the bread crumbs, pressing the crumbs on with your hands, if necessary.

Heat a little of the oil in a skillet, and fry the patties for 2–3 minutes on each side, until golden, adding more oil if necessary. Drain on paper towels and serve hot on buns with french fries, mixed salad greens, and chutney.

HELPFUL HINT
Drain the potatoes thoroughly and dry them over a very low heat before mashing with the milk and butter to ensure that the mixture is not too soft to shape.

Seared Pancetta–Wrapped Cod

SERVES 4

4 6-oz. cod fillets
4 very thin slices of pancetta
3 tbsp. capers, in vinegar
1 tbsp. vegetable or corn oil
2 tbsp. lemon juice

1 tbsp. olive oil
freshly ground black pepper
1 tbsp. freshly chopped
   parsley, to garnish

To serve:
freshly cooked vegetables
new potatoes

Wipe the cod fillets and wrap each one with the pancetta. Secure each fillet with a toothpick and set aside.

Drain the capers and soak in cold water for 10 minutes to remove any excess salt, then drain and set aside.

Heat the oil in a large skillet and sear the wrapped pieces of cod fillet for about 3 minutes on each side, turning carefully with a spatula so as not to break up the fish.

Lower the heat, then continue to cook for 2–3 minutes or until the fish is cooked thoroughly.

Meanwhile, place the remaining capers, lemon juice, and olive oil in a small saucepan. Add the black pepper.

Place the saucepan over a low heat and bring to a gentle simmer, stirring continuously for 2–3 minutes.

Once the fish is cooked, garnish with the parsley and serve with the warm caper dressing, freshly cooked vegetables, and new potatoes.

Gingered Cod Steaks

SERVES 4

1-in. piece fresh
   ginger, peeled
4 scallions
2 tsp. freshly
   chopped parsley

1 tbsp. brown sugar
4 6-oz. cod steaks
salt and freshly ground
   black pepper

¼ stick reduced-fat butter
freshly cooked vegetables,
   to serve

Preheat the broiler and line the broiler rack with a layer of foil. Coarsely grate the piece of fresh ginger. Trim the scallions and cut into thin strips.

Mix the scallions, ginger, chopped parsley, and sugar together. Add 1 tablespoon of water.

Wipe the fish steaks. Season with salt and pepper. Place onto four separate 8 x 8 inch foil squares.

Carefully spoon the scallions and ginger mixture evenly over the fish.

Cut the butter into small cubes and place over the fish.

Loosely fold the foil over the steaks to enclose the fish and to make a pocket.

Place under the preheated broiler and cook for 10–12 minutes until cooked and the flesh has turned opaque.

Place the fish pockets on individual serving plates. Serve immediately with the freshly cooked vegetables.

HELPFUL HINT

This recipe also works well with other fish steaks. Try salmon, fresh haddock or monkfish fillets. The monkfish fillets may take a little longer to cook.

Spanish Omelet with Smoked Fish

SERVES 3-4

3 tbsp. sunflower oil
2 cups peeled and
   diced potatoes
2 medium onions, peeled
   and cut into wedges
2–4 large garlic cloves,
   peeled and thinly sliced
1 large red bell pepper,
   seeded, quartered, and
   thinly sliced

¼ lb. smoked haddock
salt and freshly ground
   black pepper
2 tbsp. butter, melted
1 tbsp. heavy cream
6 large eggs, beaten
2 tbsp. freshly chopped
   Italian flat-leaf parsley
½ cup shredded
   cheddar cheese

To serve:
crusty bread
tossed green salad

Heat the oil in a large, nonstick, heavy skillet, add the potatoes, onions, and garlic, and cook gently for 10–15 minutes until golden brown, then add the red bell pepper and cook for 3 minutes.

Meanwhile, place the fish in a shallow skillet and cover with water. Season to taste with salt and pepper, and poach gently for 10 minutes. Drain and flake the fish into a bowl, toss in the melted butter and cream, adjust the seasoning, and set aside.

When the vegetables are cooked, drain off any excess oil, and stir in the beaten egg with the chopped parsley. Pour the fish mixture over the top and cook gently for 5 minutes or until the eggs become firm.

Sprinkle with the cheese and place the pan under a preheated broiler. Cook for 2–3 minutes until the cheese is golden and bubbling. Carefully slide the omelet onto a large plate, and serve immediately with plenty of bread and salad.

HELPFUL HINT

For best results, Spanish omelet should be cooked slowly until set. Finishing the dish under the broiler gives it a delicious golden look.

Saucy Cod & Pasta Bake

SERVES 4

1 lb. cod fillets, skinned
2 tbsp. sunflower oil
1 onion, peeled and chopped
4 slices smoked bacon, rind
   removed and chopped
1½ cups wiped baby
   button mushrooms
2 celery stalks, trimmed and
   thinly sliced

2 small zucchini, halved
   lengthwise and sliced
14 oz. canned chopped
   tomatoes
7 tbsp. fish stock or dry
   white wine
1 tbsp. freshly
   chopped tarragon

salt and freshly ground
   black pepper

For the pasta topping:
2–2½ cups pasta shells
2 tbsp. butter
4 tbsp all-purpose flour
1½ cups milk

Preheat the oven to 400˚F. Cut the cod into bite-sized pieces and set aside.

Heat the sunflower oil in a large pan. Add the onion and bacon and cook for 7–8 minutes. Add the mushrooms and celery, and cook for 5 minutes or until fairly soft. Add the zucchini and tomatoes to the bacon mixture, and pour in the fish stock or wine. Bring to a boil, then simmer uncovered for 5 minutes or until the sauce has thickened slightly. Remove from the heat and stir in the cod pieces and the tarragon. Season with salt and pepper, then spoon into a large, greased baking dish.

Meanwhile, bring a large pan of lightly salted water to a rolling boil. Add the pasta shells and cook according to the package directions or until tender but still firm to the bite.

For the topping, place the butter and flour in a pan, and pour in the milk. Bring to a boil slowly, whisking until thickened and smooth.

Drain the pasta thoroughly and stir into the sauce. Spoon carefully over the fish and vegetables. Place in the preheated oven and bake for 20–25 minutes until the top is lightly browned and bubbling.

HELPFUL HINT

For a speedier topping, beat together 2 eggs, 3 tablespoons plain yogurt and 3 tablespoons heavy cream; season. Add the pasta and mix. Spoon on top of the filling and bake for 15–20 minutes.

Pappardelle with Smoked Haddock & Blue Cheese Sauce

SERVES 4

12 oz. smoked haddock
2 bay leaves
1¼ cups milk
14 oz. pappardelle
   or tagliatelle
2 tbsp. butter
¼ cup all-purpose flour
⅔ cup light cream or extra milk

4 oz. Dolcelatte or
   Gorgonzola cheese, cut
   into small pieces
¼ tsp. freshly
   grated nutmeg
salt and freshly ground
   black pepper

To garnish:
⅓ cup chopped
   toasted walnuts
1 tbsp. freshly
   chopped parsley

Place the smoked haddock in a pan with 1 bay leaf and pour in the milk. Bring to a boil slowly, cover and simmer for 6–7 minutes or until the fish is opaque. Remove and roughly flake the fish, discarding the skin and any bones. Strain the milk and set aside.

Bring a large pan of lightly salted water to a rolling boil. Add the pasta and cook according to the package directions or until tender but still firm to the bite.

Meanwhile, put the butter, flour, and cream (or milk, if preferred) in a pan and stir to mix. Stir in the reserved warm milk and add the remaining bay leaf. Bring to a boil, whisking all the time, until smooth and thick. Gently simmer for 3–4 minutes, stirring frequently. Discard the bay leaf.

Add the Dolcelatte or Gorgonzola cheese to the sauce. Heat gently, stirring until melted. Add the flaked haddock and season to taste with nutmeg and salt and pepper.

Drain the pasta thoroughly and return to the pan. Add the sauce and toss gently to coat, taking care not to break up the flakes of fish. Spoon into a warmed serving bowl, sprinkle with toasted walnuts and parsley, and serve immediately.

Smoked Haddock Rösti

SERVES 4

1 lb. potatoes, peeled and
   coarsely grated
1 large onion, peeled and
   coarsely grated
2–3 garlic cloves, peeled
   and crushed
1 lb. smoked haddock

1 tbsp. olive oil
salt and freshly ground
   black pepper
2 tsp. finely grated
   lemon zest
1 tbsp. freshly
   chopped parsley

To serve:
2 tbsp. crème fraîche
lettuce leaves
lemon wedges

Dry the grated potatoes in a clean dishtowel. Rinse the grated onion thoroughly in cold water, dry in a clean dishtowel, and add to the potatoes.

Stir the garlic into the potato mixture. Skin the smoked haddock and remove as many of the tiny pin bones as possible. Cut into thin slices and set aside.

Heat the oil in a large nonstick skillet. Add half the potatoes and press down in the skillet. Season to taste with salt and pepper.

Add a layer of fish and a sprinkling of lemon zest, parsley, and a little black pepper.

Top with the remaining potatoes and press down firmly. Cover with a sheet of foil, and cook on the lowest heat for 25–30 minutes.

Preheat the broiler 2–3 minutes before the end of the cooking time. Remove the foil and place the rösti under the broiler to brown. Turn out onto a warmed serving dish, and serve immediately with spoonfuls of crème fraîche, lemon wedges, and mixed lettuce leaves.

HELPFUL HINT

Use smoked haddock fillets. Finnan or Arbroath smokies would be too bony for this dish.

Smoked Haddock Kedgeree

SERVES 4

1 lb. smoked haddock fillet
4 tbsp. butter
1 onion, peeled and
    finely chopped
2 tsp. mild curry powder
1 cup long-grain rice

2 cups fish or vegetable
    stock, heated
2 extra-large eggs, hard-
    boiled and peeled
2 tbsp. freshly
    chopped parsley

2 tbsp. whipping
    cream (optional)
salt and freshly ground
    black pepper
pinch cayenne pepper

Place the haddock in a shallow skillet, and cover with 1¼ cups water. Simmer gently for 8–10 minutes until the fish is cooked. Drain, then remove all the skin and bones from the fish, and flake into a dish. Keep warm.

Melt the butter in a saucepan and add the chopped onion and curry powder. Cook, stirring, for 3–4 minutes until the onion is soft, then stir in the rice. Cook for an additional minute, stirring continuously, then stir in the hot stock.

Cover and simmer gently for 15 minutes or until the rice has absorbed all the liquid. Cut the eggs into quarters or eighths, and add half to the mixture with half the parsley.

Carefully fold the cooked fish into the mixture and add the cream, if desired. Season to taste with salt and pepper. Heat the kedgeree until piping hot.

Transfer the mixture to a large dish, and garnish with the remaining quartered eggs and parsley, and season with a pinch of cayenne pepper. Serve immediately.

Chunky Fish Casserole

4 tbsp. butter or margarine
2 large onions, peeled and
  sliced into rings
1 red bell pepper, seeded
  and roughly chopped
1 lb. potatoes, peeled
1 lb. zucchini, trimmed and
  thickly sliced

2 tbsp. all-purpose flour
1 tbsp. paprika
2 tsp. vegetable oil
1¼ cups white wine
⅔ cup fish stock
14 oz. canned
  chopped tomatoes
2 tbsp. freshly chopped basil

salt and freshly ground
  black pepper
1 lb. firm white fish fillet,
  skinned and cut into
  1-in. cubes
fresh basil sprigs,
  to garnish
freshly cooked rice, to serve

Melt the butter or margarine in a large saucepan, add the onions and pepper, and cook for 5 minutes or until softened.

Cut the peeled potatoes into 1-in. cubes, rinse lightly, and shake dry, then add them to the onions and pepper in the saucepan. Add the zucchini and cook, stirring frequently, for an additional 2–3 minutes.

Sprinkle the flour, paprika, and vegetable oil into the saucepan and cook, stirring continuously, for 1 minute. Pour in ⅔ cup of the wine, with all the stock, and the chopped tomatoes, and bring to a boil.

Add the basil to the casserole, season to taste with salt and pepper, and cover. Simmer for 15 minutes, then add the fish and the remaining wine, and simmer very gently for an additional 5–7 minutes until the fish and vegetables are just tender. Garnish with basil sprigs and serve immediately with freshly cooked rice.

Pasta Provençale

SERVES 4

2 tbsp. olive oil
1 garlic clove, peeled
   and crushed
1 onion, peeled and
   finely chopped
1 small fennel bulb,
   trimmed, halved, and
   thinly sliced

14 oz. canned
   chopped tomatoes
1 rosemary sprig, plus extra
   sprig to garnish
12 oz. monkfish, skinned
2 tsp. lemon juice
3½ cups gnocchi pasta
½ cup pitted ripe olives

7 oz. canned flageolet beans,
   drained and rinsed
1 tbsp. freshly chopped
   oregano, plus sprig
   to garnish
salt and freshly ground
   black pepper

Heat the olive oil in a large pan. Add the garlic and onion, and cook gently for 5 minutes. Add the fennel and cook for an additional 5 minutes. Stir in the chopped tomatoes and rosemary sprig. Half-cover the pan and simmer for 10 minutes.

Cut the monkfish into bite-sized pieces and sprinkle with the lemon juice. Add to the tomatoes, cover, and simmer gently for 5 minutes or until the fish is opaque.

Meanwhile, bring a large pan of lightly salted water to a rolling boil. Add the pasta and cook according to the package directions or until the gnocchi rise to the top. Drain the pasta thoroughly and return to the saucepan.

Remove the rosemary from the tomato sauce. Stir in the ripe olives, flageolet beans, and chopped oregano, then season to taste with salt and pepper. Add the sauce to the pasta and toss gently together to coat, taking care not to break up the monkfish. Spoon into a warmed serving bowl. Garnish with rosemary and oregano sprigs, and serve immediately.

HELPFUL HINT

Only the tail of the monkfish is eaten and is usually sold skinned. It may still have a tough transparent membrane covering it, which should be carefully removed before cooking.

Mediterranean Fish Stew

SERVES 4-6

4 tbsp. olive oil
1 onion, peeled and
    finely sliced
5 garlic cloves, peeled and
    finely sliced
1 fennel bulb, trimmed and
    finely chopped
3 celery stalks, trimmed and
    finely chopped

14 oz. canned chopped
    tomatoes
1 tbsp. freshly
    chopped oregano
1 bay leaf
1 tbsp. orange zest
3 tbsp. orange juice
1 tsp. saffron strands
3 cups fish stock

3 tbsp. dry vermouth
salt and freshly ground
    black pepper
½ lb. thick haddock fillets
½ lb. sea bass fillets
2 cups shelled jumbo shrimp
crusty bread, to serve

Heat the olive oil in a large saucepan. Add the onion, garlic, fennel, and celery, and cook over a low heat for 15 minutes, stirring frequently, until the vegetables are soft and just beginning to turn brown.

Add the canned tomatoes with their juice, the oregano, bay leaf, orange zest, orange juice, and saffron strands. Bring to a boil, reduce the heat, and simmer for 5 minutes. Add the fish stock, vermouth, and season to taste with salt and pepper. Bring to a boil. Reduce the heat and simmer for 20 minutes.

Wipe or rinse the haddock and sea bass fillets and remove as many of the bones as possible. Place on a chopping board and cut into 2-inch cubes. Add to the saucepan and cook for 3 minutes. Add the shrimp and cook for an additional 5 minutes. Adjust the seasoning to taste and serve with crusty bread.

HELPFUL HINT

Use the list of fish here as a guideline – any combination of fish and shellfish that you prefer will work well in a stew such as this.

Fish Crisp

SERVES 6

1 lb. white fish fillets
1¼ cups milk
salt and freshly ground
    black pepper
1 tbsp. sunflower oil
6 tbsp. butter or margarine
1 medium onion, peeled and
    finely chopped
2 leeks, trimmed and sliced

1 medium carrot, peeled
    and diced
2 medium potatoes, peeled
    and cut into small pieces
1½ cups all-purpose flour
1½ cups fish or
    vegetable stock
2 tbsp. whipping cream
1 tsp. freshly chopped dill

For the crumble topping:
6 tbsp. butter or margarine
1½ cups all-purpose flour
¾ cup grated
    Parmesan cheese
¾ tsp. cayenne pepper

Preheat the oven to 400˚F. Grease a pie pan. Place the fish in a saucepan with the milk, salt, and pepper. Bring to a boil, cover, and simmer for 8–10 minutes until the fish is cooked. Remove with a slotted spoon, setting aside the cooking liquid. Flake the fish into the prepared dish.

Heat the oil and 1 tablespoon of the butter or margarine in a small skillet and gently fry the onion, leeks, carrot, and potatoes for 1–2 minutes. Cover tightly, and cook over a gentle heat for an additional 10 minutes until softened. Spoon the vegetables over the fish.

Melt the remaining butter or margarine in a saucepan, add the flour, and cook for 1 minute, stirring. Whisk in the cooking liquid and the stock. Cook until thickened, then stir in the cream. Remove from the heat and stir in the dill. Pour over the fish.

To make the crumble, rub the butter or margarine into the flour until the mixture resembles bread crumbs, then stir in the cheese and cayenne pepper. Sprinkle over the dish, and bake in the oven for 20 minutes.

Traditional Fish Pie

SERVES 4

1 lb. white fish
   fillets, skinned
2 cups milk
1 small onion, peeled
   and quartered
salt and freshly ground
   black pepper

5 cups peeled and coarsely
   diced potatoes
7 tbsp. butter
¼ lb. large shrimp, peeled
2 extra-large eggs, hard-
   boiled and quartered

7 oz. canned corn, drained
2 tbsp. freshly
   chopped parsley
3 tbsp. all-purpose flour
½ cup shredded
   cheddar cheese

Preheat the oven to 400°F. Place the fish in a shallow skillet, pour 1¾ cups of the milk over, and add the onion. Season to taste with salt and pepper. Bring to a boil and simmer for 8–10 minutes until the fish is cooked. Remove the fish with a slotted spoon and place in a baking dish. Strain the cooking liquid and set aside.

Boil the potatoes until soft, then mash with the 3 tablespoons of butter and 2–3 tablespoons of the remaining milk. Set aside.

Arrange the shrimp and sliced eggs on top of the fish, then sprinkle with the corn and parsley.

Melt the remaining butter in a saucepan, stir in the flour, and cook gently for 1 minute, stirring. Whisk in the cooking liquid and remaining milk. Cook for 2 minutes or until thickened, then pour over the fish mixture and cool slightly.

Spread the mashed potato over the top of the pie and sprinkle the cheese over the top. Bake in the preheated oven for 30 minutes, until golden. Serve immediately.

TASTY TIP

Any variety of white fish may be used here, including haddock, hake, pollock and whiting. You could also used smoked cod or haddock. After simmering in milk, carefully check and remove any bones.

Coconut Fish Curry

SERVES 4

2 tbsp. sunflower oil
1 medium onion, peeled and
   very finely chopped
1 yellow bell pepper, seeded
   and finely chopped
1 garlic clove, peeled
   and crushed
1 tbsp. mild curry paste
1-in. piece of ginger, peeled
   and grated

1 red chile, seeded and
   finely chopped
14 oz. canned coconut milk
1½ lb. firm white fish,
   skinned and cut
   into chunks
1⅓ cups basmati rice
1 tbsp. freshly
   chopped cilantro
1 tbsp. mango chutney

salt and freshly ground
   black pepper

To garnish
lime wedges
fresh cilantro sprigs

To serve:
plain yogurt
warm naan bread

Put 1 tablespoon of the oil into a large skillet and cook the onion, pepper, and garlic for 5 minutes or until soft. Add the remaining oil, curry paste, ginger, and chile, and cook for an additional minute.

Pour in the coconut milk and bring to a boil. Reduce the heat and simmer gently for 5 minutes, stirring occasionally. Add the fish to the pan and continue to simmer gently for 5–10 minutes or until the fish is tender, but not overcooked.

Meanwhile, cook the rice in a saucepan of salted boiling water for 15 minutes or until tender. Drain the rice thoroughly and turn out into a serving dish.

Stir the chopped cilantro and chutney gently into the fish curry, and season to taste with salt and pepper. Spoon the fish curry over the cooked rice, garnish with lime wedges and cilantro sprigs, and serve immediately with spoonfuls of plain yogurt and warm naan bread.

Crispy Shrimp Stir–Fry

3 tbsp. soy sauce
1 tsp. cornstarch
pinch sugar
6 tbsp. peanut oil
1 lb. raw shelled jumbo shrimp, halved lengthwise

2 medium carrots, peeled and cut into matchsticks
1-in. piece fresh ginger, peeled and cut into matchsticks
1 cup snow peas, trimmed and shredded

½ cup asparagus spears, cut into short lengths
¾ cup bean sprouts
¼ head Chinese cabbage or bok choy, shredded
2 tsp. sesame oil

Mix together the soy sauce, cornstarch, and sugar in a small bowl, and set aside.

Heat a large wok, then add 3 tablespoons of the oil, and heat until almost smoking. Add the shrimp and stir-fry for 4 minutes or until pink all over. Using a slotted spoon, transfer the shrimp to a plate and set aside in a warm oven.

Add the remaining oil to the wok, and when just smoking, add the carrots and ginger, and stir-fry for 1 minute or until slightly softened, then add the snow peas and stir-fry for an additional minute. Add the asparagus and stir-fry for 4 minutes or until softened.

Add the bean sprouts and Chinese cabbage, and stir-fry for 2 minutes or until the cabbage is slightly wilted. Pour in the soy sauce mixture and return the shrimp to the wok. Stir-fry over a medium heat until piping hot, then add the sesame oil, give a final stir, and serve immediately.

HELPFUL HINT

The long list of ingredients need not be daunting. Good preparation saves a lot of time. Cut everything into small, uniform pieces and have everything ready before starting to cook.

Szechuan Chili Shrimp

SERVES 4

1 lb. raw jumbo shrimp
2 tbsp. peanut oil
1 onion, peeled and sliced
1 red bell pepper, seeded
 and cut into strips
1 small red chile, seeded
 and thinly sliced

2 garlic cloves, peeled and
 finely chopped
2–3 scallions, trimmed and
 diagonally sliced
cilantro sprigs or chile
 flowers, to garnish
freshly cooked rice or
 noodles, to serve

For the chili sauce:
1 tbsp. cornstarch
4 tbsp. cold fish stock
 or water
2 tbsp. soy sauce
2 tbsp. sweet or hot chili
 sauce, or to taste
2 tsp. light brown sugar

Peel the shrimp, leaving the tails attached, if desired. Using a sharp knife, remove the black veins along the back of the shrimp. Rinse and pat dry with paper towels.

Heat a wok or large skillet, add the oil, and, when hot, add the onion, bell pepper, and chile, and stir-fry for 4–5 minutes or until the vegetables are tender but retain a bite. Stir in the garlic and cook for 30 seconds. Using a slotted spoon, transfer to a plate and set aside.

Add the shrimp to the wok, and stir-fry for 1–2 minutes or until they turn pink and opaque.

Blend all the chili sauce ingredients together in a bowl or pitcher, then stir into the shrimp. Add the vegetables and bring to a boil, stirring constantly. Cook for 1–2 minutes until the sauce is thickened and the shrimp and vegetables are well coated.

Stir in the scallions, tip onto a warmed platter, and garnish with chile flowers or cilantro sprigs. Serve immediately with freshly cooked rice or noodles.

Cheesy Vegetable & Shrimp Bake

SERVES 4

1 cup long-grain rice
salt and freshly ground
    black pepper
1 garlic clove, peeled
    and crushed
1 extra-large egg, beaten

3 tbsp. freshly
    shredded basil
4 tbsp. grated
    Parmesan cheese
¼ lb. baby asparagus spears,
    trimmed
1 cup trimmed baby carrots

1 cup trimmed green beans
¼ lb. cherry tomatoes
1 cup peeled cooked shrimp,
    thawed if frozen
¼ lb. mozzarella cheese,
    thinly sliced

Preheat the oven to 400°F. Cook the rice in lightly salted, boiling water for 12–15 minutes until tender and drain. Stir in the garlic, beaten egg, shredded basil, 2 tablespoons of the Parmesan cheese, and season to taste with salt, and pepper. Press this mixture into a greased 9-in. square, ovenproof dish and set aside.

Bring a large saucepan of water to a boil, then drop in the asparagus, carrots, and green beans. Return to a boil and cook for 3–4 minutes. Drain and let cool.

Quarter or halve the cherry tomatoes, and mix them into the cooled vegetables. Spread the prepared vegetables over the rice, and top with the shrimp. Season to taste with salt and pepper.

Cover the shrimp with the mozzarella, and sprinkle with the remaining Parmesan cheese. Bake in the preheated oven for 20–25 minutes until piping hot and golden brown in places. Serve immediately.

FOOD FACT

Mozzarella cheese
becomes stringy
when cooked, so should
be sliced as thinly as
possible here.

Scallops with Black Bean Sauce

SERVES 4

1½ lbs. scallops, with
  their coral
2 tbsp. vegetable oil
2–3 tbsp. Chinese fermented
  black beans, rinsed,
  drained, and
  coarsely chopped

2 garlic cloves, peeled and
  finely chopped
1½-in. piece ginger, peeled
  and finely chopped
4–5 scallions, thinly sliced
  diagonally
2–3 tbsp. soy sauce

1½ tbsp. Chinese rice wine or
  dry sherry
1–2 tsp. sugar
1 tbsp. fish stock or water
2–3 dashes hot pepper sauce
1 tbsp. sesame oil
freshly cooked noodles,
  to serve

Pat the scallops dry with paper towels. Carefully separate the orange coral from the scallop. Peel off and discard the membrane and thick, opaque muscle that attaches the coral to the scallop. Cut any large scallops crosswise in half, leaving the corals whole.

Heat a wok or large skillet, add the oil, and, when hot, add the white scallop meat and stir-fry for 2 minutes or until just beginning to brown on the edges. Using a slotted spoon or spatula, transfer to a plate. Set aside.

Add the black beans, garlic, and ginger, and stir-fry for 1 minute. Add the scallions, soy sauce, Chinese rice wine or sherry, sugar, fish stock or water, hot pepper sauce, and the corals, and stir until mixed.

Return the scallops and juices to the wok, and stir gently for 3 minutes or until the scallops and corals are cooked through. Add a little more stock or water if necessary. Stir in the sesame oil, and turn into a heated serving dish. Serve immediately with noodles.

Mussels Arrabbiata

SERVES 4

4 lbs. mussels
3–4 tbsp. olive oil
1 large onion, peeled
  and sliced
4 garlic cloves, peeled and
  finely chopped

1 red chile, seeded and
  finely chopped
2 lb. 10 oz. canned
  chopped tomatoes
⅔ cup white wine
1 cup halved and pitted
  ripe olives

salt and freshly ground
  black pepper
2 tbsp. freshly
  chopped parsley
crusty bread, to serve

Clean the mussels by scrubbing with a small, soft brush, removing the beard and any barnacles from the shells. Discard any mussels that are open or have damaged shells. Place in a large bowl and cover with cold water. Change the water frequently before cooking, and leave in the refrigerator until needed.

Heat the olive oil in a large saucepan and fry the onion, garlic, and chili until soft but not colored. Add the tomatoes and bring to a boil, then simmer for 15 minutes.

Add the white wine to the tomato sauce, bring the sauce to a boil, and add the mussels. Cover and carefully shake the saucepan. Cook the mussels for 5–7 minutes until the shells have opened.

Add the olives to the saucepan and cook uncovered for about 5 minutes to warm through. Season to taste with salt and pepper, and sprinkle over the chopped parsley. Discard any mussels that have not opened, and serve immediately with lots of crusty bread.

Meat

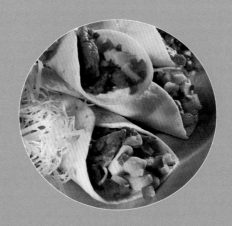

Grilled Steaks with Saffron Potatoes & Roast Tomatoes

SERVES 4

1½ lb. halved new potatoes
few strands of saffron
1¼ cups vegetable or
   beef stock
1 small onion, peeled and
   finely chopped

6 tbsp. butter
salt and freshly ground
   black pepper
2 tsp. balsamic vinegar
2 tbsp. olive oil
1 tsp. superfine sugar

8 plum tomatoes, halved
4 boneless steaks, each
   weighing ½ lb.
2 tbsp. freshly
   chopped parsley

Cook the potatoes in salted, boiling water for 8 minutes and drain well. Return the potatoes to the saucepan, along with the saffron, stock, onion, and one third of the butter. Season to taste with salt and pepper, and simmer uncovered for 10 minutes until the potatoes are tender.

Meanwhile, turn on the broiler. Mix together the vinegar, olive oil, and sugar, and season to taste. Arrange the tomatoes cut-side up in a broiler pan lined with aluminum foil, and drizzle over the dressing. Broil for 12–15 minutes, basting occasionally, until tender.

Melt the remaining butter in a large skillet. Add the steaks and cook for 4–8 minutes, to taste.

Arrange the potatoes and tomatoes on the middles of four serving plates. Top with the steaks, along with any pan juices. Sprinkle over the parsley and serve immediately.

HELPFUL HINT

You can tell how well a steak is cooked by lightly pressing on it with your fingertips – the less the resistance, the rarer the meat.

Fillet Steaks with Tomato & Garlic Sauce

SERVES 4

1½ lb. ripe tomatoes
2 garlic cloves
2 tbsp. olive oil
2 tbsp. freshly chopped basil
2 tbsp. freshly
  chopped oregano

2 tbsp. red wine
salt and freshly ground
  black pepper
½ cup chopped pitted
  ripe olives
4 fillet steaks

freshly cooked vegetables,
  to serve

Make a small cross on the top of each tomato and place in a large bowl. Cover with boiling water and leave for 2 minutes. Using a slotted spoon, remove the tomatoes and peel carefully. Repeat until all the tomatoes are peeled. Place on a chopping board, cut into quarters, remove the seeds, chop coarsely, and then set aside.

Peel and chop the garlic. Heat half the olive oil in a saucepan and cook the garlic for 30 seconds. Add the chopped tomatoes with the basil, oregano, and red wine, and season to taste with salt and pepper. Bring to a boil, then reduce the heat, cover, and simmer for 15 minutes, stirring occasionally, until the sauce is reduced and thickened. Stir the olives into the sauce and keep warm while cooking the steaks.

Meanwhile, lightly oil a heavy skillet with the remaining olive oil and cook the steaks for 2 minutes on each side to seal. Continue to cook the steaks for an additional 2–4 minutes, depending on personal preference. Serve the steaks immediately with the garlic sauce and freshly cooked vegetables.

HELPFUL HINT

Raw fillet steak should be a deep mahogany with a good marbling of fat. If the meat is bright red or the fat bright white, the meat has not been aged properly and will probably be quite tough.

Pasta with Beef, Capers & Olives

SERVES 4

2 tbsp. olive oil
11 oz. rump steak, trimmed
    and cut into strips
4 scallions, trimmed
    and sliced
2 garlic cloves, peeled
    and chopped
2 zucchini, trimmed and cut
    into strips

1 red bell pepper, seeded
    and cut into strips
2 tsp. freshly
    chopped oregano
2 tbsp. capers, drained
    and rinsed
4 tbsp. sliced pitted
    ripe olives

14 oz. canned
    chopped tomatoes
salt and freshly ground
    black pepper
1 lb. fettuccine
1 tbsp. freshly
    chopped parsley,
    to garnish

Heat the olive oil in a large skillet over a high heat. Add the steak and cook, stirring, for 3–4 minutes until browned. Remove from the pan using a slotted spoon and set aside.

Lower the heat, add the scallions and garlic to the pan, and cook for 1 minute. Add the zucchini and bell pepper, and cook for 3–4 minutes.

Add the oregano, capers, and olives to the pan with the chopped tomatoes. Season to taste with salt and pepper, then simmer for 7 minutes, stirring occasionally. Return the beef to the pan and simmer for 3–5 minutes until the sauce has thickened slightly.

Meanwhile, bring a large pan of lightly salted water to a rolling boil. Add the pasta and cook according to the package directions until tender but still firm to the bite.

Drain the pasta thoroughly. Return to the pan and add the beef sauce. Toss gently until the pasta is lightly coated. Spoon into a warmed serving dish or onto individual plates. Sprinkle with chopped parsley and serve immediately.

TASTY TIP

It is important that the beef fries rather than steams, giving a beautifully brown and caramelized outside, while keeping the middle moist and tender. Make sure that the oil in the pan is hot.

Spaghetti Bolognese

SERVES 4

1 carrot
2 celery stalks
1 onion
2 garlic cloves
2 cups lean ground beef
2 cups bacon, chopped
1 tbsp. all-purpose flour
⅔ cup red wine

14 oz. canned chopped
  tomatoes
2 tbsp. tomato paste
2 tsp. dried mixed herbs
pinch sugar
salt and freshly ground
  black pepper
4 cups spaghetti

fresh oregano sprigs,
  to garnish
Parmesan cheese shavings,
  to serve

Peel and chop the carrot, trim and chop the celery, then peel and chop the onion and garlic. Heat a large nonstick skillet and sauté the beef and bacon for 5–10 minutes, stirring occasionally until browned. Add the prepared vegetables to the skillet and cook for about 3 minutes until softened, stirring occasionally.

Add the flour and cook for 1 minute. Stir in the red wine, tomatoes, tomato paste, mixed herbs, and sugar and season to taste with salt and pepper. Bring to a boil, then cover and simmer for 45 minutes, stirring occasionally.

Meanwhile, bring a large saucepan of lightly salted water to a boil and cook the spaghetti for 10–12 minutes until tender but still firm to the bite. Drain well and divide among four serving plates. Spoon over the sauce, garnish with a few sprigs of oregano, and serve immediately with plenty of Parmesan shavings.

Traditional Lasagne

2 cups lean ground beef
¾ cup chopped pancetta
  or bacon
1 large onion, peeled
  and chopped
2 celery stalks, trimmed
  and chopped
1 cup wiped and chopped
  button mushrooms
2 garlic cloves, peeled
  and chopped
1 cup all-purpose flour
1¼ cups beef stock
1 tbsp. dried mixed herbs
5 tbsp. tomato paste
salt and freshly ground
  black pepper
6 tbsp. butter
1 tsp. mustard powder
pinch freshly grated nutmeg
3 cups milk
1¼ cups grated Parmesan
  cheese
1 cup shredded cheddar cheese
8–12 precooked
  lasagna noodles

To serve:
crusty bread
fresh green salad leaves

Preheat the oven to 400°F. Cook the beef and pancetta in a large, heavy saucepan for 10 minutes, stirring to break up any lumps. Add the onion, celery, and mushrooms, and cook for 4 minutes or until softened slightly.

Stir in the garlic and 1 tablespoon of the flour, then cook for 1 minute. Stir in the stock, herbs, and tomato paste. Season to taste with salt and pepper. Bring to a boil, then cover, reduce the heat, and simmer for 45 minutes.

Meanwhile, melt the butter in a small saucepan and stir in the remaining flour, mustard powder, and nutmeg until well blended. Cook for 2 minutes. Remove from the heat and gradually blend in the milk until smooth. Return to the heat and bring to a boil, stirring until thickened. Gradually stir in half the Parmesan and cheddar until melted. Season to taste.

Spoon half the meat mixture into the base of a large ovenproof dish. Top with a single layer of pasta. Spread over half the sauce and sprinkle with half the cheese. Repeat layers, finishing with cheese. Cook in the preheated oven for 30 minutes or until the pasta is cooked and the top is golden brown and bubbly. Serve immediately with crusty bread and a green salad.

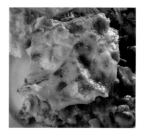

Beef Fajitas with Avocado Salsa

SERVES 3–6

2 tbsp. corn oil	8 oz. canned chopped	1 shallot, peeled and chopped
1-lb. rump steak, trimmed	tomatoes	1 large tomato, peeled,
and cut into strips	7 oz. canned red kidney	seeded, and chopped
2 garlic cloves, peeled	beans, drained	1 red chile, diced
and crushed	1 tbsp. freshly	1 tbsp. lemon juice
1 tsp. ground cumin	chopped cilantro	6 large flour tortillas
¼ tsp. cayenne pepper	1 avocado, peeled, pitted,	3–4 tbsp. sour cream
1 tbsp. paprika	and chopped	green salad, to serve

Heat the wok, add the oil, then stir-fry the beef for 3–4 minutes. Add the garlic and spices, and cook for an additional 2 minutes. Stir the tomatoes into the wok, bring to a boil, cover, and simmer gently for 5 minutes.

Meanwhile, blend the kidney beans in a food processor until slightly broken up, then add to the wok. Continue to cook for an additional 5 minutes, adding 2–3 tablespoons of water. The mixture should be thick and fairly dry. Stir in the chopped cilantro.

Mix the chopped avocado, shallot, tomato, chile, and lemon juice together. Spoon into a serving dish and set aside.

When ready to serve, warm the flour tortillas and spread with a little sour cream. Place a spoonful of the beef mixture on top, followed by a spoonful of the avocado salsa, then roll up. Repeat until all the mixture is used up. Serve immediately with a green salad.

HELPFUL HINT

Don't make the avocado salsa too far in advance, as avocado has a tendency to discolor. If you do need to make it some time ahead, cover the surface of the sauce with plastic wrap.

Chili con Carne with Crispy–Skinned Potatoes

SERVES 4

2 tbsp. vegetable oil, plus
   extra for brushing
1 large onion, peeled and
   finely chopped
1 garlic clove, peeled and
   finely chopped
1 red chile, seeded and
   finely chopped

1 lb. chuck steak, finely
   chopped, or lean
   ground beef
1 tbsp. chili powder
14 oz. canned
   chopped tomatoes
2 tbsp. tomato paste
4 large baking potatoes

coarse salt and freshly
   ground black pepper
14 oz. canned red kidney
   beans, drained and rinsed

To serve:
guacamole
sour cream

Preheat the oven to 300°F. Heat the oil in a large flameproof casserole and add the onion. Cook gently for 10 minutes until soft and lightly browned. Add the garlic and chile, and cook briefly. Increase the heat. Add the steak or ground beef and cook for an additional 10 minutes, stirring occasionally, until browned.

Add the chili powder and stir well. Cook for about 2 minutes, then add the chopped tomatoes and tomato paste. Bring slowly to a boil. Cover and cook in the preheated oven for 1½ hours.

Meanwhile, brush a little vegetable oil all over the potatoes and rub on some coarse salt. Put the potatoes in the oven alongside the chili.

To serve, remove the chili from the oven and stir in the kidney beans. Return to the oven for an additional 15 minutes. Cut a cross in each potato, then squeeze to open slightly, and season to taste with salt and pepper. Serve with the chili, guacamole, and sour cream.

TASTY TIP

To make guacamole, mash 1 large peeled, stoned avocado in a bowl with 2 tablespoons each of lemon juice and crème fraîche, ¼ teaspoon Tabasco, 1 crushed garlic clove, and salt and pepper.

Spicy Chili Beef

2 tbsp. olive oil
1 onion, peeled and
   finely chopped
1 red bell pepper, seeded
   and sliced
5 cups ground beef
2 garlic cloves, peeled
   and crushed

2 red chiles, seeded and
   finely sliced
salt and freshly ground
   black pepper
14 oz. canned
   chopped tomatoes
2 tbsp. tomato paste
14 oz. canned red kidney
   beans, drained

2 oz. good-quality dark
   chocolate, grated
3 cups dried fusilli
pat of butter
2 tbsp. freshly chopped
   Italian flat-leaf parsley
paprika, to garnish
sour cream, to serve

Heat the olive oil in a large heavy pan. Add the onion and red bell pepper, and cook for 5 minutes or until beginning to soften. Add the ground beef and cook over a high heat for 5–8 minutes until the meat is browned. Stir with a wooden spoon during cooking to break up any lumps in the meat. Add the garlic and chiles, fry for 1 minute, then season to taste.

Add the chopped tomatoes, tomato paste, and the kidney beans to the pan. Bring to a boil, lower the heat, and simmer covered for at least 40 minutes, stirring occasionally. Stir in the grated chocolate and cook for 3 minutes or until melted.

Meanwhile, bring a large pan of lightly salted water to a rolling boil. Add the fusilli and cook according to the package directions until tender but still firm to the bite.

Drain the pasta, return to the pan, and toss with the butter and parsley. Spoon into a warmed serving dish or spoon onto individual plates. Spoon the sauce over the pasta. Sprinkle with paprika and serve immediately with spoonfuls of sour cream.

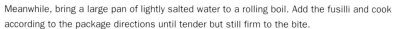

Beef Teriyaki with Green & Black Rice

SERVES 4

3 tbsp. sake (Japanese rice wine)
3 tbsp. dry sherry
3 tbsp. dark soy sauce
1½ tbsp. brown sugar

4 trimmed steaks, each weighing 6 oz.
2 cups mixed long-grain and wild rice
1-in. piece ginger
½ lb. snow peas

salt
6 scallions, trimmed and cut into fine strips

In a small saucepan, gently heat the sake, dry sherry, dark soy sauce, and sugar until the sugar has dissolved. Increase the heat and bring to a boil. Remove from the heat and leave until cold. Lightly wipe the steaks, place in a shallow dish, and pour the sake mixture over. Cover loosely and marinate in the refrigerator for at least 1 hour, spooning the marinade over the steaks occasionally.

Cook the rice with the ginger, according to the package's instructions. Drain well, then remove and discard the piece of ginger.

Slice the snow peas thinly lengthwise into fine shreds. Plunge into a saucepan of salted, boiling water, return the water to a boil, and drain immediately. Stir the drained snow peas and scallions into the hot rice.

Meanwhile, heat a griddle until almost smoking. Remove the steaks from the marinade and cook on the hot griddle for 3–4 minutes each side, depending on the thickness.

Place the remaining marinade in a saucepan and bring to a boil. Simmer rapidly for 2 minutes and remove from the heat. When the steaks are cooked as desired, allow to rest for 2–3 minutes, then slice thinly and serve with the rice and the hot marinade.

Beef with Paprika

SERVES 4

1½-lb. rump steak
3 tbsp. all-purpose flour
salt and freshly ground
    black pepper
1 tbsp. paprika
1½ cups long-grain rice
6 tbsp. butter

1 tsp. oil
1 onion, peeled and thinly
    sliced into rings
2 cups wiped and sliced
    button mushrooms
2 tsp. dry sherry
⅔ cup sour cream

2 tbsp. freshly cut chives
chive bundles, to garnish

Beat the steak until very thin, then trim off and discard the fat and cut into thin strips. Season the flour with the salt, pepper, and paprika, then toss the steak in the flour until coated.

Meanwhile place the rice in a saucepan of boiling salted water, and simmer for 15 minutes until tender or according to the package directions. Drain the rice, then return to the saucepan, add ¼ stick of the butter, cover and keep warm.

Heat the wok, then add the oil and ¼ stick of the butter. When hot, stir-fry the meat for 3–5 minutes until sealed. Remove from the wok with a slotted spoon and set aside. Add the remaining butter to the wok and stir-fry the onion rings and button mushrooms for 3–4 minutes.

Add the sherry while the wok is very hot, then turn down the heat. Return the steak to the wok with the sour cream and seasoning to taste. Heat through until piping hot, then sprinkle with the cut chives. Garnish with bundles of chives, and serve immediately with the cooked rice.

TASTY TIP

The button mushrooms in this recipe could be replaced by exotic or wild mushrooms. Chanterelles go particularly well with beef, as do porcini.

Leek & Ham Risotto

1 tbsp. olive oil
2 tbsp. butter
1 medium onion, peeled and
   finely chopped
4 leeks, trimmed and
   thinly sliced

1½ tbsp. freshly
   chopped thyme
2 cups Arborio rice
5½ cups vegetable or chicken
   stock, heated
½ lb. cooked ham

1¼ cups peas, thawed
   if frozen
½ cup grated
   Parmesan cheese
salt and freshly ground
   black pepper

Heat the oil and half the butter together in a large saucepan. Add the onion and leeks, and cook over a medium heat for 6–8 minutes, stirring occasionally, until soft and beginning to color. Stir in the thyme and cook briefly.

Add the rice and stir well. Continue stirring over a medium heat for about 1 minute until the rice is glossy. Add a ladleful or two of the stock, and stir well until the stock is absorbed. Continue adding stock, a ladleful at a time, stirring well between additions, until about two thirds of the stock has been added.

Meanwhile, either chop or finely shred the ham, then add to the saucepan of rice, together with the peas. Continue adding ladlefuls of stock, until the rice is tender and the ham is heated through completely.

Add the remaining butter, sprinkle with the Parmesan cheese, and season to taste with salt and pepper. When the butter has melted and the cheese has softened, stir well to incorporate. Taste and adjust the seasoning, then serve immediately.

Risi e Bisi

SERVES 4

2 tbsp. unsalted butter
1 tsp. olive oil
3 slices pancetta or
    bacon, chopped
1 small onion, peeled and
    finely chopped
1 garlic clove, peeled and
    finely chopped
5¼ cups vegetable stock

pinch sugar
1 tsp. lemon juice
1 bay leaf
1½ cups peas, thawed
    if frozen
1 cup risotto rice
3 tbsp. freshly chopped
    parsley

½ cup finely grated
    Parmesan cheese
salt and freshly ground
    black pepper

To garnish:
fresh parsley sprig
julienned orange rind strips

Melt the butter and olive oil together in a large, heavy saucepan. Add the chopped pancetta or bacon, the chopped onion and garlic, and gently cook for about 10 minutes or until the onion is softened and is just beginning to brown.

Pour in the vegetable stock, then add the sugar, lemon juice, and bay leaf. Add the fresh peas, if using. Bring the mixture to a fast boil.

Add the rice, stir, and simmer uncovered for about 20 minutes until the rice is tender. Occasionally, stir the mixture gently while it cooks. If using frozen peas, stir them into the rice about 2 minutes before the end of the cooking time.

When the rice is cooked, remove the bay leaf and discard. Stir in 2½ tablespoons of the chopped parsley and the Parmesan cheese. Season to taste with salt and pepper.

Transfer the rice to a large serving dish. Garnish with the remaining chopped parsley, a sprig of fresh parsley, and julienned strips of orange rind. Serve immediately while piping hot.

Italian Risotto

1 onion, peeled
2 garlic cloves, peeled
1 tbsp. olive oil
2 cups chopped
   Italian salami
½ cup asparagus tips
1½ cups risotto rice

1¼ cups dry white wine
4 cups chicken
   stock, warmed
¾ cup frozen fava
   beans, thawed
1 cup diced dolcelatte or
   blue cheese

3 tbsp. freshly chopped
   mixed herbs, such as
   parsley and basil
salt and freshly ground
   black pepper

Chop the onion and garlic, and set aside. Heat the olive oil in a large skillet, and cook the salami for 3–5 minutes until golden. Transfer to a plate and keep warm. Add the asparagus and stir-fry for 2–3 minutes until just wilted. Transfer to the plate with the salami. Add the onion and garlic, and cook for 5 minutes or until softened.

Add the rice to the skillet and cook for 2 minutes. Add the wine, bring to a boil, then simmer, stirring until the wine has been absorbed. Add half the stock and return to a boil. Simmer, stirring, until the liquid has been absorbed.

Add half of the remaining stock and the fava beans to the rice mixture. Bring to a boil, then simmer for an additional 5–10 minutes until all of the liquid has been absorbed.

Add the remaining stock, bring to a boil, then simmer until all the liquid is absorbed and the rice is tender. Stir in the remaining ingredients until the cheese has just melted. Serve immediately.

Prosciutto & Gruyère Carbonara

SERVES 4

3 large egg yolks
½ cup shredded
  Gruyère cheese
2 tbsp. olive oil
2 garlic cloves, peeled
  and crushed

2 shallots, peeled and
  finely chopped
7 oz. prosciutto ham, cut
  into strips
4 tbsp. dry vermouth
1 lb. spaghetti

salt and freshly ground
  black pepper
1 tbsp. butter
1 tbsp. freshly shredded
  basil leaves
basil sprigs, to garnish

Place the egg yolks with 6 tablespoons of the Gruyère cheese in a bowl and mix lightly until well blended, then set aside.

Heat the olive oil in a large pan, and cook the garlic and shallots for 5 minutes or until golden-brown. Add the prosciutto ham, then cook for an additional minute. Pour in the dry vermouth and simmer for 2 minutes, then remove from the heat. Season to taste with salt and pepper and keep warm.

Meanwhile, bring a large pan of lightly salted water to a rolling boil. Add the pasta and cook according to the package directions until tender but still firm to the bite. Drain thoroughly, setting aside 4 tablespoons of the water, and return the pasta to the pan.

Remove from the heat, then add the egg and cheese mixture with the butter to the pasta; toss lightly until coated. Add the prosciutto mixture and toss again, adding the pasta water, if needed, to moisten. Season to taste and sprinkle with the remaining Gruyère cheese and the shredded basil leaves. Garnish with basil sprigs and serve immediately.

Special Rösti

SERVES 4

1½ lb. potatoes, scrubbed but not peeled
salt and freshly ground black pepper
6 tbsp. butter
1 large onion, peeled and finely chopped

1 garlic clove, peeled and crushed
2 tbsp. freshly chopped parsley
1 tbsp. olive oil
scant ¼ lb. prosciutto, thinly sliced

½ cup chopped sun-dried tomatoes
1½ cups shredded Emmentaler cheese
mixed green salad, to serve

Cook the potatoes in a large saucepan of salted, boiling water for about 10 minutes until just tender. Drain in a colander, then rinse in cold water. Drain again. Leave until cool enough to handle, then peel off the skins.

Melt the butter in a large skillet and gently fry the onion and garlic for about 3 minutes until softened and beginning to color. Remove from the heat.

Shred the potatoes into a large bowl, then stir in the onion and garlic mixture. Sprinkle over the parsley and stir well to mix. Season to taste with salt and pepper.

Heat the oil in the frying pan and cover the bottom of the pan with half the potato mixture. Lay the slices of prosciutto on top. Sprinkle with the chopped sun-dried tomatoes first, then with the Emmentaler cheese.

Finally, top with the remaining potato mixture. Cook over a low heat, pressing down with a palette knife from time to time, for 10–15 minutes until the bottom is golden brown. Carefully invert the rösti onto a large plate, then carefully slide it back into the pan and cook the other side until golden. Serve cut into wedges, with a mixed green salad.

HELPFUL HINT

To make sure the rösti is the right thickness, you will need a heavy, nonstick skillet with a diameter of about 9 in.

Gnocchi & Prosciutto Bake

SERVES 4

3 tbsp. olive oil
1 red onion, peeled
   and sliced
2 garlic cloves, peeled
3 plum tomatoes, skinned
   and quartered
2 tbsp. sun-dried
   tomato paste

1 cup mascarpone cheese
salt and freshly ground
   black pepper
1 tbsp. freshly
   chopped tarragon
11 oz. fresh gnocchi
1 cup grated cheddar or
   Parmesan cheese

1 cup fresh white
   bread crumbs
2 oz. prosciutto, sliced
10 pitted green
   olives, halved
sprigs of Italian flat-leaf
   parsley, to garnish

Heat the oven to 350˚F. Heat 2 tablespoons of the olive oil in a large skillet and cook the onion and garlic for 5 minutes or until softened. Stir in the tomatoes, sun-dried tomato paste, and mascarpone cheese. Season to taste with salt and pepper. Add half the tarragon. Bring to a boil, then lower the heat immediately and simmer for 5 minutes.

Meanwhile, bring 8 cups water to a boil in a large pan. Add the remaining olive oil and a good pinch of salt. Add the gnocchi and cook for 1–2 minutes or until they rise to the surface.

Drain the gnocchi thoroughly and transfer to a large ovenproof dish. Add the tomato sauce and toss gently to coat the pasta. Combine the cheddar or Parmesan cheese with the bread crumbs and remaining tarragon and spread over the pasta mixture. Top with the prosciutto and olives and season again.

Cook in the preheated oven for 20–25 minutes until golden and bubbling. Serve immediately, garnished with parsley sprigs.

HELPFUL HINT

Use a large pan of boiling water so that the gnocchi have plenty of room to move around, otherwise they will stick together during cooking. Alternatively, cook the gnocchi in two batches.

Chorizo with Pasta in a Tomato Sauce

SERVES 4

2 tbsp. butter
2 tbsp. olive oil
2 large onions, peeled and
    finely sliced
1 tsp. brown sugar
2 garlic cloves, peeled
    and crushed

8 oz. chorizo, sliced
1 chile, seeded and
    finely sliced
14 oz. canned
    chopped tomatoes
1 tbsp. sun-dried
    tomato paste

⅔ cup red wine
salt and freshly ground
    black pepper
4 cups rigatoni
freshly chopped parsley,
    to garnish

Melt the butter with the olive oil in a large heavy pan. Add the onions and sugar, and cook over a very low heat, stirring occasionally, for 15 minutes or until soft and starting to caramelize.

Add the garlic and chorizo to the pan and cook for 5 minutes. Stir in the chile, chopped tomatoes, and tomato paste, and pour in the wine. Season well with salt and pepper. Bring to a boil, cover, reduce the heat, and simmer for 30 minutes, stirring occasionally. Remove the lid and simmer for an additional 10 minutes or until the sauce starts to thicken.

Meanwhile, bring a large pan of lightly salted water to a rolling boil. Add the pasta and cook according to the package directions until tender but still firm to the bite.

Drain the pasta, setting aside 2 tablespoons of the water, and return to the pan. Add the chorizo sauce with the cooking water, and toss gently until the pasta is evenly covered. Spoon into a warmed serving dish, sprinkle with the parsley, and serve immediately.

HELPFUL HINT

Take care when preparing chiles, as the volatile oils in the seeds and the membrane can cause irritation – wash your hands thoroughly afterwards and avoid touching your eyes.

Crispy Baked Potatoes
with Prosciutto

SERVES 4

4 large baking potatoes
4 tsp. crème fraîche
salt and freshly ground
    black pepper
¼ cup cooked diced carrots

2 slices lean serrano ham or
    prosciutto, with
    fat removed
1 cup cooked baby
    fava beans

1 cup cooked peas
½ cup shredded hard cheese,
    such as cheddar
fresh green salad, to serve

Preheat the oven to 400°F. Scrub the potatoes dry. Prick with a fork and place on a baking sheet. Cook for 1–1½ hours or until tender when squeezed. Use oven mitts to pick up the potatoes, as they will be very hot.

Cut the potatoes in half horizontally and scoop out all the flesh into a bowl.

Spoon the crème fraîche into the bowl and mix thoroughly with the potatoes. Season to taste with a little salt and pepper.

Cut the ham or prosciutto into fine strips, and carefully stir into the potato mixture with the fava beans, carrots, and peas.

Pile the mixture back into the 8 potato shells and sprinkle a little shredded cheese over the top. Place under a hot broiler and cook until golden and heated through. Serve immediately with a fresh green salad.

Pasta & Pork Ragù

SERVES 4

1 tbsp. sunflower oil
1 leek, trimmed and
   thinly sliced
2½ cups diced
   pork tenderloin
1 garlic clove, peeled
   and crushed
2 tsp. paprika

¼ tsp. cayenne pepper
⅔ cup white wine
2½ cups vegetable stock
14 oz. canned cranberry
   beans, drained and rinsed
2 carrots, peeled and diced
salt and freshly ground
   black pepper

8 oz. fresh egg tagliatelle
1 tbsp. freshly
   chopped parsley,
   to garnish
crème fraîche, to serve

Heat the sunflower oil in a large skillet. Add the sliced leek and cook, stirring frequently, for 5 minutes or until softened. Add the pork and cook, stirring, for 4 minutes or until sealed.

Add the crushed garlic and the paprika and cayenne peppers to the pan. Stir until all the pork is lightly coated in the garlic and pepper mixture.

Pour in the wine and 1¾ cups of the vegetable stock. Add the cranberry beans and carrots, and season to taste with salt and pepper. Bring the sauce to a boil, then lower the heat and simmer for 5 minutes.

Meanwhile, place the egg tagliatelle in a large saucepan of lightly salted boiling water, cover, and simmer for 5 minutes or until the pasta is tender but still firm to the bite.

Drain the pasta, then add to the pork ragù; toss well. Adjust the seasoning, then spoon into a warmed serving dish. Sprinkle with chopped parsley and serve with a little crème fraîche.

HELPFUL HINT

Pork fillet, also known as tenderloin, is a very lean and tender cut of pork. It needs little cooking time, and is perfect for this quick and simple dish.

Pork in Peanut Sauce

1 lb. pork fillet
2 tbsp. light soy sauce
1 tbsp. vinegar
1 tsp. sugar
1 tsp. Chinese five
  spice powder
2–4 garlic cloves, peeled
  and crushed
2 tbsp. peanut oil

1 large onion, peeled and
  finely sliced
2 medium carrots, peeled
  and cut into matchsticks
2 celery stalks, trimmed and
  sliced
¾ cup trimmed and halved
  green beans
3 tbsp. smooth peanut butter

1 tbsp. freshly chopped
  Italian flat-leaf parsley

To serve:
freshly cooked basmati and
  wild rice
green salad

Remove any fat or sinew from the pork fillet, cut into thin strips, and set aside. Blend the soy sauce, vinegar, sugar, Chinese five spice powder, and garlic in a bowl, and add the pork. Cover and allow to marinate in the refrigerator for at least 30 minutes.

Drain the pork, setting aside any marinade. Heat the wok, then add the oil and, when hot, stir-fry the pork for 3–4 minutes or until sealed.

Add the onion, carrots, celery, and beans to the wok, and stir-fry for 4–5 minutes until the meat is tender and the vegetables are softened.

Blend the marinade, peanut butter, and 2 tablespoons of hot water together. When smooth, stir into the wok and cook for several minutes more until the sauce is thick and the pork is piping hot. Sprinkle with the chopped parsley and serve immediately with the basmati and wild rice, and a green salad.

Pork Goulash & Rice

SERVES 4

1½ lb. boneless pork
   rib chops
1 tbsp. olive oil
2 onions, peeled and
   roughly chopped
1 red bell pepper, seeded
   and thinly sliced

1 garlic clove, peeled
   and crushed
1 tbsp. all-purpose flour
1 rounded tbsp. paprika
14 oz. canned
   chopped tomatoes
salt and freshly ground
   black pepper

1½ cups long-grain
   white rice
2 cups chicken stock
⅔ cup sour cream
fresh Italian flat-leaf parsley
   sprigs, to garnish

Preheat the oven to 275°F. Cut the pork into large cubes, about 1½ in. square. Heat the oil in a large flameproof casserole and brown the pork in batches over a high heat, transferring the cubes to a plate as they brown.

Over a medium heat, add the onions and pepper, and cook for about 5 minutes, stirring regularly, until they begin to brown. Add the garlic, and return the meat to the casserole along with any juices on the plate. Sprinkle in the flour and paprika, and stir well.

Add the tomatoes and season to taste with salt and pepper. Bring slowly to a boil, cover with a tight-fitting lid, and cook in the preheated oven for 1½ hours.

Meanwhile, rinse the rice in several changes of water until the water remains relatively clear. Drain well and put into a saucepan with the chicken stock or water and a little salt. Cover tightly and bring to a boil. Turn the heat down as low as possible and cook for 10 minutes, without removing the lid. After 10 minutes, remove from the heat, and leave for an additional 10 minutes, without removing the lid. Fluff with a fork.

When the meat is tender, lightly stir in the sour cream to create a marbled effect, or serve separately. Garnish with parsley, and serve with the rice.

Pork Cabbage Pockets

8 large, green
cabbage leaves
1 tbsp. vegetable oil
2 celery sticks, trimmed
and chopped
1 carrot, peeled and
thinly sliced
¼ lb. fresh ground pork
button mushrooms, wiped
and sliced

1 tsp. Chinese five
spice powder
⅓ cup cooked
long-grain rice
juice of 1 lemon
1 tbsp. soy sauce
⅔ cup chicken stock

For the tomato sauce:
1 tbsp. vegetable oil
1 bunch scallions, trimmed
and chopped
14 oz. canned
chopped tomatoes
1 tbsp. light soy sauce
1 tbsp. freshly chopped mint
freshly ground black pepper

Preheat the oven to 350˚F. To make the sauce, heat the oil in a heavy saucepan, add the scallions, and cook for 2 minutes or until softened.

Add the tomatoes, soy sauce, and mint to the saucepan, bring to a boil, cover, then simmer for 10 minutes. Season to taste with pepper. Reheat when needed.

Meanwhile, blanch the cabbage leaves in a large saucepan of lightly salted water for 3 minutes. Drain under cold running water. Pat dry with paper towels, and set aside.

Heat the oil in a small saucepan, add the celery, carrot, and ground pork, and cook for 3 minutes. Add the mushrooms and cook for 3 minutes. Stir in the Chinese five spice powder, rice, lemon juice, and soy sauce, and heat through.

Place some of the filling in the center of each cabbage leaf, and fold to enclose the filling. Place in a shallow ovenproof dish seam-side down. Pour over the stock, and cook in the preheated oven for 30 minutes. Serve immediately with the reheated tomato sauce.

Sweet & Sour Pork

1 lb. pork fillet
1 large egg white
4 tsp. cornstarch
salt and freshly ground
    black pepper
1 cup peanut oil
1 small onion, peeled and
    finely sliced

2 medium carrots,
    peeled and cut into
    matchsticks
1-in. piece ginger, peeled
    and cut into strips
⅔ cup orange juice
⅔ cup chicken stock
1 tbsp. light soy sauce

7 oz. canned pineapple
    pieces, drained, with juice
    set aside
1 tbsp. white wine vinegar
1 tbsp. freshly
    chopped parsley
freshly cooked rice, to serve

Trim, then cut the pork fillet into small cubes. In a bowl, beat the egg white and cornstarch with a little seasoning, then add the pork to the egg white mixture and stir until the cubes are well coated.

Heat the wok, then add the oil. Heat until very hot before adding the pork and stir-frying for 30 seconds. Turn off the heat and continue to stir for 3 minutes. The meat should be white and sealed. Drain off the oil, set the pork aside, and wipe the wok clean.

Pour 2 teaspoons of the drained peanut oil back into the wok and cook the onion, carrots, and ginger for 2–3 minutes. Blend the orange juice with the chicken stock and soy sauce, and make up to 1¼ cups with the pineapple juice.

Return the pork to the wok with the juice mixture, and simmer for 3–4 minutes. Stir in the pineapple pieces and vinegar. Heat through, then sprinkle with the chopped parsley and serve immediately with freshly cooked rice.

Pork with Spring Vegetables & Sweet Chili Sauce

SERVES 4

1 lb. pork fillet
2 tbsp. corn oil
2 garlic cloves, peeled
   and crushed
1-in. piece fresh ginger,
   peeled and grated

2 medium carrots, peeled
   and cut into matchsticks
4 scallions, trimmed
1 cup snow peas
1 cup baby corn
2 tbsp. sweet chili sauce
2 tbsp. light soy sauce

1 tbsp. vinegar
½ tsp. sugar, or to taste
¾ cup bean sprouts
1 tbsp. grated orange zest
freshly cooked rice, to serve

Trim, then cut the pork fillet into thin strips and set aside. Heat a wok and pour in the oil. When hot, add the garlic and ginger, and stir-fry for 30 seconds. Add the carrots to the wok and continue to stir-fry for about 1–2 minutes until they start to soften.

Slice the scallions lengthwise, then cut into three lengths. Trim the snow peas and the baby corn. Add the scalllions, snow peas, and corn to the wok, and stir-fry for 30 seconds.

Add the pork to the wok and continue to stir-fry for 2–3 minutes until the meat is sealed and browned all over. Blend the sweet chili sauce, soy sauce, vinegar, and sugar together, then stir into the wok with the bean sprouts.

Continue to stir-fry until the meat is cooked, and the vegetables are tender but still crisp. Sprinkle with the orange zest and serve immediately with the freshly cooked rice.

TASTY TIP

Sweet chili sauce can still have a good hot kick. It is wise to taste a little before adding it to the sauce and adjust the quantity according to preference.

Pork Sausages with Onion Gravy & Best–Ever Mashed Potatoes

SERVES 4

4 tbsp. butter
1 tbsp. olive oil
2 large onions, peeled and
    thinly sliced
pinch sugar
1 tbsp. freshly
    chopped thyme
1 tbsp. all-purpose flour

½ cup Madeira
¾ cup vegetable stock
8–12 good-quality pork
    sausages, depending
    on size

For the mashed potatoes:
2 lb. floury potatoes, peeled
6 tbsp. butter
4 tbsp. crème fraîche or
    sour cream
salt and freshly ground
    black pepper

Melt the butter with the oil and add the onions. Cover and cook gently for about 20 minutes until the onions have collapsed. Add the sugar and stir well. Uncover and continue to cook, stirring often, until the onions are very soft and golden. Add the thyme, stir well, then add the flour while stirring. Gradually add the Madeira and the stock. Bring to a boil and simmer gently for 10 minutes.

Meanwhile, put the sausages in a large skillet, and cook over a medium heat for about 15–20 minutes, turning often, until golden brown and slightly sticky all over.

For the mashed potatoes, boil the potatoes in plenty of lightly salted water for 15–18 minutes until tender. Drain well and return to the saucepan. Put over a low heat to allow to dry. Remove from the heat and add the butter, crème fraîche or sour cream, and salt and pepper. Mash thoroughly. Serve the mashed potatoes topped with the sausages and onion gravy.

HELPFUL HINT

Sausages should always be cooked slowly over a gentle heat to ensure that they are cooked through.

Sausage & Redcurrant Pasta Bake

1 lb. good-quality, thick pork sausages
2 tsp. sunflower oil
2 tbsp. butter
1 onion, peeled and sliced
2 tbsp. all-purpose flour
1¾ cups chicken stock

⅔ cup port or good-quality red wine
1 tbsp. freshly chopped thyme leaves, plus sprigs to garnish
1 bay leaf
4 tbsp. red currant jelly

salt and freshly ground black pepper
3 cups fresh penne
¾ cup shredded Gruyère cheese

Preheat the oven to 425°F. Prick the sausages, place in a shallow ovenproof dish, and toss in the sunflower oil. Cook in the oven for 25–30 minutes or until golden brown.

Meanwhile, melt the butter in a skillet. Add the sliced onion and fry for 5 minutes or until golden brown. Stir in the flour and cook for 2 minutes. Remove the pan from the heat and gradually stir in the chicken stock with the port or red wine.

Return the pan to the heat and bring to a boil, stirring continuously until the sauce starts to thicken. Add the thyme, bay leaf, and red currant jelly, and season well with salt and pepper. Simmer the sauce for 5 minutes.

Bring a large pan of salted water to a rolling boil. Add the pasta and cook for about 4 minutes until tender but still firm to the bite. Drain thoroughly and set aside.

Lower the oven temperature to 400°F. Remove the sausages from the oven, drain off any excess fat, and return the sausages to the dish. Add the pasta. Pour over the sauce, discarding the bay leaf, and toss together. Sprinkle with the Gruyère cheese and return to the oven for 15–20 minutes until bubbling and golden brown. Serve immediately, garnished with thyme sprigs.

Oven–Baked Pork Balls with Peppers

SERVES 4

For the garlic bread:
2–4 garlic cloves, peeled
4 tbsp. butter, softened
1 tbsp. freshly
   chopped parsley
2–3 tsp. lemon juice
1 focaccia loaf

For the pork balls:
2 cups fresh ground pork

4 tbsp. freshly chopped basil
2 garlic cloves, peeled
   and chopped
3 sun-dried tomatoes,
   chopped
salt and freshly ground
   black pepper
3 tbsp. olive oil
1 medium red bell pepper,
   seeded and cut into chunks

1 medium green bell pepper,
   seeded and cut into chunks
1 medium yellow bell
   pepper, seeded and cut
   into chunks
2 cups cherry tomatoes
2 tbsp. balsamic vinegar

Preheat the oven to 400°F. Crush the garlic, then blend with the softened butter, the parsley, and enough lemon juice to give a soft consistency. Shape into a roll, wrap in baking parchment, and chill in the refrigerator for at least 30 minutes.

Mix together the pork, basil, 1 chopped garlic clove, sun-dried tomatoes, and seasoning until well combined. With damp hands, roll into 16 balls and set aside.

Spoon the olive oil into a large roasting pan, and place in the preheated oven for about 3 minutes until very hot. Remove from the heat and stir in the pork balls, the remaining chopped garlic, and bell peppers. Cook for about 15 minutes. Remove from the oven, stir in the cherry tomatoes, and season to taste with plenty of salt and pepper. Cook for an additional 20 minutes.

Just before the pork balls are ready, slice the bread, toast lightly, and spread with the prepared garlic butter. Remove the pork balls from the oven, stir in the vinegar, and serve immediately with the garlic bread.

HELPFUL HINT

You can prepare the garlic butter ahead. Refrigerate for up to 1 week or freeze for up to 2 months.

Italian Meatballs in Tomato Sauce

SERVES 4

For the tomato sauce:
4 tbsp. olive oil
1 large onion, peeled and
   finely chopped
2 garlic cloves, peeled
   and chopped
14 oz. canned
   chopped tomatoes
1 tbsp. sun-dried

tomato paste
1 tbsp. dried mixed herbs
⅔ cup red wine
salt and freshly ground
   black pepper

For the meatballs:
2 cups fresh ground pork
½ cup fresh bread crumbs

1 large egg yolk
¾ cup Parmesan
   cheese, grated
20 small stuffed green olives
freshly cut chives, to garnish
freshly cooked pasta,
   to serve

To make the tomato sauce, heat half the olive oil in a saucepan and cook half the chopped onion for 5 minutes until softened. Add the garlic, chopped tomatoes, tomato paste, mixed herbs, and red wine to the saucepan, and season to taste with salt and pepper. Stir well until blended. Bring to a boil, then cover and simmer for 15 minutes.

To make the meatballs, place the pork, bread crumbs, remaining onion, egg yolk, and half the Parmesan cheese in a large bowl. Season well and mix together with your hands. Divide the mixture into 20 balls.

Flatten one ball out in the palm of your hands, place an olive in the center, then squeeze the meat around the olive to enclose completely. Repeat with remaining mixture and olives. Place the meatballs on a baking sheet, cover with plastic wrap, and chill in the refrigerator for 30 minutes.

Heat the remaining oil in a large skillet, and cook the meatballs for 8–10 minutes, turning occasionally, until golden brown. Pour in the sauce and heat through. Sprinkle with chives and the remaining Parmesan. Serve immediately with the freshly cooked pasta.

Shepherd's Pie

SERVES 4

2 tbsp. vegetable or olive oil
1 onion, peeled and
    finely chopped
1 carrot, peeled and
    finely chopped
1 celery stalk, trimmed and
    finely chopped
1 tbsp. sprigs of fresh thyme

5 cups finely chopped
    leftover roast lamb
⅔ cup red wine
⅔ cup lamb or
    vegetable stock
2 tbsp. tomato paste
salt and freshly ground
    black pepper

4 cups roughly
    chopped potatoes
2 tbsp. butter
6 tbsp. milk
1 tbsp. freshly
    chopped parsley
fresh herbs, to garnish

Preheat the oven to 400°F about 15 minutes before cooking. Heat the oil in a large saucepan and add the onion, carrot, and celery. Cook over a medium heat for 8–10 minutes until softened and starting to brown.

Add the thyme and cook briefly, then add the cooked lamb, wine, stock, and tomato paste. Season to taste with salt and pepper, and simmer gently for 25–30 minutes until reduced and thickened. Remove from the heat to cool slightly and season again.

Meanwhile, boil the potatoes in plenty of salted water for 12–15 minutes until tender. Drain and return to the saucepan over a low heat to dry out. Remove from the heat and add the butter, milk, and parsley. Mash until creamy, adding a little more milk if necessary. Season.

Transfer the lamb mixture to a shallow ovenproof dish. Spoon the mashed potatoes over the filling, spreading evenly to cover completely. Fork the surface, then cook in the preheated oven for 25–30 minutes until the potato topping is browned and the filling is piping hot. Garnish and serve.

TASTY TIP

You can make this with minced lamb if preferred. Simply dry-fry 1 lb. lean meat over a high heat until well browned, then follow the recipe as before.

Lamb Arrabbiata

SERVES 4

4 tbsp. olive oil
1 lb. lamb fillets, cubed
1 large onion, peeled
and sliced
4 garlic cloves, peeled and
finely chopped

1 red chile, seeded and
finely chopped
14 oz. canned
chopped tomatoes
1½ cups pitted and
halved ripe olives
⅔ cup white wine

salt and freshly ground
black pepper
2½ cups farfalle
1 tsp. butter
4 tbsp. freshly chopped
parsley, plus1 tbsp.
to garnish

Heat 2 tablespoons of the olive oil in a large skillet and cook the lamb for 5–7 minutes until sealed. Remove from the skillet using a slotted spoon and set aside.

Heat the remaining oil in the skillet. Add the onion, garlic, and chile, and cook until softened. Add the tomatoes and bring to a boil, then simmer for 10 minutes.

Return the browned lamb to the skillet with the olives and pour in the wine. Bring the sauce back to a boil, then reduce the heat and simmer, uncovered, for 15 minutes or until the lamb is tender. Season to taste with salt and pepper.

Meanwhile, bring a large pan of lightly salted water to a rolling boil. Add the pasta and cook according to the package directions until tender but still firm to the bite.

Drain the pasta. Toss in the butter, then add to the sauce and mix. Stir in 4 tablespoons of the chopped parsley, then spoon into a warmed serving dish. Sprinkle with the remaining parsley and serve immediately.

FOOD FACT

When cooking pasta, remember to use a very large saucepan so that the pasta has plenty of room to move around freely.

Lamb with Stir–Fried Vegetables

1¼ lb. lamb fillet, cut
  into strips
1-in. piece ginger, peeled
  and thinly sliced
2 garlic cloves, peeled
  and chopped
4 tbsp. soy sauce
2 tbsp. dry sherry
2 tsp. cornstarch

4 tbsp. peanut oil
½ cup trimmed and halved
  green beans
2 medium carrots, peeled
  and thinly sliced
1 red bell pepper, seeded
  and cut into chunks
1 yellow bell pepper, seeded
  and cut into chunks

8 oz. canned water chestnuts,
  drained and halved
3 tomatoes, chopped
freshly cooked sticky rice in
  banana leaves, to
  serve (optional)

Place the lamb strips in a shallow dish. Mix together the ginger and half the garlic in a small bowl. Pour over the soy sauce and sherry, and stir well. Pour over the lamb, and stir until coated lightly. Cover with plastic wrap, and leave to marinate for at least 30 minutes, occasionally spooning the marinade over the lamb.

Using a slotted spoon, lift the lamb from the marinade and place on a plate. Blend the cornstarch and the marinade together until smooth, and set aside.

Heat a wok or large skillet, add 2 tablespoons of the oil, and, when hot, add the remaining garlic, green beans, carrots, and bell peppers, and stir-fry for 5 minutes. Using a slotted spoon, transfer the vegetables to a plate, and keep warm.

Heat the remaining oil in the wok, add the lamb, and stir-fry for 2 minutes or until tender. Return the vegetables to the wok with the water chestnuts, tomatoes, and marinade mixture. Bring to a boil, then simmer for 1 minute. Serve immediately, with freshly cooked sticky rice in banana leaves, if desired.

Poultry

Chicken & Baby Vegetable Stir-Fry

SERVES 4

2 tbsp. peanut oil
1 small red chile, seeded and finely chopped
⅓ lb. chicken breast or thigh meat, skinned and cut into cubes
2 baby leeks, trimmed and sliced
12 asparagus spears, halved

1 cup trimmed snow peas
8 baby carrots, trimmed and halved lengthwise
¾ cup trimmed and diagonally sliced green beans
1 cup diagonally halved baby corn
¼ cup chicken stock

2 tsp. light soy sauce
1 tbsp. dry sherry
1 tsp. sesame oil
toasted sesame seeds, to garnish

Heat the wok until very hot and add the oil. Add the chopped chile and chicken, and stir-fry for 4–5 minutes until the chicken is cooked and golden.

Increase the heat, add the leeks to the chicken, and stir-fry for 2 minutes. Add the asparagus spears, snow peas, baby carrots, green beans, and baby corn. Stir-fry for 3–4 minutes until the vegetables soften slightly but still retain a slight crispness.

In a small bowl, mix together the chicken stock, soy sauce, dry sherry, and sesame oil. Pour into the wok, stir, and cook until heated through. Sprinkle with the toasted sesame seeds and serve immediately.

HELPFUL HINT

Look for packages of mixed baby vegetables in the supermarket. They are often available ready to eat, which will save a lot of time.

Braised Chicken with Eggplant

SERVES 4

3 tbsp. vegetable oil
12 chicken thighs
2 large eggplants, trimmed and cubed
4 garlic cloves, peeled and crushed
2 tsp. freshly shredded ginger

3¾ cups vegetable stock
2 tbsp. light soy sauce
2 tbsp. Chinese preserved black beans
6 scallions, trimmed and thinly sliced diagonally
1 tbsp. cornstarch
1 tbsp. sesame oil

scallion tassels, to garnish
freshly cooked noodles or rice, to serve

Heat a wok or large skillet, add the oil, and, when hot, add the chicken thighs and cook over a medium-high heat for 5 minutes or until browned all over. Transfer to a large plate and keep warm.

Add the eggplant to the wok, and cook over a high heat for 5 minutes or until browned, turning occasionally. Add the garlic and ginger, and stir-fry for 1 minute.

Return the chicken to the wok, pour in the stock, and add the soy sauce and black beans. Bring to a boil, then simmer for 20 minutes or until the chicken is tender. Add the scallions after 10 minutes.

Blend the cornstarch with 2 tablespoons of water. Stir into the wok, and simmer until the sauce has thickened. Stir in the sesame oil, heat for 30 seconds, then remove from the heat. Garnish with scallion tassels, and serve immediately with noodles or rice.

Pan–Cooked Chicken with Thai Spices

SERVES 4

4 kaffir lime leaves
2-in. piece fresh ginger, peeled and chopped
1¼ cups chicken stock, boiling
4 ½-lb. chicken breasts
2 tsp. peanut oil
5 tbsp. coconut milk

1 tbsp. fish sauce
2 red chiles, seeded and finely chopped
1 cup Thai jasmine rice
1 tbsp. lime juice
3 tbsp. freshly chopped cilantro

salt and freshly ground black pepper

To garnish:
lime wedges
freshly chopped cilantro

Lightly bruise the kaffir lime leaves and put in a bowl with the chopped ginger. Pour in the chicken stock, cover, and allow to infuse for 30 minutes.

Meanwhile, cut each chicken breast into 2 pieces. Heat the oil in a large nonstick skillet or flameproof casserole dish, and brown the chicken pieces for 2–3 minutes on each side.

Strain the infused chicken stock into the skillet. Half-cover the skillet with a lid, and gently simmer for 10 minutes.

Stir in the coconut milk, fish sauce, and chopped chiles. Simmer uncovered for 5–6 minutes until the chicken is tender and cooked through, and the sauce has reduced slightly.

Meanwhile, cook the rice in boiling, salted water according to the package instructions. Drain the rice thoroughly.

Stir the lime juice and chopped cilantro into the sauce. Season to taste with salt and pepper. Serve the dish on a bed of rice. Garnish with wedges of lime and freshly chopped cilantro and serve immediately.

FOOD FACT

Kaffir lime leaves can be found, usually frozen, in Asian food stores. Most supermarkets now stock dried kaffir lime leaves. If using dried, crumble lightly and use as above.

Stir-Fried Chicken with Basil

SERVES 4

3 tbsp. corn oil
3 tbsp. green curry paste
1 lb. skinless, boneless
   chicken breast fillets,
   trimmed and cut
   into cubes
8 cherry tomatoes

½ cup coconut cream
2 tbsp. brown sugar
2 tbsp. Thai fish sauce
1 red chile, seeded and
   thinly sliced
1 green chile, seeded and
   thinly sliced

6 tbsp. fresh torn
   basil leaves
freshly steamed white rice,
   to serve
fresh cilantro sprigs,
   to garnish

Heat the wok, then add the oil and heat for 1 minute. Add the green curry paste and cook, stirring for 1 minute to release the flavor and cook the paste. Add the chicken and stir-fry over a high heat for 2 minutes, making sure the chicken is coated thoroughly with the green curry paste.

Reduce the heat under the wok, then add the cherry tomatoes and cook, stirring gently for 2–3 minutes until the tomatoes burst and begin to disintegrate into the green curry paste.

Add half the coconut cream and add to the wok with the brown sugar, Thai fish sauce, and the red and green chiles. Stir-fry gently for 5 minutes or until the sauce is mixed and the chicken is cooked thoroughly.

Just before serving, sprinkle the chicken with the torn basil leaves and add the remaining coconut cream, then serve immediately with freshly steamed white rice garnished with fresh cilantro sprigs.

Spicy Chicken Skewers with Mango Tabbouleh

SERVES 4

¾ lb. chicken breast fillet
1 cup low-fat plain yogurt
1 garlic clove, peeled
   and crushed
1 small red chile, seeded
   and finely chopped
½ tsp. turmeric
2 tsp. finely grated
   lemon zest
2 tsp. lemon juice

fresh mint sprigs,
   to garnish

For the mango tabbouleh:
1 cup bulgur
1 tsp. olive oil
1 tbsp. lemon juice
½ red onion, finely chopped
1 ripe mango, halved, pitted,
   peeled, and chopped

¼ cucumber, finely diced
2 tbsp. freshly
   chopped parsley
2 tbsp. freshly torn mint
salt and finely ground
   black pepper

If using wooden skewers, presoak them in cold water for 30 minutes. This keeps them from burning during broiling. Cut the chicken into 2 x ½ inch strips, and place in a shallow dish. Mix together the yogurt, garlic, chile, turmeric, lemon zest, and juice. Pour over the chicken and toss to coat. Cover and leave to marinate in the refrigerator for up to 8 hours.

To make the tabbouleh, put the bulgur in a bowl. Pour in enough boiling water to cover. Put a plate over the bowl. Allow to soak for 20 minutes. Whisk together the oil and lemon juice in a bowl. Add the red onion and leave to marinate for 10 minutes. Drain the bulgur and squeeze out any excess moisture in a clean dishtowel. Add to the red onion with the mango, cucumber, herbs, and season to taste with salt and pepper. Toss together to mix thoroughly.

Thread the chicken strips onto eight wooden or metal skewers. Cook under a hot broiler for 8 minutes. Turn and brush with the marinade until the chicken is lightly browned and cooked through.

Spoon the tabbouleh onto individual plates. Arrange the chicken skewers on top, and garnish with the sprigs of mint. Serve warm or cold.

Aromatic Chicken Curry

⅔ cup red lentils
2 tsp. ground coriander
½ tsp. cumin seeds
2 tsp. mild curry paste
1 bay leaf
small strip of lemon rind

2½ cups chicken or
   vegetable stock
8 chicken thighs, skinned
¾ cup spinach leaves, rinsed
   and shredded
1 tbsp. freshly
   chopped cilantro

2 tsp. lemon juice
salt and freshly ground
   black pepper

To serve:
freshly cooked rice
low-fat plain yogurt

Put the lentils in a sieve and rinse thoroughly under cold running water.

Fry the ground coriander and cumin seeds in a large saucepan over a low heat for about 30 seconds. Stir in the curry paste.

Add the lentils to the saucepan with the bay leaf and lemon rind, then pour in the stock.

Stir, then slowly bring to a boil. Turn down the heat, half-cover the saucepan with a lid, and simmer gently for 5 minutes, stirring occasionally.

Secure the chicken thighs with toothpicks to hold their shape. Place in the saucepan and half-cover. Simmer for 15 minutes.

Stir in the shredded spinach, and cook for an additional 25 minutes or until the chicken is very tender, and the sauce is thick.

Remove the bay leaf and lemon rind. Stir in the cilantro and lemon juice, then season to taste with salt and pepper. Serve immediately with the rice and some plain yogurt.

Red Chicken Curry

SERVES 4

1 cup coconut cream
2 tbsp. vegetable oil
2 garlic cloves, peeled and
    finely chopped
2 tbsp. Thai red curry paste
2 tbsp. Thai fish sauce

2 tsp. sugar
1½ cups finely sliced
    boneless, skinless
    chicken breast
2 cups chicken stock
2 lime leaves, shredded

chopped red chile,
    to garnish
freshly boiled rice or
    steamed Thai fragrant
    rice, to serve

Pour the coconut cream into a small saucepan and heat gently. Meanwhile, heat a wok or large skillet and add the oil. When the oil is very hot, swirl it around the wok until the wok is lightly coated, then add the garlic and stir-fry for about 10–20 seconds until the garlic begins to brown. Add the curry paste and stir-fry for a few more seconds, then pour in the warmed coconut cream.

Cook the coconut cream mixture for 5 minutes or until the cream has curdled and thickened. Stir in the fish sauce and sugar. Add the finely sliced chicken breast, and cook for 3–4 minutes until the chicken has turned white.

Pour the stock into the wok, bring to a boil, then simmer for 1–2 minutes until the chicken is cooked through. Stir in the shredded lime leaves. Turn into a warmed serving dish, garnish with chopped red chile, and serve immediately with rice.

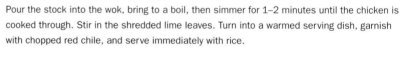

Persian Chicken Pilaf

2–3 tbsp. vegetable oil
1½ lbs. boneless skinless chicken pieces (breast and thighs), cut into 1-in. pieces
2 medium onions, peeled and coarsely chopped
1 tsp. ground cumin

heaping 1 cup long-grain white rice
1 tbsp. tomato paste
1 tsp. saffron strands
salt and freshly ground black pepper
1 cup pomegranate juice
3¾ cups chicken stock

1 cup halved and pitted dried apricots or prunes
2 tbsp. raisins
2 tbsp. freshly chopped mint or parsley
pomegranate seeds, to garnish (optional)

Heat the oil in a large, heavy saucepan over a medium-high heat. Cook the chicken pieces in batches until lightly browned. Return all the browned chicken to the saucepan.

Add the onions to the saucepan, reduce the heat to medium, and cook for 3–5 minutes, stirring frequently, until the onions begin to soften. Add the cumin and rice, and stir to coat the rice. Cook for about 2 minutes until the rice is golden and translucent. Stir in the tomato paste and the saffron strands, then season to taste with salt and pepper.

Add the pomegranate juice and stock, and bring to a boil, stirring once or twice. Add the apricots and raisins, and stir gently. Reduce the heat to low and cook for 30 minutes until the chicken and rice are tender and the liquid is absorbed.

Turn into a shallow serving dish and sprinkle with the chopped mint or parsley. Serve immediately, garnished with pomegranate seeds, if desired.

HELPFUL HINT

Pomegranate juice is available from Middle Eastern groceries and some speciality shops. Substitute unsweetened grape or apple juice if you cannot find pomegranate juice.

Pad Thai

SERVES 4

For the sauce:
3 tbsp. Thai fish sauce
2–3 tbsp. rice vinegar or
    cider vinegar
1 tbsp. oyster sauce
1 tbsp. toasted sesame oil
1 tbsp. light brown sugar
1 red chile, seeded and
    thinly sliced

For the noodles:
½ lb. flat rice noodles
2 tbsp. vegetable oil
½ lb. boneless chicken
    breast, skinned and
    thinly sliced
4 shallots, peeled and
    thinly sliced
2 garlic cloves, peeled and
    finely chopped

4 scallions, trimmed and cut
    diagonally into 2-in. pieces
¾ lb. fresh white crabmeat or
    tiny shrimp
1½ cups rinsed and drained
    fresh bean sprouts
2 tbsp. preserved or fresh
    radish, chopped
2–3 tbsp. roasted peanuts,
    chopped (optional)

To make the sauce, whisk all the sauce ingredients in a bowl and set aside. Put the rice noodles in a large bowl and pour over enough hot water to cover. Let stand for about 15 minutes until softened. Drain and rinse, then drain again.

Heat the oil in a wok over a high heat until hot, but not smoking. Add the chicken strips and stir-fry constantly until they begin to color. Using a slotted spoon, transfer to a plate. Reduce the heat to medium-high. Add the shallots, garlic, and scallions, and stir-fry for 1 minute. Stir in the rice noodles, then the sauce; mix well.

Add the chicken strips with the crabmeat, bean sprouts, and radish, and stir well. Cook for about 5 minutes, stirring frequently, until heated through. If the noodles begin to stick, add a little water.

Turn into a large shallow serving dish and sprinkle with the chopped peanuts, if desired. Serve immediately.

Chicken with Porcini Mushrooms & Cream

SERVES 4

2 tbsp. olive oil
4 boneless chicken breasts
2 garlic cloves, peeled
  and crushed
⅔ cup dry vermouth or dry
  white wine

salt and freshly ground
  black pepper
2 tbsp. butter
4 cups thickly sliced porcini
  or wild mushrooms

1 tbsp. freshly
  chopped oregano
fresh basil sprigs,
  to garnish
freshly cooked rice, to serve

Heat the olive oil in a large, heavy skillet, then add the chicken breasts, skin-side down, and cook for about 10 minutes or until they are well browned. Remove the chicken breasts and set aside. Add the garlic, stir into the juices, and cook for 1 minute.

Pour the vermouth or white wine into the skillet, and season to taste with salt and pepper. Return the chicken to the skillet. Bring to a boil, reduce the heat to low, and simmer for about 20 minutes until tender.

In another large skillet, heat the butter and add the sliced porcini or wild mushrooms. Stir-fry for about 5 minutes or until the mushrooms are golden and tender.

Add the porcini or wild mushrooms and any juices to the chicken. Season to taste with salt and pepper, then add the chopped oregano. Stir together gently and cook for 1 minute longer. Transfer to a large serving plate, and garnish with sprigs of fresh basil, if desired. Serve immediately with rice.

Chicken Pockets with Zucchini & Pasta

SERVES 4

2 tbsp. olive oil
1 cup farfalle pasta or pasta shapes
1 onion, peeled and thinly sliced
1 garlic clove, peeled and finely chopped

2 medium zucchini, trimmed and thinly sliced
salt and freshly ground black pepper
2 tbsp. freshly chopped oregano

4 plum tomatoes, seeded and coarsely chopped
4 boneless, skinless chicken breasts
⅔ cup Italian white wine

Preheat the oven to 400°F. Lightly brush four large sheets of nonstick baking parchment with half the oil. Bring a saucepan of lightly salted water to a boil, and cook the pasta for 10 minutes or until tender but still firm to the bite. Drain and set aside.

Heat the remaining oil in a skillet and cook the onion for 2–3 minutes. Add the garlic and cook for 1 minute. Add the zucchini and cook for 1 minute, then remove from the heat, season to taste with salt and pepper, and add half the oregano.

Divide the cooked pasta equally among the four sheets of baking parchment, positioning the pasta in the center. Top the pasta with equal amounts of the vegetable mixture, and sprinkle a quarter of the chopped tomatoes over each.

Score the surface of each chicken breast about ½ inch deep. Place a chicken breast on top of the pasta, and sprinkle each with the remaining oregano and the white wine. Fold the edges of the paper along the top and then along each side, creating a sealed envelope.

Cook in the preheated oven for 30–35 minutes until cooked. Serve immediately. Be careful when opening the pouches, as the steam will be very hot.

Lemon Chicken with Potatoes, Rosemary & Olives

SERVES 6

12 skinless boneless
chicken thighs
1 large lemon
½ cup extra-virgin olive oil
6 garlic cloves, peeled
and sliced
2 onions, peeled and
thinly sliced

1 bunch fresh rosemary
2½ lbs. potatoes, peeled and
cut into 1½-inch pieces
salt and freshly ground
black pepper
18–24 pitted ripe olives

To serve:
steamed carrots
and zucchini

Preheat the oven to 400°F. Trim the chicken thighs and place in a shallow baking dish large enough to hold them in a single layer. Remove the zest from the lemon with a zester, or if using a peeler, julienne. Set half aside and add the remainder to the chicken. Squeeze the lemon juice over the chicken, toss to coat well, and let stand for 10 minutes.

Transfer the chicken to a large roasting pan. Add the remaining lemon zest or strips, olive oil, sliced garlic, onions, and half of the rosemary sprigs. Toss gently and leave for about 20 minutes.

Cover the potatoes with lightly salted water and bring to a boil. Cook for 2 minutes, then drain well and add to the chicken. Season to taste with salt and pepper.

Roast the chicken in the preheated oven for 50 minutes, turning frequently and basting, or until the chicken is cooked. Just before the end of cooking time, discard the rosemary, and add fresh sprigs of rosemary. Add the olives and stir. Serve immediately with steamed carrots and zucchini.

HELPFUL HINT

It is worth seeking out unwaxed lemons for any recipe in which the zest is to be eaten. If unwaxed fruit are not available, pour hot water over them and scrub well before removing the zest.

Chicken Pie with Sweet Potato Topping

SERVES 4

4 cups peeled and coarsely
diced sweet potatoes
1½ cups peeled and coarsely
diced potatoes
salt and freshly ground
black pepper
⅔ cup milk
2 tbsp. butter
2 tsp. brown sugar

grated zest of 1 orange
4 skinless chicken breast
fillets, diced
1 medium onion, peeled and
coarsely chopped
¼ lb. baby mushrooms,
stems trimmed
2 leeks, trimmed and
thickly sliced

⅔ cup dry white wine
1 chicken bouillon cube
1 tbsp. freshly
chopped parsley
¼ cup crème fraîche or thick
heavy cream
green vegetables, to serve

Preheat the oven to 375˚F. Cook the sweet and regular potatoes together in lightly salted, boiling water until tender. Drain well, then return to the saucepan, and mash until creamy, gradually adding the milk, then the butter, sugar, and orange zest. Season to taste and set aside.

Place the chicken in a saucepan with the onion, mushrooms, leeks, wine, bouillon cube, and seasoning to taste. Simmer covered until the chicken and vegetables are tender. Using a slotted spoon, transfer the chicken and vegetables to a pie dish. Add the parsley and crème fraîche to the liquid in the pan, and bring to a boil. Simmer until thickened and smooth, stirring constantly. Pour over the chicken in the pie dish, mix, and cool.

HELPFUL HINT

There are two types of sweet potato: one has a creamy-coloured flesh, the other orange. The former has a drier texture, so, if using, you may need a little more milk.

Spread the mashed potatoes over the chicken filling, and swirl the surface into decorative peaks. Bake in the preheated oven for 35 minutes or until the top is golden and the chicken is heated through. Serve immediately with fresh green vegetables.

Chicken & Asparagus with Tagliatelle

SERVES 4

2 cups fresh
   asparagus stalks
4 tbsp. butter
4 scallions, trimmed and
   coarsely chopped

¾ lb. boneless, skinless
   chicken breast,
   thinly sliced
2 tbsp. white vermouth
1 cup heavy cream

2 tbsp. freshly chopped chives
4½ cups fresh tagliatelle
½ cup grated Parmesan or
   pecorino cheese
cut chives, to garnish

Using a swivel-bladed vegetable peeler, lightly peel the asparagus stalks and then cook in lightly salted, boiling water for 2–3 minutes or until just tender. Drain and rinse in cold water, then cut into 1½-inch pieces and set aside.

Melt the butter in a large skillet, then add the scallions and the chicken slices, and cook for 4 minutes. Add the vermouth and allow to reduce until the liquid has evaporated. Pour in the cream and half the chives. Cook gently for 5–7 minutes until the sauce has thickened and the chicken is tender.

Bring a large saucepan of lightly salted water to a boil and cook the tagliatelle for 4–5 minutes until tender but still firm to the bite. Drain and immediately add to the chicken and cream sauce.

Using a pair of spaghetti tongs or kitchen forks, lightly toss the sauce and pasta until it is mixed thoroughly. Add the remaining chives and the Parmesan cheese, and toss gently. Garnish with cut chives and serve immediately, with extra Parmesan cheese, if desired.

HELPFUL HINT

Freshly made pasta will cook in 30–60 seconds. It is cooked when it rises to the surface. Bought fresh pasta will take 2–3 minutes. Dried pasta takes 4–10 minutes, depending on the variety.

Chicken Marengo

SERVES 4

2 tbsp. all-purpose flour	1 Spanish onion, peeled	3 tbsp. freshly chopped basil
salt and freshly ground	and chopped	3 tbsp. freshly
black pepper	1 garlic clove, peeled	chopped thyme
4 boneless and skinless	and chopped	½ cup dry white wine or
chicken breasts, cut into	14 oz. canned	chicken stock
bite-sized pieces	chopped tomatoes	3 cups rigatoni
4 tbsp. olive oil	2 tbsp. sun-dried	3 tbsp. freshly chopped
	tomato paste	Italian flat-leaf parsely

Season the flour with salt and pepper and toss the chicken in the flour to coat. Heat 2 tablespoons of the olive oil in a large skillet and cook the chicken for 7 minutes or until browned, turning occasionally. Remove from the skillet using a slotted spoon and keep warm.

Add the remaining oil to the skillet, then add the onion and cook, stirring occasionally, for 5 minutes or until softened and starting to brown. Add the garlic, tomatoes, tomato paste, basil, and thyme. Pour in the wine or chicken stock and season well. Bring to a boil. Stir in the chicken pieces, and simmer for 15 minutes or until the chicken is tender and the sauce has thickened.

Meanwhile, bring a large pan of lightly salted water to a boil. Add the rigatoni and cook according to the package directions until tender but still firm to the bite.

Drain the rigatoni thoroughly, then return to the pan and stir in the chopped parsley. Tip the pasta into a large, warmed serving dish or spoon onto individual plates. Spoon the chicken sauce over the pasta and serve immediately.

Warm Chicken & Potato Salad with Peas & Mint

SERVES 4-6

1 lb. new potatoes, peeled or scrubbed and cut into bite-sized pieces
salt and freshly ground black pepper
2 tbsp. cider vinegar
1¼ cups frozen peas, thawed

1 small ripe avocado
4 cooked chicken breasts, about 1 lb. in weight, skinned and diced
2 tbsp. freshly chopped mint
2 heads romaine lettuce
fresh mint sprigs, to garnish

For the dressing:
2 tbsp. raspberry or sherry vinegar
2 tsp. Dijon mustard
1 tsp. honey
¼ cup sunflower oil
¼ cup extra-virgin olive oil

Cook the potatoes in lightly salted, boiling water for 15 minutes or until just tender when pierced with the tip of a sharp knife; do not overcook. Rinse under cold running water to cool slightly, then drain and turn into a large bowl. Sprinkle with the cider vinegar and toss gently.

Run the peas under hot water to ensure that they are thawed, pat dry with paper towels, and add to the potatoes.

Cut the avocado in half lengthwise and remove the pit. Peel and cut the avocado into cubes, and add to the potatoes and peas. Add the chicken and stir together lightly.

To make the dressing, place all the ingredients in a screw-top jar with a little salt and pepper. Shake well to mix; add a little more oil if the flavor is too sharp. Pour over the salad and toss gently to coat. Sprinkle in half the mint and stir lightly.

Separate the lettuce leaves and spread onto a large shallow serving plate. Spoon the salad on top and sprinkle with the remaining mint. Garnish with mint sprigs and serve.

Spicy Chicken & Pasta Salad

SERVES 6

4 cups pasta shells
2 tbsp. butter
1 onion, peeled
   and chopped
2 tbsp. mild curry paste
1 cup chopped
   dried apricots

2 tbsp. tomato paste
3 tbsp. mango chutney
1¼ cups mayonnaise
15 oz. canned pineapple
   slices in juice
salt and freshly ground
   black pepper

1 lb. skinned, boned, cooked
   chicken, cut into
   bite-size pieces
2 tbsp. almond slivers,
   flaked and toasted
cilantro sprigs, to garnish

Bring a large pan of lightly salted water to a rolling boil. Add the pasta shells and cook according to the package directions until tender but still firm to the bite. Drain and refresh under cold running water, then drain thoroughly and place in a large serving bowl.

Meanwhile, melt the butter in a heavy pan, then add the onion and cook for 5 minutes or until softened. Add the curry paste and cook, stirring, for 2 minutes. Stir in the apricots and tomato paste, then cook for 1 minute. Remove from the heat and let cool.

Blend the mango chutney and mayonnaise together in a small bowl. Drain the pineapple slices, adding 2 tablespoons of the pineapple juice to the mayonnaise mixture; set aside the pineapple slices. Season the mayonnaise to taste with salt and pepper.

Cut the pineapple slices into chunks and stir into the pasta together with the mayonnaise mixture, curry paste, and cooked chicken pieces. Toss lightly together to coat the pasta. Sprinkle with the almond slivers, then garnish with cilantro sprigs and serve.

Pasta & Pepper Salad

SERVES 4

4 tbsp. olive oil
1 each red, orange, and
   yellow bell pepper,
   seeded and cut into chunks
1 large zucchini, trimmed
   and cut into chunks
1 medium eggplant,
   trimmed and diced

2½ cups fusilli
4 plum tomatoes, quartered
1 bunch fresh basil leaves,
   coarsely chopped
2 tbsp. pesto
2 garlic cloves, peeled and
   coarsely chopped
1 tbsp. lemon juice

8 oz. boneless and skinless
   roasted chicken breast
salt and freshly ground
   black pepper
1 cup crumbled feta cheese
fresh, crusty bread, to serve

Preheat the oven to 400°F. Spoon the olive oil into a roasting pan and heat in the oven for 2 minutes or until almost smoking. Remove from the oven, then add the bell peppers, zucchini, and eggplant, and stir until coated. Bake for 30 minutes or until charred, stirring occasionally.

Bring a large pan of lightly salted water to a boil. Add the pasta and cook according to the package directions until tender but still firm to the bite. Drain and refresh under cold running water. Drain thoroughly, then place in a large salad bowl and set aside.

Remove the cooked vegetables from the oven and let cool. Add to the cooled pasta, together with the quartered tomatoes, chopped basil leaves, pesto, garlic, and lemon juice. Toss lightly to mix.

Shred the chicken coarsely into small pieces and stir into the pasta and vegetable mixture. Season to taste with salt and pepper, then sprinkle the crumbled feta cheese over the pasta and stir gently. Cover the dish and let marinate for 30 minutes, stirring occasionally. Serve the salad with fresh, crusty bread.

Mixed Vegetable & Chicken Pasta

SERVES 4

3 boneless and skinless
  chicken breasts
2 leeks
1 red onion
3 cups pasta shells
2 tbsp. butter
2 tbsp. olive oil

1 garlic clove, peeled
  and chopped
6 oz. cherry
  tomatoes, halved
¾ cup heavy cream
15 oz. canned asparagus
  tips, drained

salt and freshly ground
  black pepper
1 cup crumbled Double
  Gloucester cheese
  with chives, or cheddar
green salad, to serve

Preheat the broiler just before using. Cut the chicken into thin strips. Trim the leeks, leaving some of the dark green tops, then shred and wash in cold water. Peel the onion and cut into thin wedges.

Bring a large pan of lightly salted water to a rolling boil. Add the pasta and cook according to the package directions until tender but still firm to the bite.

Meanwhile, melt the butter with the olive oil in a large heavy pan. Add the chicken and cook, stirring occasionally, for 8 minutes or until browned all over. Add the leeks and onion, and cook for 5 minutes or until softened. Add the garlic and cherry tomatoes, and cook for an additional 2 minutes.

Stir the cream and asparagus tips into the chicken and vegetable mixture, and bring to a boil slowly, then remove from the heat. Drain the pasta and return to the pan. Pour the sauce over the pasta, and season to taste with salt and pepper, then toss lightly.

Spoon the mixture into a gratin dish and sprinkle with the cheese. Cook under the preheated broiler for 5 minutes or until bubbling and golden, turning the dish occasionally. Serve with a green salad.

TASTY TIP

Fresh asparagus is in season during late spring, and can be used in place of canned. Tie in small bundles and cook in lightly salted, boiling water for 5–8 minutes.

Chicken & White Wine Risotto

SERVES 4-6

2 tbsp. oil	3¼ cups chicken	2 tbsp. freshly chopped dill
½ cup (1 stick) butter	stock, heated	or parsley
2 shallots, peeled and	¾ lb. skinless chicken breast	salt and freshly ground
finely chopped	fillets, thinly sliced	black pepper
1¾ cups Arborio rice	½ cup grated	
2½ cups dry white wine	Parmesan cheese	

Heat the oil and half the butter in a large heavy saucepan over a medium-high heat. Add the shallots and cook for 2 minutes or until softened, stirring frequently. Add the rice and cook for 2–3 minutes, stirring frequently, until the rice is translucent and well coated.

Pour in half the wine; it will bubble and steam rapidly. Cook, stirring constantly, until the liquid is absorbed. Add a ladleful of the hot stock and cook until the liquid is absorbed. Carefully stir in the chicken.

Continue adding the stock, about half a ladleful at a time, allowing each addition to be absorbed before adding the next; never allow the rice to cook dry. This process should take about 20 minutes. The risotto should have a creamy consistency, and the rice should be tender, but firm to the bite.

HELPFUL HINT

Keep the stock to be added to the risotto at a low simmer in a separate saucepan, so that it is piping hot when added to the rice. This will help to achieve a perfect creamy texture.

Stir in the remaining wine and cook for 2–3 minutes. Remove from the heat and stir in the remaining butter with the Parmesan cheese and half the chopped herbs. Season to taste with salt and pepper. Spoon into warmed shallow bowls and sprinkle each with the remaining chopped herbs. Serve immediately.

Cheesy Chicken Burgers

SERVES 6

1 tbsp. corn oil
1 small onion, peeled and
finely chopped
1 garlic clove, peeled
and crushed
½ red bell pepper, seeded
and finely chopped
1 lb. fresh ground chicken
2 tbsp. nonfat plain yogurt
½ cup whole-wheat
bread crumbs

1 tbsp. freshly chopped
herbs, such as parsley
or tarragon
½ cup crumbled
cheddar cheese
salt and freshly ground
black pepper

**For the corn and
carrot relish:**
7 oz. canned corn, drained

1 carrot, peeled and shredded
½ green chile, seeded and
finely chopped
2 tsp. cider vinegar
2 tsp. light brown sugar

To serve:
whole-wheat rolls
lettuce
sliced tomatoes
mixed lettuce leaves

Preheat the broiler. Heat the oil in a skillet and gently cook the onion and garlic for 5 minutes. Add the red bell pepper and cook for 5 minutes. Transfer into a bowl and set aside.

Add the chicken, yogurt, bread crumbs, herbs, and cheese, and season to taste with salt and pepper. Mix well. Divide and shape the mixture into six burgers. Cover and chill in the refrigerator for at least 20 minutes.

To make the relish, put all the ingredients in a small saucepan with 1 tablespoon of water, and heat gently, stirring occasionally, until all the sugar has dissolved. Cover and cook over a low heat for 2 minutes, then uncover and cook for an additional minute or until the relish is thick.

Place the burgers on a lightly greased broiler pan, and broil under a medium heat for 8–10 minutes on each side until browned and cooked through.

Warm the rolls, if desired, then split in half and fill with the burgers, lettuce, sliced tomatoes, and relish, serving some mixed lettuce leaves on the side.

Cheesy Baked Chicken Macaroni

SERVES 4

1 tbsp. olive oil
3¾ cups diced boneless and
　skinless chicken breasts
⅛ cup diced pancetta
1 onion, peeled
　and chopped
1 garlic clove, peeled
　and chopped
1½ cups tomato sauce

14 oz. canned chopped
　tomatoes
2 tbsp. freshly chopped
　basil, plus leaves
　to garnish
salt and freshly ground
　black pepper
3 cups macaroni

1¼ cups drained
　and chopped
　mozzarella cheese
½ cup grated Gruyère cheese
½ cup freshly grated
　Parmesan cheese

Preheat the broiler just before cooking. Heat the oil in a large skillet, and cook the chicken for 8 minutes or until browned, stirring occasionally. Drain on paper towels and set aside. Add the diced pancetta to the skillet, and fry until browned and crispy. Remove from the skillet and set aside. Add the onion and garlic to the skillet, and cook for 5 minutes or until softened. Stir in the tomato sauce, chopped tomatoes, and basil, and season to taste with salt and pepper. Bring to a boil, lower the heat, and simmer the sauce for about 5 minutes.

Meanwhile, bring a large pan of lightly salted water to a boil. Add the macaroni and cook according to the package directions until tender but still firm to the bite.

Drain the macaroni thoroughly, then return to the pan and stir in the sauce, chicken, and mozzarella. Spoon into a shallow ovenproof dish.

Sprinkle the pancetta over the macaroni. Sprinkle the Gruyère and Parmesan cheeses on top. Place under the preheated broiler and cook for 5–10 minutes until golden-brown; turn the dish occasionally. Garnish and serve immediately.

FOOD FACT

Pancetta (unsmoked cured bacon) imparts a wonderful flavor to a dish; it is available from Italian delicatessens and supermarkets.

Sweet & Sour Turkey

2 tbsp. peanut oil
2 garlic cloves, peeled
and chopped
1 tbsp. freshly grated ginger
4 scallions, trimmed and cut
into 1½-in. lengths
1 lb. turkey breast, skinned
and cut into strips

1 red bell pepper, seeded
and cut into 1-in. squares
8 oz. canned water
chestnuts, drained
⅔ cup chicken stock
2 tbsp. Chinese rice wine
3 tbsp. light soy sauce
2 tsp. dark soy sauce
2 tbsp. tomato paste

2 tbsp. white wine vinegar
1 tbsp. sugar
1 tbsp. cornstarch
egg-fried rice, to serve

Heat the wok over a high heat, add the oil, and, when hot, add the garlic, ginger, and scallions, and stir-fry for about 20 seconds.

Add the turkey to the wok and stir-fry for 2 minutes or until beginning to color. Add the bell peppers and water chestnuts, and stir-fry for an additional 2 minutes.

Mix the chicken stock, Chinese rice wine, light and dark soy sauces, tomato paste, white wine vinegar, and the sugar together in a small bowl. Add the mixture to the wok, stir, and bring the sauce to a boil.

Mix together the cornstarch with 2 tablespoons of water, and add to the wok. Reduce the heat and simmer for 3 minutes or until the turkey is cooked thoroughly and the sauce is slightly thickened and glossy. Serve immediately with egg-fried rice.

Green Turkey Curry

SERVES 4

4 baby eggplants, trimmed and quartered
1 tsp. salt
2 tbsp. sunflower oil
4 shallots, peeled and halved, or quartered if large
2 garlic cloves, peeled and sliced

2 tbsp. Thai green curry paste
⅔ cup chicken stock
1 tbsp. Thai fish sauce
1 tbsp. lemon juice
1½ cups cubed, boneless, skinless turkey breast
1 red bell pepper, seeded and sliced

¾ cup trimmed and halved green beans
⅛ cup creamed coconut
freshly boiled rice or steamed Thai fragrant rice, to serve

Place the eggplants into a colander, and sprinkle with the salt. Set over a plate or in the sink to drain, and leave for 30 minutes. Rinse under cold running water, and pat dry on paper towels.

Heat a wok or large skillet, add the sunflower oil, and, when hot, add the shallots and garlic, and stir-fry for 3 minutes or until beginning to brown. Add the curry paste and stir-fry for 1–2 minutes. Pour in the stock, fish sauce, and lemon juice, and simmer for 10 minutes.

Add the turkey, red bell pepper, and green beans to the wok with the eggplants. Return to a boil, then simmer for 10–15 minutes until the turkey and vegetables are tender. Add the creamed coconut, and stir until melted and the sauce has thickened. Turn into a warmed serving dish, and serve immediately with rice.

Creamy Turkey & Tomato Pasta

SERVES 4

4 tbsp. olive oil
1 lb. turkey breasts, cut into
   bite-sized pieces
1¼ lb. cherry tomatoes, on
   the vine

2 garlic cloves, peeled
   and chopped
4 tbsp. balsamic vinegar
salt and freshly ground
   black pepper

12 oz. tagliatelle
4 tbsp. freshly chopped basil
¾ cup crème fraîche
shaved Parmesan cheese,
   to garnish

Preheat the oven to 400°F. Heat 2 tablespoons of the olive oil in a large skillet. Add the turkey and cook for 5 minutes or until sealed, turning occasionally. Transfer to a roasting pan and add the remaining olive oil, the vine tomatoes, garlic, and balsamic vinegar. Stir well and season to taste with salt and pepper. Cook in the preheated oven for 30 minutes or until the turkey is tender, turning the tomatoes and turkey once.

Meanwhile, bring a large pan of lightly salted water to a rolling boil. Add the pasta and cook according to the package directions until tender but still firm to the bite. Drain, return to the pan, and keep warm. Stir the basil and seasoning into the crème fraîche.

Remove the roasting pan from the oven and discard the vines. Stir the crème fraîche and basil mix into the turkey and tomato mixture and return to the oven for 1–2 minutes until thoroughly heated through.

Stir the turkey and tomato mixture into the pasta and toss lightly together. Spoon into a warmed serving dish. Garnish with Parmesan cheese shavings and serve immediately.

Turkey & Tomato Tagine

SERVES 4

For the meatballs:
1 lb. fresh ground turkey
1 small onion, peeled and very finely chopped
1 garlic clove, peeled and crushed
1 tbsp. freshly chopped cilantro
1 tsp. cumin
1 tbsp. olive oil

salt and freshly ground black pepper

For the sauce:
1 onion, peeled and finely chopped
1 garlic clove, peeled and crushed
⅔ cup turkey stock

14 oz. canned chopped tomatoes
½ tsp. ground cumin
½ tsp. ground cinnamon
pinch cayenne pepper
freshly chopped parsley
freshly chopped herbs, to garnish
couscous or rice, to serve

Preheat the oven to 375˚F. Put all the ingredients (except for the oil) for the meatballs in a bowl, and mix well. Season to taste with salt and pepper. Shape into 20 balls, about the size of walnuts. Put on a tray, cover lightly, and chill in the refrigerator while making the sauce. Put the onion and garlic in a saucepan with ½ cup of the stock. Cook over a low heat until all the stock has evaporated. Continue cooking for 1 minute or until the onions start to brown.

Add the remaining stock to the pan with the tomatoes, cumin, cinnamon, and cayenne pepper. Simmer for 10 minutes until slightly thickened and reduced. Stir in the parsley and season to taste. Heat the oil in a large nonstick skillet, and cook the meatballs in two batches until lightly browned all over.

Using a slotted spoon, lift the meatballs out, and drain on absorbent paper towels.

Pour the sauce into a tagine or an ovenproof casserole dish. Top with the meatballs, cover, and cook in the preheated oven for 25–30 minutes until the meatballs are cooked through and the sauce is bubbling. Garnish with freshly chopped herbs, and serve immediately with couscous or plain boiled rice.

Turkey Cutlets with Apricot Chutney

SERVES 4

4 turkey steaks, ¼ lb. each
1 tbsp. all-purpose flour
salt and freshly ground
    black pepper
1 tbsp. olive oil
Italian flat-leaf parsely
    sprigs, to garnish
orange wedges, to serve

For the apricot chutney:
⅔ cup chopped
    dried apricots
1 red onion, peeled and
    finely chopped
1 tsp. freshly grated ginger
2 tbsp. superfine sugar
½ tbsp. grated orange zest

½ cup fresh orange juice
½ cup ruby port
1 whole clove
1 tbsp. freshly
    chopped cilantro

Put a turkey steak onto a sheet of plastic wrap or nonstick baking parchment. Cover with a second sheet. Using a rolling pin, gently pound the turkey until the meat is flattened to about ¼ inch thick. Repeat to make four cutlets.

Mix the flour with the salt and pepper, and use to lightly dust the turkey cutlets. Put the turkey cutlets on a board or cookie sheet, and cover with a piece of plastic wrap or nonstick baking parchment. Chill in the refrigerator until ready to cook.

For the apricot chutney, put the apricots, onion, ginger, sugar, orange zest, orange juice, port, and clove into a saucepan. Slowly bring to a boil and simmer uncovered for 10 minutes, stirring occasionally, until thick and syrupy.

Remove the clove and stir in the chopped cilantro. Heat the oil in a griddle pan, and cook the turkey cutlets (in two batches if necessary) for 3–4 minutes on each side until golden brown and tender.

Spoon the chutney onto four individual serving plates. Place a turkey cutlet on top of each spoonful of chutney. Garnish with sprigs of parsley, and serve immediately with orange wedges.

Turkey & Pesto Rice Roulades

SERVES 4

cooked white rice, at
  room temperature
1 garlic clove, peeled
  and crushed
1–2 tbsp. grated
  Parmesan cheese
2 tbsp. prepared pesto sauce

2 tbsp. pine nuts, lightly
  toasted and chopped
4 turkey steaks, each
  weighing about 5 oz.
salt and freshly ground
  black pepper
4 slices prosciutto
2 tbsp. olive oil

¼ cup white wine
2 tbsp. butter, chilled

To serve:
freshly cooked spinach
freshly cooked pasta

Put the rice in a bowl and add the garlic, Parmesan cheese, pesto, and pine nuts. Stir to combine the ingredients, then set aside.

Place the turkey steaks on a chopping board and, using a sharp knife, slice horizontally through each steak, without cutting all the way through. Fold back the top slice and cover with baking parchment. Flatten slightly by pounding with a meat mallet or rolling pin.

Season each steak with salt and pepper. Divide the stuffing equally among the steaks, spreading evenly over one half. Fold the steaks in half to enclose the filling, then wrap each steak in a slice of prosciutto and secure with wooden toothpicks.

Heat the oil in a large skillet over medium heat. Cook the steaks for 5 minutes or until golden on one side. Turn and cook for an additional 2 minutes. Push the steaks to the side and pour in the wine. Allow the wine to bubble and evaporate. Add the butter a little at a time, whisking constantly until the sauce is smooth. Discard the toothpicks, then serve the steaks, drizzled with the sauce, with spinach and pasta.

Turkey Tetrazzini

3¾ cups green and
    white tagliatelle
4 tbsp. butter
4 slices bacon, diced
1 onion, peeled and
    finely chopped
1½ cups thinly sliced
    mushrooms
½ cup all-purpose flour

2 cups chicken stock
½ cup heavy cream
2 tbsp. sherry
5 cups bite-sized pieces
    cooked turkey meat
1 tbsp. freshly
    chopped parsley
freshly grated nutmeg

salt and freshly ground
    black pepper
¼ cup grated Parmesan
    cheese

To garnish:
freshly chopped parsley
Parmesan cheese, grated

Preheat the oven to 350°F. Lightly grease a large ovenproof dish. Bring a large saucepan of lightly salted water to a boil. Add the tagliatelle and cook for 7–9 minutes until tender but still firm to the bite. Drain well and set aside.

In a heavy saucepan, heat the butter and add the bacon. Cook for 2–3 minutes or until crisp and golden. Add the onion and mushrooms, and cook for 3–4 minutes until the vegetables are tender.

Stir in the flour and cook for 2 minutes. Remove from the heat and slowly stir in the stock. Return to the heat and cook, stirring, until a smooth, thick sauce has formed. Add the tagliatelle, then pour in the cream and sherry. Add the turkey and parsley. Season to taste with the nutmeg, salt, and pepper. Toss well to coat.

Turn the mixture into the prepared dish, spreading evenly. Sprinkle the top with the Parmesan cheese, and cook in the preheated oven for 30–35 minutes until crisp, golden, and bubbling. Garnish with chopped parsley and Parmesan cheese. Serve straight from the dish.

Turkey Hash with Potato & Beet

SERVES 4-6

2 tbsp. vegetable oil
4 tbsp. butter
4 slices bacon, diced
   or sliced
1 medium onion, peeled and
   finely chopped

2¼ cups diced
   cooked turkey
2½ cups finely chopped
   cooked potatoes
2–3 tbsp. freshly
   chopped parsley

2 tbsp. all-purpose flour
1¾ cups diced,
   cooked beets
green salad, to serve

In a large, heavy skillet, heat the oil and half the butter over a medium heat until sizzling. Add the bacon and cook for 4 minutes or until crisp and golden, stirring occasionally. Using a slotted spoon, transfer to a large bowl. Add the onion to the pan and cook for 3–4 minutes or until soft and golden, stirring frequently.

Meanwhile, add the turkey, potatoes, parsley, and flour to the cooked bacon in the bowl. Stir and toss gently, then fold in the diced beet.

Add half the remaining butter to the skillet and then the turkey-vegetable mixture. Stir, then spread the mixture to evenly cover the bottom of the pan. Cook for 15 minutes or until the underside is crisp and brown, pressing the hash firmly with a spatula. Remove from the heat.

Place a large plate over the skillet and, holding the plate and pan together with an oven mitt, invert the hash out onto the plate. Heat the remaining butter in the pan, slide the hash back into the pan, and cook for 4 minutes or until crisp and brown on the other side. Invert onto the plate again and serve immediately with a green salad.

TASTY TIP

Make sure that you buy plainly cooked beetroot, rather than the type preserved in vinegar.

Stir–Fried Duck with Cashews

1 lb. duck breast, skinned
3 tbsp. peanut or
   vegetable oil
1 garlic clove, peeled and
   finely chopped
1 tsp. freshly
   shredded ginger

1 carrot, peeled and sliced
¾ cup trimmed snow peas
2 tsp. Chinese rice wine or
   dry sherry
1 tbsp. light soy sauce
1 tsp. cornstarch

½ cup unsalted
   roasted cashews
1 scallion, trimmed and
   finely chopped
1 scallion, shredded
boiled or steamed rice,
   to serve

Trim the duck breasts, discarding any fat, and slice thickly. Heat the wok, add 2 tablespoons of the oil, and, when hot, add the sliced duck breast. Cook for 3–4 minutes until sealed. Using a slotted spoon, remove from the wok, and let drain on paper towels.

Wipe the wok clean and return to the heat. Add the remaining oil, and, when hot, add the garlic and ginger. Stir-fry for 30 seconds, then add the sliced carrots and snow peas. Stir-fry for an additional 2 minutes, then pour in the Chinese rice wine or sherry and soy sauce.

Blend the cornstarch with 1 teaspoon of water, and stir into the wok. Mix well and bring to a boil. Return the duck slices to the wok, and simmer for 5 minutes or until the meat and vegetables are tender. Add the cashews, then remove the wok from the heat.

Sprinkle with the chopped and shredded scallions, and serve immediately with plain boiled or steamed rice.

HELPFUL HINT

To prepare the snow peas, simply top and tail, pulling away as much string from the edges as you can. Dry-fry the cashew nuts in the wok before starting to seal the duck breasts. Take care that the nuts do not burn.

Vegetable Dishes

Spring Vegetable & Herb Risotto

SERVES 2-3

4 cups vegetable stock
½ cup trimmed
    asparagus tips
1 cup scrubbed baby carrots
½ cup fresh or frozen peas
½ cup trimmed green beans
1 tbsp. olive oil

1 onion, peeled and
    finely chopped
1 garlic clove, peeled and
    finely chopped
2 tsp. freshly
    chopped thyme
1 cup risotto rice

⅔ cup white wine
1 tbsp. each freshly chopped
    basil, chives, and parsley
1 tbsp. lemon zest
3 tbsp. crème fraîche
salt and freshly ground
    black pepper

Bring the vegetable stock to a boil in a large saucepan and add the asparagus, baby carrots, peas, and beans. Bring the stock back to a boil, and using a slotted spoon, remove the vegetables at once. Rinse under cold running water. Drain again and set aside. Keep the stock hot.

Heat the oil in a large, deep skillet and add the onion. Cook over a medium heat for 4–5 minutes until starting to brown. Add the garlic and thyme, and cook for a few seconds. Add the rice and stir well for a minute until the rice is hot and coated in oil.

Add the white wine and stir constantly until the wine is almost completely absorbed by the rice. Begin adding the stock, a ladleful at a time, stirring well and waiting until the last ladleful has been absorbed before stirring in the next. Add the vegetables after using about half of the stock. Continue until all the stock is used. This will take 20–25 minutes. The rice and vegetables should both be tender.

Remove the skillet from the heat. Stir in the herbs, lemon zest, and crème fraîche. Season to taste with salt and pepper, and serve immediately.

Roast Butternut Squash Risotto

1 medium butternut squash
2 tbsp. olive oil
1 garlic bulb, cloves
  separated but unpeeled
1 tbsp. unsalted butter
1¼ cups risotto rice
large pinch of
  saffron strands

⅔ cup dry white wine
4 cups vegetable stock
1 tbsp. freshly
  chopped parsley
1 tbsp. freshly
  chopped oregano
½ cup finely grated
  Parmesan cheese

salt and freshly ground
  black pepper
fresh oregano sprigs,
  to garnish
extra Parmesan cheese,
  to serve

Preheat the oven to 375°F. Cut the butternut squash in half, thickly peel, then scoop out the seeds and discard. Cut the flesh into ¾-inch cubes. Pour the oil into a large roasting pan, and heat in the preheated oven for 5 minutes. Add the butternut squash and garlic cloves. Turn in the oil to coat, then roast in the oven for about 25–30 minutes until golden brown and very tender, turning the vegetables halfway through the cooking time.

Melt the butter in a large saucepan. Add the rice and stir over a high heat for a few seconds. Add the saffron and the wine, and boil fiercely until almost totally reduced, stirring frequently. At the same time, heat the stock in a separate saucepan and keep at a steady simmer.

Reduce the heat under the rice to low. Add a ladleful of stock to the saucepan and simmer, stirring until absorbed. Continue adding the stock in this way until the rice is tender. This will take about 20 minutes and it may not be necessary to add all the stock.

Turn off the heat and stir in the herbs, Parmesan cheese, and seasoning. Cover and allow to stand for 2–3 minutes. Quickly remove the skins from the roasted garlic. Add to the risotto with the butternut squash and mix gently. Garnish with sprigs of oregano, and serve immediately with Parmesan cheese.

Adzuki Bean & Rice Burgers

SERVES 4

2½ tbsp. sunflower oil
1 medium onion, peeled and
   very finely chopped
1 garlic clove, peeled
   and crushed
1 tsp. curry paste
1⅓ cups basmati rice
14 oz. canned adzuki beans,
   drained and rinsed
   (kidney beans may also
   be used)

1 cup vegetable stock
¼ lb. firm tofu, crumbled
1 tsp. garam masala
2 tbsp. freshly
   chopped cilantro
salt and freshly ground
   black pepper

For the carrot raita:
2 large carrots, peeled
   and shredded
½ cucumber, diced
⅔ cup Greek-style yogurt

To serve:
whole-wheat
   hamburger buns
tomato slices
lettuce leaves

Heat 1 tablespoon of the oil in a saucepan and gently cook the onion for 10 minutes until soft. Add the garlic and curry paste, and cook for a few more seconds. Stir in the rice and beans.

Pour in the stock, bring to a boil, and simmer for 12 minutes or until all the stock has been absorbed—do not lift the lid for the first 10 minutes of cooking. Set aside.

Lightly mash the tofu. Add to the rice mixture with the garam masala, cilantro, salt, and pepper. Mix. Shape the mixture into eight patties. Chill in the refrigerator for 30 minutes.

Meanwhile, make the raita. Mix together the carrots, cucumber, and yogurt. Spoon into a small bowl and chill in the refrigerator until ready to serve.

Heat the remaining oil in a large skillet. Fry the patties, in batches if necessary, for 4–5 minutes on each side until lightly browned. Serve in the buns with tomato slices and lettuce. Accompany with the raita.

Mediterranean Feast

SERVES 4

1 small head of lettuce
1½ cups green beans
8 oz. baby new
   potatoes, scrubbed
4 large eggs
1 green bell pepper
1 medium onion, peeled
7 oz. canned tuna in water,
   drained and flaked into
   small pieces

½ cup small cubes hard
   cheese, such as cheddar
8 ripe but firm cherry
   tomatoes, quartered
5 tbsp. pitted ripe
   olives, halved
freshly chopped basil,
   to garnish

For the lime vinaigrette:
3 tbsp. light olive oil
2 tbsp. white wine vinegar
4 tbsp. lime juice
2 tsp. grated lime zest
1 tsp. mustard
1–2 tsp. sugar
salt and freshly ground
   black pepper

Quarter the lettuce and remove the hard core. Tear into bite-size pieces and arrange on a large serving platter or four individual plates.

Cook the green beans in boiling, salted water for 8 minutes, and the potatoes for 10 minutes or until tender. Drain and rinse in cold water until cool, then cut both the beans and potatoes in half with a sharp knife.

Boil the eggs for 10 minutes, then rinse thoroughly under cold running water until cool. Remove the shells under the water, then cut each egg into four.

Remove the seeds from the bell pepper and cut into thin strips. Finely chop the onion. Arrange the beans, potatoes, eggs, bell peppers, and onion on top of the lettuce. Add the tuna, cheese, and tomatoes. Sprinkle with the olives and garnish with the basil.

To make the vinaigrette, place all the ingredients in a screw-top jar, and shake vigorously until everything is mixed thoroughly. Spoon 4 tablespoons over the top of the prepared salad, and serve the remainder separately.

Carrot, Celeriac & Sesame Seed Salad

SERVES 6

1 head celeriac
2 medium carrots, peeled
5 tbsp. seedless raisins
2 tbsp. sesame seeds
freshly chopped parsley,
    to garnish

**For the lemon and
    chile dressing:**
1 tbsp. grated lemon zest
4 tbsp. lemon juice
2 tbsp. corn oil
2 tbsp. honey

1 red Thai chile, seeded and
    finely chopped
salt and freshly ground
    black pepper

Slice the celeriac into thin matchsticks. Place in a small saucepan of boiling, salted water, and boil for 2 minutes.

Drain and rinse the celeriac in cold water, and place in a mixing bowl.

Finely grate the carrot. Add the carrot and the raisins to the celeriac in the bowl.

Place the sesame seeds under a hot broiler or fry in a skillet for 1–2 minutes until golden brown, then allow to cool.

Make the dressing by beating together the lemon zest, lemon juice, oil, honey, chile, and seasoning, or by shaking thoroughly in a screw-top jar.

Pour 2 tablespoons of the dressing over the salad and toss well. Turn into a serving dish, and sprinkle over the toasted sesame seeds and chopped parsley. Serve the remaining dressing separately.

FOOD FACT

Celeriac is a root vegetable that is similar in taste to celery, but with a texture closer to parsnip. This versatile vegetable has a creamy taste and is also delicious in soups and gratins.

Indonesian Salad with Peanut Dressing

SERVES 4

½ lb. new
potatoes, scrubbed
1 large carrot, peeled and
thinly sliced
¾ cup trimmed
green beans
½ lb. tiny cauliflower florets
¾ cup cucumber,
thinly sliced

1½ cups fresh bean sprouts
3 large eggs, hard-boiled
and quartered

For the peanut dressing:
2 tbsp. sesame oil
1 garlic clove, peeled
and crushed

1 red chile, seeded and
finely chopped
⅔ cup crunchy
peanut butter
6 tbsp. hot vegetable stock
2 tsp. light brown sugar
2 tsp. dark soy sauce
1 tbsp. lime juice

Cook the potatoes in a saucepan of salted, boiling water for 15–20 minutes until tender. Remove with a slotted spoon and slice thickly into a large bowl. Keep the saucepan of water boiling.

Add the carrot, green beans, and cauliflower to the water, return to a boil, and cook for 2 minutes or until just tender. Drain and rinse under cold running water, then drain well. Add to the potatoes with the cucumber and bean sprouts.

To make the dressing, gently heat the sesame oil in a small saucepan. Add the garlic and chile and cook for a few seconds, then remove from the heat. Stir in the peanut butter.

Stir in the stock, a little at a time. Add the remaining ingredients and mix together to make a thick, creamy dressing.

Divide the vegetables between four plates and arrange the eggs on top. Drizzle the dressing over the salad and serve immediately.

Chinese Salad with Soy & Ginger Dressing

SERVES 4

1 head of Chinese cabbage
7 oz. canned water
  chestnuts, drained
6 scallions, trimmed
4 ripe but firm cherry
  tomatoes
1 cup snow peas
¾ cup bean sprouts

2 tbsp. freshly
  chopped cilantro

**For the soy and
  ginger dressing:**
2 tbsp. corn oil
4 tbsp. light soy sauce

1-in. piece ginger, peeled
  and grated
2 tbsp. lemon zest
1 tbsp. lemon juice
salt and freshly ground
  black pepper
crusty white bread, to serve

Rinse and finely shred the Chinese cabbage and place in a serving dish.

Slice the water chestnuts into small slivers and cut the scallions diagonally into 1-inch lengths, then split lengthwise into thin strips.

Cut the tomatoes in half, then slice each half into 3 wedges, and set aside.

Simmer the snow peas in boiling water for 2 minutes until beginning to soften, drain, and cut in half diagonally.

Arrange the water chestnuts, scallions, snow peas, tomatoes, and bean sprouts on top of the shredded Chinese cabbage. Garnish with the freshly chopped cilantro.

Make the dressing by whisking all the ingredients together in a small bowl until mixed thoroughly. Serve with the bread and the salad.

Vegetables in Coconut Milk with Rice Noodles

⅓ cup creamed coconut
1 tsp. salt
2 tbsp. sunflower oil
2 garlic cloves, peeled and finely chopped
2 red bell peppers, seeded

and cut into thin strips
1-in. piece of ginger, peeled and cut into thin strips
¼ lb. baby corn
2 tsp. cornstarch
2 avocados, medium-ripe

but firm
1 small head Romaine lettuce, cut into thick strips
freshly cooked rice noodles, to serve

Roughly chop the creamed coconut, place in a bowl with the salt, then pour in 2½ cups of boiling water. Stir until the coconut has dissolved completely, and set aside.

Heat a wok or large skillet, add the oil, and, when hot, add the chopped garlic, sliced bell peppers, and ginger. Cook for 30 seconds, then cover and cook very gently for 10 minutes or until the peppers are soft.

Pour in the coconut milk and bring to a boil. Stir in the baby corn, cover, and simmer for 5 minutes. Blend the cornstarch with 2 teaspoons of water, pour into the wok, and cook, stirring, for 2 minutes or until thickened slightly.

Cut the avocados in half, peel, pit, and slice. Add to the wok with the lettuce strips, and stir until well mixed and heated through. Serve immediately on a bed of rice noodles.

FOOD FACT

Dried flat rice noodles, rice sticks and stir-fry rice noodles are all made from rice flour and come in varying thicknesses. Check the packet for cooking instructions.

Mixed Vegetables Stir–Fry

SERVES 4

2 tbsp. peanut oil
4 garlic cloves, peeled and
   finely sliced
1-in. piece ginger, peeled
   and finely sliced
¾ cup broccoli florets
heaping ½ cup trimmed
   snow peas

1 carrot, peeled and
   thinly sliced
1 green bell pepper, seeded
   and cut into strips
1 red bell pepper, seeded
   and cut into strips
1 tbsp. soy sauce
1 tbsp. hoisin sauce

1 tsp. sugar
salt and freshly ground
   black pepper
4 scallions, trimmed and
   shredded, to garnish

Heat a wok, add the oil, and, when hot, add the garlic and ginger slices, and stir-fry for 1 minute.

Add the broccoli florets to the wok, stir-fry for 1 minute, then add the snow peas, carrots, and the green and red bell peppers, and stir-fry for an additional 3–4 minutes or until tender but still crisp.

Blend the soy sauce, hoisin sauce, and sugar in a small bowl. Stir well, season to taste with salt and pepper, and pour into the wok. Transfer the vegetables to a warmed serving dish. Garnish with shredded scallions and serve immediately with a selection of other Thai dishes.

HELPFUL HINT

Vary the combination of vegetables—try asparagus spears cut into short lengths, sliced mushrooms, green beans, red onion wedges, or cauliflower florets.

Bean & Cashew Stir-Fry

SERVES 4

3 tbsp. sunflower oil
1 onion, peeled and
   finely chopped
1 celery stalk, trimmed
   and chopped
1-in. piece ginger, peeled
   and grated
2 garlic cloves, peeled
   and crushed

1 red chile, seeded and
   finely chopped
1 cup trimmed and halved
   green beans
1¼ cups diagonally sliced
   snow peas (thirds)
2⅓ cups unsalted cashews
1 tsp. brown sugar
½ cup vegetable stock
2 tbsp. dry sherry

1 tbsp. light soy sauce
1 tsp. red wine vinegar
salt and freshly ground
   black pepper
freshly chopped cilantro,
   to garnish

Heat a wok or large skillet, add the oil, and, when hot, add the onion and celery, and stir-fry gently for 3–4 minutes or until softened.

Add the ginger, garlic, and chile to the wok, and stir-fry for 30 seconds. Stir in the green beans, snow peas, and cashews, and continue to stir-fry for 1–2 minutes or until the nuts are golden brown.

Dissolve the sugar in the stock, then blend with the sherry, soy sauce, and vinegar. Stir into the bean mixture, and bring to a boil. Simmer gently, stirring occasionally, for 3–4 minutes or until the beans and snow peas are tender but still crisp, and the sauce has thickened slightly. Season to taste with salt and pepper. Transfer to a warmed serving bowl, or spoon onto individual plates. Sprinkle with freshly chopped cilantro and serve immediately.

Thai Fried Noodles

1 lb. tofu
2 tbsp. dry sherry
4 oz. medium egg noodles
¾ cup halved snow peas
3 tbsp. peanut oil
1 onion, peeled and
   finely sliced
1 garlic clove, peeled and
   finely sliced

1-in. piece fresh root ginger,
   peeled and finely sliced
2 cups bean sprouts
1 tbsp. Thai fish sauce
2 tbsp. light soy sauce
½ tsp. sugar
salt and freshly ground
   black pepper
½ zucchini, thinly sliced

To garnish:
2 tbsp. roasted peanuts,
   roughly chopped
fresh basil sprigs

Cut the tofu into cubes and place in a bowl. Sprinkle with the sherry, and toss to coat. Cover loosely, and let marinate in the refrigerator for 30 minutes.

Bring a large saucepan of lightly salted water to a boil, and add the noodles and snow peas. Simmer for 3 minutes, or according to the package instructions, then drain, and rinse under cold, running water. Leave to drain again.

Heat a wok or large skillet, add the oil, and, when hot, add the onion and stir-fry for 2–3 minutes. Add the garlic and ginger, and stir-fry for 30 seconds. Add the bean sprouts and tofu, then stir in the Thai fish sauce, soy sauce, and sugar, and season to taste.

Stir-fry the tofu mixture over a medium heat for 2–3 minutes, then add the zucchini, noodles, and snow peas, and stir-fry for an additional 1–2 minutes. Tip into a warmed serving dish, or spoon onto individual plates. Sprinkle with the peanuts, add a sprig of basil, and serve immediately.

Thai Noodles & Vegetables with Tofu

SERVES 4

¼ lb. firm tofu
2 tbsp. soy sauce
2 tsp. grated lime zest
2 lemongrass stalks
1 red chile
4 cups vegetable stock
2 slices fresh ginger, peeled
2 garlic cloves, peeled
2 fresh cilantro sprigs

2½ cups dried egg noodles
1¾ cups shiitake or button
   mushrooms, sliced
   if large
2 carrots, peeled and cut
   into matchsticks
1 cup snow peas
2½ cups bok choy or other
   Chinese cabbage

1 tbsp. freshly
   chopped cilantro
salt and freshly ground
   black pepper
fresh cilantro sprigs,
   to garnish

Drain the tofu well and cut into cubes. Put into a shallow dish with the soy sauce and lime zest. Stir well to coat, and leave to marinate for 30 minutes.

Meanwhile, put the lemongrass and chile on a chopping board and bruise with the side of a large knife, ensuring the blade is pointing away from your body. Put the vegetable stock in a large saucepan, and add the lemongrass, chile, ginger, garlic, and cilantro. Bring to a boil, cover, and simmer gently for 20 minutes.

Strain the stock into a clean saucepan. Return to a boil and add the noodles, tofu and its marinade, and the mushrooms. Simmer gently for 4 minutes.

Add the carrots, snow peas, bok choy, and cilantro, and simmer for an additional 3–4 minutes until the vegetables are just tender. Season to taste with salt and pepper. Garnish with cilantro sprigs and serve immediately.

Pad Thai Noodles with Mushrooms

SERVES 4

2 cups flat rice noodles or rice vermicelli
1 tbsp. vegetable oil
2 garlic cloves, peeled and finely chopped
1 medium egg, lightly beaten
2 cups mixed mushrooms, such as shiitake, oyster, field, brown, and wild mushrooms
2 tbsp. lemon juice
1½ tbsp. Thai fish sauce
½ tsp. sugar
½ tsp. cayenne pepper

2 scallions, trimmed and cut into 1-in. pieces
¼ cup fresh bean sprouts

To garnish:
chopped roasted peanuts
freshly chopped cilantro

Cook the noodles according to the package instructions. Drain well and set aside.

Heat a wok or large skillet. Add the oil and garlic. Cook until just golden. Add the egg and stir quickly to break it up.

Cook for a few seconds before adding the noodles and mushrooms. Scrape down the sides of the skillet to ensure they mix with the egg and garlic.

Add the lemon juice, fish sauce, sugar, cayenne pepper, scallions, and half of the bean sprouts, stirring quickly all the time.

Cook over a high heat for an additional 2–3 minutes until everything is heated through.

Turn onto a serving plate. Sprinkle with the remaining bean sprouts. Garnish with the chopped peanuts and cilantro, and serve immediately.

TASTY TIP

An aromatic alternative for this dish is to use lemongrass. Discard the outer leaves, finely chop and add instead of the lemon juice.

Coconut–Baked Zucchini

SERVES 4

3 tbsp. peanut oil
1 onion, peeled and
   finely sliced
4 garlic cloves, peeled
   and crushed

½ tsp. chili powder
1 tsp. ground coriander
6–8 tbsp. unsweetened
   shredded dry coconut
1 tbsp. tomato paste

1½ lbs. zucchini,
   thinly sliced
freshly chopped parsley,
   to garnish

Preheat the oven to 350˚F. Lightly grease a large, shallow ovenproof dish. Heat a wok, add the oil, and, when hot, add the onion, and stir-fry for 2–3 minutes until softened. Add the garlic, chili powder and coriander, and stir-fry for 1–2 minutes.

Pour 1¼ cups cold water into the wok, and bring to a boil. Add the shredded coconut and tomato paste, and simmer for 3–4 minutes; most of the water will evaporate by this stage. Spoon 4 tablespoons of the spice and coconut mixture into a small bowl, and set aside.

Stir the zucchini into the remaining spice and coconut mixture, coating well. Spoon the zucchini into the greased dish, and sprinkle the spice and coconut mixture evenly over the top. Bake uncovered in the preheated oven for 15–20 minutes until golden. Garnish with chopped parsley, and serve immediately.

HELPFUL HINT

Dry shredded coconut has a relatively short shelf life. Unless you use it in large quantities, buy it in small packets, checking the sell-by date. Once opened, it should be used within 2 months.

Zucchini Lasagne

SERVES 8

2 tbsp. olive oil
1 medium onion, peeled and
    finely chopped
4 cups wiped and thinly
    sliced mushrooms
3–4 zucchini, trimmed and
    thinly sliced
2 garlic cloves, peeled and
    finely chopped

½ tsp. dried thyme
1–2 tbsp. freshly chopped
    basil or Italian
    flat-leaf parsley
salt and freshly ground
    black pepper
1 quantity prepared white
    sauce, (*see* page 187)

12 oz. lasagna
    noodles, cooked
2 cups shredded
    mozzarella cheese
½ cup grated
    Parmesan cheese
14 oz. canned chopped
    tomatoes, drained

Preheat the oven to 400˚F. Heat the oil in a large skillet, then add the onion and cook for 3–5 minutes. Add the mushrooms and cook for 2 minutes. Add the zucchini and cook for an additional 3–4 minutes until tender. Stir in the garlic, thyme, and basil or parsley, then season to taste with salt and pepper. Remove from the heat and set aside.

Spoon one third of the white sauce onto the base of a lightly greased large baking dish. Arrange a layer of lasagna noodles over the sauce. Spread half the zucchini mixture over the pasta, then sprinkle with some of the mozzarella and some of the Parmesan cheese. Repeat with more white sauce and another layer of lasagna, then cover with half the drained tomatoes.

Cover the tomatoes with lasagna noodles, the remaining zucchini mixture, and some mozzarella and Parmesan cheese. Repeat the layers, ending with a layer of lasagna noodles, white sauce, and the remaining Parmesan cheese. Bake in the preheated oven for 35 minutes or until golden. Serve immediately.

Fusilli with Zucchini & Sun–Dried Tomatoes

SERVES 6

5 tbsp. olive oil
1 large onion, peeled and
  thinly sliced
2 garlic cloves, peeled and
  finely chopped
1½ lbs. zucchini, trimmed
  and sliced

14 oz. canned chopped
  plum tomatoes
12 sun-dried tomatoes, cut
  into thin strips
salt and freshly ground
  black pepper
4 cups fusilli

2 tbsp. butter, diced
2 tbsp. freshly chopped basil
  or Italian flat-leaf parsley
grated Parmesan or
  pecorino cheese,
  for serving

Heat 2 tablespoons of the olive oil in a large skillet, then add the onion and cook for 5-7 minutes until softened. Add the chopped garlic and zucchini slices, and cook for an additional 5 minutes, stirring occasionally.

Stir the chopped tomatoes and the sun-dried tomatoes into the skillet, and season to taste with salt and pepper. Cook until the zucchini are just tender and the sauce is slightly thickened.

Bring a large pan of lightly salted water to a rolling boil. Add the fusilli and cook according to the package directions until tender but still firm to the bite.

Drain the fusilli thoroughly and return to the pan. Add the butter and remaining oil, and toss to coat. Stir the chopped basil or parsley into the zucchini mixture and pour over the fusilli. Toss and spoon into a warmed serving dish. Serve with grated Parmesan or pecorino cheese.

Pasta with Zucchini, Rosemary & Lemon

SERVES 4

4½ cups dried pasta shapes, such as rigatoni
1½ tbsp. extra-virgin olive oil
2 garlic cloves, peeled and finely chopped
4 medium zucchini, thinly sliced

1 tbsp. freshly chopped rosemary
1 tbsp. freshly chopped parsley
2 tbsp. lemon zest
5 tbsp. lemon juice
2 tbsp. pitted ripe olives, coarsely chopped

2 tbsp. pitted green olives, coarsely chopped
salt and freshly ground black pepper

To garnish:
lemon slices
fresh rosemary sprigs

Bring a large saucepan of salted water to a boil and add the dried pasta.

Return to a boil and cook according to the package instructions until tender but still firm to the bite.

Meanwhile, when the pasta is almost done, heat the oil in a large skillet and add the garlic.

Cook over a medium heat until the garlic just begins to brown. Be careful not to overcook the garlic at this stage or it will become bitter.

Add the zucchini, rosemary, parsley, lemon zest, and juice. Cook for 3–4 minutes until the zucchini are just tender.

Add the olives to the skillet and stir well. Season to taste with salt and pepper, and remove from the heat.

Drain the pasta well and add to the skillet. Stir until combined thoroughly. Garnish with lemon and sprigs of fresh rosemary, and serve immediately.

Vegetarian Spaghetti Bolognese

SERVES 4

2 tbsp. olive oil
1 onion, peeled and
  finely chopped
1 carrot, peeled and
  finely chopped
1 celery stick, trimmed and
  finely chopped

¼ lb. ground soy meat
  substitute
½ cup red wine
1¼ cups vegetable stock
1 tsp. ketchup
4 tbsp. tomato paste
4 cups dried spaghetti

4 tbsp. crème fraîche
salt and freshly ground
  black pepper
1 tbsp. freshly
  chopped parsley

Heat the oil in a large saucepan, and add the onion, carrot, and celery. Cook gently for 10 minutes, adding a little water if necessary, until softened and starting to brown.

Add the soy and cook an additional 2–3 minutes before adding the red wine. Increase the heat and simmer gently until nearly all the wine has evaporated.

Mix the vegetable stock and ketchup together, and add about half to the soy mixture, along with the tomato paste. Cover and simmer gently for about 45 minutes, adding the remaining stock as necessary.

Meanwhile, bring a large saucepan of salted water to a boil and add the spaghetti. Cook according to the package instructions until tender but still firm to the bite. Drain well. Remove from the heat, add the crème fraîche, and season to taste with salt and pepper. Stir in the parsley, and serve immediately with the pasta.

Creamy Vegetable Korma

SERVES 4-6

2 tbsp. ghee or vegetable oil
1 large onion, peeled
   and chopped
2 garlic cloves, peeled
   and crushed
1-in. piece of ginger, peeled
   and grated
4 green cardamom pods
2 tsp. ground coriander
1 tsp. ground cumin
1 tsp. ground turmeric

finely grated zest and juice
   of ½ lemon
½ cup ground almonds
1¾ cups vegetable stock
2⅔ cups peeled and
   diced potatoes
1 lb. mixed vegetables,
   such as cauliflower,
   carrots, and turnips,
   cut into chunks
⅔ cup heavy cream

3 tbsp. freshly
   chopped cilantro
salt and freshly ground
   black pepper
naan bread, to serve

Heat the ghee or oil in a large saucepan. Add the onion and cook for 5 minutes. Stir in the garlic and ginger, and cook for an additional 5 minutes or until soft and just beginning to brown.

Stir in the cardamom, coriander, cumin, and turmeric. Continue cooking over a low heat for 1 minute, while stirring.

Stir in the lemon zest and juice, and almonds. Blend in the vegetable stock. Slowly bring to a boil, stirring occasionally.

Add the potatoes and vegetables. Bring back to a boil, then reduce the heat, cover, and simmer for 35–40 minutes until the vegetables are just tender. Check after 25 minutes and add more stock if needed.

Slowly stir in the cream and chopped cilantro. Season to taste with salt and pepper. Cook very gently until heated through, but do not boil. Serve immediately with naan bread.

Pumpkin & Chickpea Curry

SERVES 4

1 tbsp. vegetable oil
1 small onion, peeled
   and sliced
2 garlic cloves, peeled and
   finely chopped
1-in. piece ginger, peeled
   and grated
1 tsp. ground coriander
½ tsp. ground cumin
½ tsp. ground turmeric

¼ tsp. ground cinnamon
2 tomatoes, chopped
2 red Thai chiles, seeded
   and finely chopped
2½ cups cubed pumpkin or
   butternut squash flesh
1 tbsp. hot curry paste
1¼ cups vegetable stock
1 large, firm banana

14 oz. canned chickpeas,
   drained and rinsed
salt and freshly ground
   black pepper
1 tbsp. freshly
   chopped cilantro
fresh cilantro sprigs,
   to garnish
rice or naan bread, to serve

Heat 1 tablespoon of the oil in a saucepan and add the onion. Cook gently for 5 minutes until softened.

Add the garlic, ginger, and spices, and cook for an additional minute. Add the chopped tomatoes and chiles, and cook for another minute.

Add the pumpkin and curry paste and cook for 3–4 minutes before adding the stock.

Stir well, bring to a boil, and simmer for 20 minutes until the pumpkin is tender.

Thickly slice the banana and add to the pumpkin along with the chickpeas. Simmer for an additional 5 minutes.

Season to taste with salt and pepper, and add the chopped cilantro. Serve immediately, garnished with cilantro sprigs and some rice or naan bread.

HELPFUL HINT

Curry pastes come in mild, medium, and hot varieties. Although hot curry paste is recommended in this recipe, use whichever one you prefer.

Mushroom Stew

SERVES 4

¼ cup dried porcini mushrooms

2 lbs. assorted fresh mushrooms, wiped

2 tbsp. good-quality virgin olive oil

1 onion, peeled and finely chopped

2 garlic cloves, peeled and finely chopped

1 tbsp. fresh thyme leaves

pinch ground cloves

salt and freshly ground black pepper

2¼ cups peeled, seeded, and chopped tomatoes

2 cups instant polenta

2½ cups vegetable stock

3 tbsp. freshly chopped mixed herbs

parsley sprigs, to garnish

Soak the porcini mushrooms in a small bowl of hot water for 20 minutes. Drain and set them aside along with their their soaking liquid. Cut the fresh mushrooms in half and set aside.

In a saucepan, heat the oil and add the onion. Cook gently for 5–7 minutes until softened. Add the garlic, thyme, and cloves, and continue cooking for 2 minutes.

Add all the mushrooms and cook for 8–10 minutes until the mushrooms have softened, stirring often. Season to taste with salt and pepper, and add the tomatoes and the soaking liquid. Simmer, partly covered, over a low heat for about 20 minutes until thickened. Adjust the seasoning to taste.

Meanwhile, cook the polenta according to the package instructions using the vegetable stock. Stir in the herbs and divide among four dishes.

Spoon the mushrooms over the polenta, garnish with the parsley, and serve immediately.

Pasta Shells with Broccoli & Capers

SERVES 4

3½ cups conchiglie (shells)
1 lb. broccoli florets, cut into
    small pieces
5 tbsp. olive oil
1 large onion, peeled and
    finely chopped

4 tbsp. capers in brine,
    rinsed and drained
½ tsp. dried pepper
    flakes (optional)
¾ cup freshly grated
    Parmesan cheese, plus
    extra to serve

¼ cup grated
    pecorino cheese
salt and freshly ground
    black pepper
2 tbsp. freshly chopped
    Italian flat-leaf parsley,
    to garnish

Bring a large pan of lightly salted water to a rolling boil. Add the conchiglie, then return to a boil and cook for 2 minutes. Add the broccoli to the pan. Return to a boil and continue cooking for 8–10 minutes until the conchiglie are tender but still firm to the bite.

Meanwhile, heat the olive oil in a large skillet, then add the onion and cook for 5 minutes or until softened, stirring frequently. Stir in the capers and pepper flakes, and cook for an additional 2 minutes.

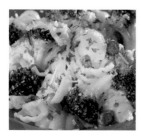

Drain the pasta and broccoli and add to the skillet. Toss the ingredients to mix thoroughly. Sprinkle over the cheeses, then stir until the cheeses have just melted. Season to taste with salt and pepper, then spoon into a warmed serving dish. Garnish with chopped parsley and serve immediately with extra Parmesan cheese.

Fusilli Pasta with Spicy Tomato Salsa

6 large, ripe tomatoes
2 tbsp. lemon juice
2 tbsp. lime juice
2 tsp. grated lime zest
2 shallots, peeled and

finely chopped
2 garlic cloves, peeled and
  finely chopped
1–2 red chiles
1–2 green chiles

6 cups fresh fusilli pasta
4 tbsp. crème fraîche
2 tbsp. freshly chopped basil
oregano sprigs, to garnish

Place the tomatoes in a bowl and cover with boiling water. Allow to stand until the skins start to peel away.

Remove the skins from the tomatoes, quarter each, and remove all the seeds. Dice the flesh and put in a small saucepan. Add the lemon and lime juice and the lime zest, and stir well.

Add the chopped shallots and garlic. Remove the seeds carefully from the chiles, chop finely, and add to the saucepan.

Bring to a boil, and simmer gently for 5–10 minutes until the salsa has thickened slightly.

Set the salsa aside to allow the flavors to develop while the pasta is cooking.

Bring a large saucepan of water to a boil and add the pasta. Simmer for 3–4 minutes or until the pasta is just tender.

Drain the pasta and rinse in boiling water. Mix in the salsa, then divide among four dishes. Top each with a small spoonful of crème fraîche. Garnish with the chopped basil and oregano sprigs, and serve immediately.

Tortellini, Cherry Tomato & Mozzarella Skewers

SERVES 6

9 oz. mixed green and plain cheese- or vegetable-filled fresh tortellini
⅔ cup extra-virgin olive oil
2 garlic cloves, peeled and crushed

pinch dried thyme or basil
salt and freshly ground black pepper
8 oz. cherry tomatoes
1 lb. mozzarella, cut into 1-in. cubes

basil leaves, to garnish
dressed lettuce leaves, to serve

Preheat the broiler and line a broiler pan with foil, just before cooking. Bring a large pan of lightly salted water to a rolling boil. Add the tortellini and cook according to the package directions until tender but still firm to the bite. Drain and rinse under cold running water. Drain again and toss with 2 tablespoons of the olive oil and set aside.

Pour the remaining olive oil into a small bowl. Add the crushed garlic and thyme or basil, then blend well. Season to taste with salt and black pepper and set aside.

To assemble the skewers, thread the tortellini alternately with the cherry tomatoes and cubes of mozzarella. Arrange the skewers on the broiler pan and brush generously on all sides with the olive oil mixture.

Cook the skewers under the preheated broiler for about 5 minutes or until they begin to turn golden, turning them halfway through cooking. Arrange two skewers on each plate and garnish with a few basil leaves. Serve immediately with dressed lettuce leaves.

HELPFUL HINT

If using wooden skewers for this recipe, soak them in cold water for at least 30 minutes before cooking to prevent them scorching. The skewer tips may be protected with small pieces of foil.

Marinated Vegetable Kebabs

SERVES 4

2 small zucchini, cut into
    ¾-in. pieces
½ green bell pepper, seeded
    and cut into
    1-in. pieces
½ red bell pepper, seeded
    and cut into 1-in. pieces
½ yellow bell pepper, seeded
    and cut into
    1-in. pieces

8 baby onions, peeled
8 button mushrooms
8 cherry tomatoes
freshly chopped parsley,
    to garnish
couscous, to serve

For the marinade:
1 tbsp. light olive oil
4 tbsp. dry sherry

2 tbsp. light soy sauce
1 red chile, seeded and
    finely chopped
2 garlic cloves, peeled
    and crushed
1-in. piece ginger, peeled
    and finely grated

Place the zucchini, bell peppers, and baby onions in a saucepan of just-boiled water. Bring back to a boil, and simmer for about 30 seconds.

Drain and rinse the cooked vegetables in cold water, and dry on absorbent paper towels.

Thread the cooked vegetables, mushrooms, and tomatoes alternately onto skewers and place in a large, shallow dish.

Make the marinade by beating all the ingredients together until blended thoroughly. Pour the marinade evenly over the kebabs, then chill in the refrigerator for at least 1 hour. Spoon the marinade over the kebabs occasionally during this time.

Place the kebabs in a hot griddle pan or on a hot barbecue, and cook gently for 10–12 minutes. Turn the kebabs frequently, and brush with the marinade when needed. When the vegetables are tender, sprinkle with chopped parsley, and serve immediately with couscous.

TASTY TIP

Although these kebabs use only vegetables, large chunks of fish, such as cod, or indeed tiger shrimp could be added alternately between the vegetables and cooked in the same way.

Spanish Baked Tomatoes

SERVES 4

¾ cup brown rice
2½ cups vegetable stock
2 tsp. corn oil
2 shallots, peeled and finely chopped
1 garlic clove, peeled and crushed

1 green bell pepper, seeded and diced
1 red chile, seeded and finely chopped
½ cup finely chopped button mushrooms
1 tbsp. freshly chopped oregano

salt and freshly ground black pepper
4 large ripe tomatoes
1 extra-large egg, beaten
1 tsp. sugar
basil leaves, to garnish
crusty bread, to serve

Preheat the oven to 350°F. Place the rice in a saucepan, pour in the vegetable stock, and bring to a boil. Simmer gently for 30 minutes or until the rice is tender. Drain and turn into a large bowl.

Add 1 teaspoon of corn oil to a small nonstick skillet and cook the shallots, garlic, bell pepper, chile, and mushrooms for 2 minutes. Add to the rice, along with the chopped oregano. Season with salt and pepper.

Slice the top off each tomato. Cut and scoop out the flesh, removing the hard core. Pass the tomato flesh through a strainer. Add 1 tablespoon of the juice to the rice mixture. Stir in the beaten egg, and mix. Sprinkle sugar in the base of each tomato. Pile the rice mixture into the shells.

Place the tomatoes in a baking dish and pour a little cold water around them. Replace their lids and drizzle a few drops of corn oil over the tops.

Cook in the preheated oven for about 25 minutes. Garnish with the basil leaves and season with black pepper. Serve immediately with crusty bread.

Stuffed Onions with Pine Nuts

SERVES 4

4 medium onions, peeled
2 garlic cloves, peeled and crushed
2 tbsp. fresh whole-wheat bread crumbs
2 tbsp. fresh white bread crumbs

2 tbsp. golden raisins
4 tbsp. pine nuts
½ cup shredded hard cheese, such as cheddar, plus extra for sprinkling
2 tbsp. freshly chopped parsley

1 large egg, beaten
salt and freshly ground black pepper
lettuce leaves, to serve

Preheat the oven to 400˚F. Bring a saucepan of water to a boil, then add the onions and cook gently for about 15 minutes.

Drain well. Let the onions cool, then slice each one in half horizontally.

Scoop out most of the onion flesh, but leave a reasonably firm shell.

Chop up 4 tablespoons of the onion flesh and place in a bowl with the garlic, bread crumbs, golden raisins, pine nuts, shredded cheese, and parsley.

Mix the bread-crumb mixture together thoroughly. Bind together with as much of the beaten egg as necessary to make a firm filling. Season to taste with salt and pepper.

Pile the mixture back into the onion shells, and sprinkle with some shredded cheese. Place on a greased baking sheet and cook in the preheated oven for 20–30 minutes until golden brown. Serve immediately with the lettuce leaves.

TASTY TIP

While this dish is delicious on its own, it also complements barbecued meat and fish. The onion takes on a mellow, nutty flavour when baked.

Melanzane Parmigiana

SERVES 4

2 lbs. eggplant
salt and freshly ground
   black pepper
⅓ cup olive oil
1 red onion, peeled
   and chopped
½ tsp. mild paprika pepper

⅔ cup dry red wine
⅔ cup vegetable stock
14 oz. canned
   chopped tomatoes
1 tsp. tomato paste
1 tbsp. freshly
   chopped oregano

1½ cups thinly sliced
   mozzarella cheese
½ cup coarsely grated
   Parmesan cheese
fresh basil sprig,
   to garnish

Preheat the oven to 400°F. Cut the eggplants lengthwise into thin slices. Sprinkle with salt and allow to drain in a strainer over a bowl for 30 minutes.

Meanwhile, heat 1 tablespoon of the olive oil in a saucepan, and cook the onion for 10 minutes until softened. Add the paprika and cook for 1 minute. Stir in the wine, stock, tomatoes, and tomato paste. Simmer uncovered for 25 minutes or until fairly thick. Stir in the oregano, and season to taste with salt and pepper. Remove from the heat.

Rinse the eggplant slices thoroughly under cold water and pat dry on paper towels. Heat 2 tablespoons of the oil in a frying pan, and cook the eggplants in batches for 3 minutes on each side until golden. Drain well on paper towels.

Pour half of the tomato sauce into the base of a large ovenproof dish. Cover with half the eggplant slices, then top with the mozzarella. Cover with the remaining eggplant slices, and pour over the remaining tomato sauce. Sprinkle with the grated Parmesan cheese.

Cook in the preheated oven for 30 minutes or until the eggplants are tender and the sauce is bubbling. Garnish with a sprig of fresh basil, and cool for a few minutes before serving.

HELPFUL HINT

Salting the eggplant draws out some of the moisture, so you'll need less oil when frying.

Light Ratatouille

SERVES 4

1 red bell pepper
2 zucchini, trimmed
1 small eggplant, trimmed
1 onion, peeled

2 ripe tomatoes
1½ cups wiped and halved or
　quartered button
　mushrooms

¾ cup tomato juice
1 tbsp. freshly chopped basil
salt and freshly ground
　black pepper

Seed the pepper, remove the membrane with a small sharp knife, and dice. Thickly slice the zucchini and dice the eggplant. Slice the onion into rings.

Place the tomatoes in boiling water until their skins begin to peel away.

Remove the skins from the tomatoes, cut into quarters, and remove the seeds.

Place all the vegetables in a saucepan with the tomato juice and basil. Season to taste with salt and pepper.

Bring to a boil, cover, and simmer for 15 minutes or until the vegetables are tender.

Remove the vegetables with a slotted spoon and arrange in a serving dish.

Bring the liquid in the saucepan to a boil and boil for 20 seconds or until it is slightly thickened. Season the sauce to taste with salt and pepper.

Pass the sauce through a strainer to remove some of the seeds, and pour over the vegetables. Serve the ratatouille hot or cold.

TASTY TIP

This dish would be perfect served as an accompaniment to any baked fish dish. It is also delicious in an omelet or as a jacket potato filling.

Rigatoni with Oven–Dried Cherry Tomatoes & Mascarpone

SERVES 4

3 cups red cherry tomatoes
1 tsp. sugar
salt and freshly ground
    black pepper
2 tbsp. olive oil

5¼ cups dried rigatoni
1 cup frozen peas
2 tbsp. mascarpone cheese
1 tbsp. freshly chopped mint

1 tbsp. freshly
    chopped parsley
fresh mint sprigs,
    to garnish

Preheat the oven to 275˚F. Halve the cherry tomatoes and place close together on a nonstick baking sheet, cut-side up. Sprinkle lightly with the sugar, and then with a little salt and pepper. Cook in the preheated oven for 1¼ hours or until dry but not beginning to brown. Let cool on the baking sheet. Put in a bowl, drizzle over the olive oil, and toss to coat.

Bring a large saucepan of lightly salted water to a boil, and cook the pasta for about 10 minutes until tender but still firm to the bite. Add the frozen peas 2–3 minutes before the end of the cooking time. Drain thoroughly and return the pasta and the peas to the saucepan.

Add the mascarpone to the saucepan. When melted, add the tomatoes, mint, parsley, and a little black pepper. Toss gently together, then transfer to a warmed serving dish or individual plates, and garnish with sprigs of fresh mint. Serve immediately.

Spaghetti alla Puttanesca

SERVES 4

4 tbsp. olive oil
2 oz. anchovy fillets in olive
   oil, drained and
   coarsely chopped
2 garlic cloves, peeled and
   finely chopped
½ tsp. dried pepper flakes
14 oz. canned chopped
   plum tomatoes

1 cup pitted ripe olives,
   cut in half
2 tbsp. capers, rinsed
   and drained
1 tsp. freshly
   chopped oregano
1 tbsp. tomato paste
salt and freshly ground
   black pepper

14 oz. spaghetti
2 tbsp. freshly
   chopped parsley

Heat the olive oil in a large skillet, then add the anchovies and cook, stirring with a wooden spoon and crushing the anchovies until they disintegrate. Add the garlic and dried pepper flakes, and cook for 1 minute, stirring frequently.

Add the tomatoes, olives, capers, oregano, and tomato paste, and cook, stirring occasionally, for 15 minutes or until the liquid has evaporated and the sauce is thickened. Season the tomato sauce to taste with salt and pepper.

Meanwhile, bring a large pan of lightly salted water to a boil. Add the spaghetti and cook according to the package directions until tender but still firm to the bite.

Drain the spaghetti thoroughly, setting aside 1–2 tablespoons of the the cooking water. Return the spaghetti with the reserved water to the pan. Pour the tomato sauce over the spaghetti, then add the chopped parsley and toss to coat. Spoon into a warmed serving dish or onto individual plates and serve immediately.

HELPFUL HINT

For a less salty dish, drain the anchovies and soak in a little milk for about 20 minutes before using. You can, of course, omit the anchovies to make a vegetarian dish.

Baked Macaroni & Cheese

SERVES 8

4 cups macaroni
6 tbsp. butter
1 onion, peeled and
    finely chopped
3 tbsp. all-purpose flour
4 cups milk
1–2 dried bay leaves
½ tsp. dried thyme

salt and freshly ground
    black pepper
cayenne pepper
freshly grated nutmeg
2 small leeks, trimmed,
    finely chopped, cooked,
    and drained
1 tbsp. Dijon mustard

3½ cups shredded
    cheddar cheese
2 tbsp. dried bread crumbs
2 tbsp. freshly grated
    Parmesan cheese
basil sprig, to garnish

Preheat the oven to 375 °F. Bring a large heavy pan of lightly salted water to a rolling boil. Add the macaroni and cook according to the package directions or until tender but still firm to the bite. Drain the pasta thoroughly and set aside.

Meanwhile, melt ½ cup of the butter in a large heavy pan, then add the onion and cook, stirring frequently, for 5–7 minutes until softened. Sprinkle in the flour and cook, stirring constantly, for about 2 minutes. Remove the pan from the heat and stir in the milk, then return to the heat and cook, stirring, until a smooth sauce has formed.

Add the bay leaf and thyme to the sauce, and season to taste with salt, pepper, cayenne pepper, and freshly grated nutmeg. Simmer for about 15 minutes, stirring frequently, until thickened and smooth.

Remove the sauce from the heat. Add the leeks, mustard, and cheddar cheese, and stir until the cheese has melted. Stir in the macaroni, then spoon into a lightly greased baking dish.

Sprinkle the bread crumbs and Parmesan cheese over the macaroni. Dot with the remaining butter, then bake in the preheated oven for 1 hour or until golden. Garnish with a basil sprig and serve immediately.

HELPFUL HINT

Make sure that you simmer the macaroni only until just tender but still firm to the bite and drain straight away, because it will be further cooked in the oven.

Four-Cheese Tagliatelle

SERVES 4

1¼ cups whipping cream
4 garlic cloves, peeled and
   lightly bruised
¾ cup diced fontina cheese
¾ cup grated Gruyère cheese

¾ cup diced
   mozzarella cheese
¼ cup grated Parmesan
   cheese, plus extra
   to serve

salt and freshly ground
   black pepper
10 oz. fresh green tagliatelle
1–2 tbsp. freshly cut chives
fresh basil leaves, to garnish

Place the whipping cream with the garlic cloves in a medium pan, and heat gently until small bubbles begin to form around the edge of the pan. Using a slotted spoon, remove and discard the garlic cloves.

Add all the cheeses to the pan and stir until melted. Season with a little salt and a lot of black pepper. Keep the sauce warm over a low heat, but do not let it come to a boil.

Meanwhile, bring a large pan of lightly salted water to a boil. Add the tagliatelle, then return to a boil and cook for 2–3 minutes until tender but still firm to the bite.

Drain the pasta and return it to the pan. Pour the sauce over the pasta, then add the chives and toss lightly until well-coated. Spoon into a warmed serving dish or spoon onto individual plates. Garnish with a few basil leaves and serve immediately with extra Parmesan cheese.

Rigatoni with Gorgonzola & Walnuts

SERVES 4

3½ cups rigatoni
2 tbsp. butter
1 cup crumbled
    Gorgonzola cheese
2 tbsp. brandy, optional
¾ cup whipping or
    heavy cream

½ cup lightly toasted and
    coarsely chopped
    walnut pieces
1 tbsp. freshly chopped basil
½ cup freshly grated
    Parmesan cheese
salt and freshly ground
    black pepper

To serve:
cherry tomatoes
fresh green salad leaves

Bring a large pan of lightly salted water to a rolling boil. Add the rigatoni and cook according to the package directions until tender but still firm to the bite. Drain the pasta thoroughly, then set aside and keep warm.

Melt the butter in a large pan or wok over a medium heat. Add the Gorgonzola cheese and stir until just melted. Add the brandy (if desired) and cook for 30 seconds, then pour in the whipping or heavy cream and cook for 1–2 minutes, stirring until the sauce is smooth.

Stir in the walnut pieces, basil, and half the Parmesan cheese, then add the rigatoni. Season with salt and pepper. Return to the heat, stirring frequently, until heated through. Divide the pasta among four warmed bowls, then sprinkle with the remaining Parmesan cheese and serve immediately with cherry tomatoes and fresh green salad leaves.

TASTY TIP

Either whipping or heavy cream may be used here; heavy cream is higher in fat, so it will give a richer, creamier finish. If preferred, you could use sour cream, but heat it gently to avoid curdling.

Spinach Dumplings with Rich Tomato Sauce

For the sauce:
2 tbsp. olive oil
1 onion, peeled
   and chopped
1 garlic clove, peeled
   and crushed
1 red chile, seeded
   and chopped
⅔ cup dry white wine

14 oz. canned tomatoes
pared strip of lemon rind

For the dumplings:
10 cups fresh spinach leaves
¼ cup ricotta cheese
¼ cup fresh white
   bread crumbs
¼ cup grated
   Parmesan cheese

1 large egg yolk
¼ tsp. freshly
   grated nutmeg
salt and freshly ground
   black pepper
5 tbsp. all-purpose flour
2 tbsp. olive oil, for cooking
fresh basil leaves, to garnish
freshly cooked tagliatelle,
   to serve

To make the tomato sauce, heat the olive oil in a large saucepan, and cook the onion for 5 minutes. Add the garlic and chile, and cook for an additional 5 minutes until softened.

Stir in the wine, chopped tomatoes, and lemon rind. Bring to a boil, cover, and simmer for 20 minutes, then uncover and simmer for 15 minutes or until the sauce has thickened. Remove the lemon rind and season to taste with salt and pepper.

To make the spinach dumplings, wash the spinach thoroughly and remove any tough stalks. Cover and cook in a large saucepan over a low heat with just the water clinging to the leaves. Drain, then squeeze out all the excess water. Finely chop and put in a large bowl.

Add the ricotta, bread crumbs, Parmesan cheese, and egg yolk to the spinach. Season with nutmeg, salt, and pepper. Mix together and shape into 20 walnut-size balls.

Toss the spinach balls in the flour. Heat the olive oil in a large nonstick skillet, and cook the balls gently for 5–6 minutes, turning occasionally. Garnish with fresh basil leaves, and serve immediately with the tomato sauce and tagliatelle.

HELPFUL HINT

It is very important to squeeze out all the excess water from the cooked spinach, otherwise the dumplings will fall apart when they are fried.

Vegetable Frittata

SERVES 2

6 large eggs
2 tbsp. freshly
   chopped parsley
1 tbsp. freshly
   chopped tarragon
¼ cup finely grated pecorino
   or Parmesan cheese
freshly ground black pepper

1¼ cups tiny new potatoes
2 small carrots, peeled
   and sliced
1¼ cups small
   broccoli florets
1 zucchini, about ¾
   cup, sliced
2 tbsp. olive oil

4 scallions, trimmed and
   thinly sliced

To serve:
mixed green salad
crusty Italian bread

Preheat the broiler just before cooking. Lightly beat the eggs with the parsley, tarragon, and half the cheese. Season to taste with pepper and set aside. Salt is not needed, as the pecorino is very salty. Bring a large saucepan of lightly salted water to a boil. Add the new potatoes and cook for 8 minutes. Add the carrots and cook for 4 minutes. Then add the broccoli florets and the zucchini, and cook for an additional 3–4 minutes until all the vegetables are barely tender. Drain well.

Heat the oil in an 8-inch heavy skillet. Add the scallions and cook for 3–4 minutes until softened. Add all the vegetables, cook for a few seconds, then pour in the beaten egg mixture. Stir gently for about a minute, then cook for an additional 1–2 minutes until the bottom of the frittata is set and golden brown.

Place the skillet under a hot broiler for 1 minute or until almost set and just beginning to brown. Sprinkle with the remaining cheese, and broil for an additional 1 minute or until it is lightly browned.

Loosen the edges and slide out of the skillet. Cut into wedges and serve hot or warm with a mixed green salad and crusty Italian bread.

Crispy Pancake Rolls

MAKES 8

1¼ cups all-purpose flour
pinch salt
1 large egg
4 tsp. sunflower oil
2 tbsp. light olive oil
¾-in. piece ginger, peeled
 and finely grated

1 garlic clove, peeled
 and crushed
½ lb. tofu, drained
 and diced
2 tbsp. soy sauce
1 tbsp. dry sherry
1½ cups wiped and chopped
 button mushrooms

1 celery stalk, trimmed and
 finely chopped
2 scallions, trimmed and
 finely chopped
2 tbsp. peanut oil
fresh cilantro and sliced
 scallion, to garnish

Sift 1 cup of the flour with the salt into a large bowl, make a well in the center, and drop in the egg. Beat to form a smooth, thin batter, gradually adding 1¼ cups of water and drawing in the flour from the sides of the bowl. Mix the remaining flour with 1–2 tablespoons of water to make a thick paste. Set aside.

Heat a little sunflower oil in an 8-in. omelet pan or skillet, and pour in 2 tablespoons of the batter. Cook for 1–2 minutes, flip over, and cook for an additional 1–2 minutes until firm. Slide from the pan and keep warm. Make more pancakes with the remaining batter.

Heat a wok or large skillet, add the olive oil, and, when hot, add the ginger, garlic, and tofu, stir-fry for 30 seconds, then pour in the soy sauce and sherry. Add the mushrooms, celery, and scallions. Stir-fry for 1–2 minutes, then remove from the wok and let cool.

Place a little filling in the center of each pancake. Brush the edges with the flour paste, fold in the edges, then roll up into pockets. Heat the peanut oil to 350°F in the wok. Fry the pancake rolls for 2–3 minutes until golden. Serve immediately, garnished with scallions and cilantro.

Desserts & Cakes

Creamy Puddings with Mixed Berry Compote

SERVES 6

1 cup heavy cream
9 oz. ricotta cheese
¼ cup superfine sugar
4 oz. white chocolate,
    broken into pieces

2 cups mixed summer fruits
    such as strawberries,
    blueberries, and
    raspberries
2 tbsp. Cointreau

Beat the cream until soft peaks form. Fold in the ricotta cheese and half the sugar.

Place the chocolate in a bowl set over a saucepan of simmering water. Stir until melted.

Remove from the heat and allow to cool, stirring occasionally. Stir into the cheese mixture until well blended.

Spoon the mixture into six custard cups and level the surface of each pudding with the back of a spoon. Place in the freezer and freeze for 4 hours.

Place the fruits and remaining sugar in a saucepan and heat, stirring occasionally, until the sugar has dissolved and the juices are beginning to run. Stir in the Cointreau to taste.

Dip the cups in hot water for 30 seconds and invert onto six serving plates. Spoon the fruit compote over the desserts and serve immediately.

Rice Pudding

SERVES 4

¾ cup pudding rice
¼ cup granulated sugar
14 oz. canned light
   evaporated milk

1¼ cups low-fat milk
pinch freshly
   grated nutmeg

2 tbsp. butter
jelly, to decorate

Preheat the oven to 300°F. Lightly grease a large ovenproof dish.

Sprinkle the rice and sugar into the dish, and mix together.

Bring the evaporated milk and milk to a boil in a small saucepan, stirring occasionally.

Stir the milks into the rice and mix well until the rice is coated thoroughly.

Sprinkle with the nutmeg, cover with foil, and cook in the preheated oven for 30 minutes.

Remove the pudding from the oven and stir well, breaking up any lumps.

Cover with the same foil and cook for an additional 30 minutes. Remove from the oven and stir well again.

Dot the pudding with butter and cook for an additional 45–60 minutes until the rice is tender and the skin is browned.

Divide the pudding among four individual serving bowls. Top with a large spoonful of the jelly and serve immediately.

TASTY TIP

The main trick to achieving traditional creamy rice pudding is long, slow cooking at a low temperature.

Crunchy Rhubarb Crisp

1 cup all-purpose flour
4 tbsp. softened butter
⅔ cup rolled oats
4 tbsp. turbinado (raw) sugar

1 tbsp. sesame seeds
½ tsp. ground cinnamon
1 lb. fresh rhubarb
4 tbsp. superfine sugar

custard or cream,
  to serve

Preheat the oven to 350°F. Place the flour in a large bowl and cut the butter into cubes. Add to the flour and rub in with your fingertips until the mixture looks like fine bread crumbs, or blend for a few seconds in a food processor.

Stir in the rolled oats, brown sugar, sesame seeds, and cinnamon. Mix well and set aside.

Prepare the rhubarb by removing the thick ends of the stems and cut diagonally into 1-inch chunks. Wash thoroughly under cold running water and pat dry with a clean dishtowel. Place the rhubarb in a 1-quart casserole dish.

Sprinkle the sugar over the rhubarb and top with the crisp mixture. Level the top of the crisp so that all the fruit is well covered, and press down firmly. If desired, sprinkle a little extra granulated sugar on the top.

Place on a cookie sheet and bake in the preheated oven for 40–50 minutes until the fruit is soft and the topping is golden brown. Sprinkle the dessert with some more granulated sugar and serve hot with custard or cream.

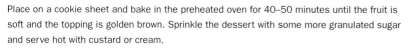

Osborne Pudding

SERVES 4

8 slices white bread
4 tbsp. butter
2 tbsp. marmalade
⅓ cup mixed dried fruits
2 tbsp. fresh orange juice
3 tbsp. superfine sugar

2 extra-large eggs
2 cups milk
⅔ cup whipping cream

For the marmalade sauce:
zest and juice of 1 orange
2 tbsp. thick-cut
    orange marmalade
1 tbsp. brandy (optional)
2 tsp. cornstarch

Preheat the oven to 325°F. Lightly grease a 1-quart baking dish.

Remove the crusts from the bread, and spread thickly with butter and marmalade. Cut the bread into small triangles. Place half the bread in the base of the dish, and sprinkle over the dried fruit, 1 tablespoon of the orange juice, and half the sugar. Top with the remaining bread and marmalade, buttered-side up, and pour over the remaining orange juice. Sprinkle over the remaining sugar.

Beat the eggs with the milk and cream, and pour over the pudding. Set aside for about 30 minutes to allow the bread to absorb the liquid.

Place in a roasting pan and pour in enough boiling water to come halfway up the sides of the dish. Bake in the preheated oven for 50–60 minutes until the pudding is set and the top is crisp and golden.

TASTY TIP

To make an orange sauce, omit the marmalade and add the juice of 3 more oranges and a squeeze of lemon juice to make 1 cup. Follow the recipe as before but increase the cornstarch to 1½ tablespoons.

Meanwhile, make the marmalade sauce. Heat the orange zest and juice with the marmalade and brandy, if using. Mix 1 tablespoon of water with the cornstarch, and mix together well. Add to the saucepan and cook on a low heat, stirring until warmed through and thickened. Serve the pudding hot with the marmalade sauce.

Tipsy Tropical Fruit

SERVES 4

8 oz. canned pineapple
    chunks in natural juice
2 guavas
1 papaya
2 passion fruit
2 tbsp. unsalted butter

1 tbsp. orange juice
¼ cup chopped
    creamed coconut
¼ cup firmly packed light
    brown sugar
2 tbsp. white rum

vanilla ice cream, to serve
fresh mint sprigs,
    to decorate

Drain the pineapple chunks, setting aside the juice. Pat the pineapple dry on absorbent paper towels. Peel the guavas and cut into wedges. Halve the papaya and scoop out the black seeds. Peel and cut into 1-inch chunks. Halve the passion fruit and scoop out the seeds into a small bowl.

Heat the butter in a wok, add the pineapple, and stir-fry over a high heat for 30 seconds. Turn down the heat and add the guavas and papaya. Drizzle over the orange juice and cook for 2 minutes, stirring occasionally, taking care not to break up the fruit.

Using a slotted spoon, remove the fruit from the wok, leaving any juices behind, and transfer to a warmed serving dish. Add the creamed coconut to the wok with the sugar and pineapple juice. Simmer for 2–3 minutes, stirring until the coconut has melted.

Add the white rum to the wok and heat through, then pour over the fruit. Spoon the passion fruit pulp on top and serve hot with spoonfuls of ice cream decorated with a sprig of mint.

Stir–Fried Bananas & Peaches with Rum Butterscotch Sauce

SERVES 4

2 medium-firm bananas
1 tbsp. superfine sugar
2 tsp. lime juice
4 firm, ripe peaches
  or nectarines
1 tbsp. corn oil

**For the rum
  butterscotch sauce:**
4 tbsp. unsalted butter
¼ cup firmly packed light
  brown sugar
½ cup turbinado (raw) sugar

½ cup heavy cream
2 tbsp. dark rum

Peel the bananas and cut into 1-inch diagonal slices. Place in a bowl and sprinkle with the sugar and lime juice, and stir until lightly coated. Set aside.

Place the peaches or nectarines in a large bowl and add enough boiling water to cover. Leave for 30 seconds, then plunge them into cold water and peel off their skins. Cut each one into eight thick slices, discarding the pit.

Heat a wok, add the oil, and swirl it around the wok to coat the sides. Add the fruit and cook for 3–4 minutes, shaking the wok and gently turning the fruit until lightly browned. Spoon the fruit into a warmed serving bowl and clean the wok with absorbent paper towels.

Add the butter and sugars to the wok, and stir continuously over a very low heat until the sugar has dissolved. Remove from the heat and let cool for 2–3 minutes.

Stir the cream and rum into the sugar syrup and return to the heat. Bring to a boil and simmer for 2 minutes, stirring continuously until smooth. Leave for 2–3 minutes to cool slightly, then serve warm with the stir-fried peaches and bananas.

Sweet-Stewed Dried Fruits

SERVES 4

1 lb. package mixed dried fruits	2 tbsp. brandy	**To decorate:**
2 cups apple juice	1 lemon	crème fraîche
2 tbsp. honey	1 orange	fine strips of pared orange zest

Place the fruits, apple juice, honey, and brandy in a small saucepan.

Using a small, sharp knife or a zester, carefully remove the zest from the lemon and orange and place in the saucepan.

Squeeze the juice from the lemon and oranges and add to the saucepan.

Bring the fruit mixture to a boil, and simmer for about 1 minute. Remove the saucepan from the heat and let the mixture cool completely.

Transfer the mixture to a large bowl, cover with plastic wrap, and chill in the refrigerator overnight to allow the flavors to blend.

Spoon the stewed fruit into four shallow dessert dishes. Decorate with a large spoonful of crème fraîche and a few strips of the pared orange zest, and serve.

Poached Pears

SERVES 4

2 small cinnamon sticks
½ cup superfine sugar
1¼ cups red wine
⅔ cup water

1 tbsp. thinly pared
  orange rind
1 tbsp. orange juice
4 firm pears

orange slices, to decorate
frozen vanilla yogurt or ice
  cream, to serve

Place the cinnamon sticks on the clean work surface, and with a rolling pin, slowly roll down the side of the cinnamon stick to bruise. Place in a large, heavy saucepan.

Add the sugar, wine, water, pared orange rind, and juice to the saucepan, and bring slowly to a boil, stirring occasionally until the sugar has dissolved.

Meanwhile, peel the pears, leaving the stalks on. Cut out the cores from the bottoms, and level them so that they stand upright.

Stand the pears in the syrup, cover the saucepan, and simmer for 20 minutes or until tender. Remove the saucepan from the heat and let the pears cool in the syrup, turning them occasionally.

Arrange the pears on serving plates and spoon over the syrup. Decorate with the orange slices and serve with the yogurt or ice cream and any remaining juices.

Coconut Rice Served with Stewed Ginger Fruits

SERVES 6-8

1 vanilla pod
2 cups coconut milk
5 cups low-fat milk
2½ cups heavy cream
⅔ cup superfine sugar
2 star anise

8 tbsp. toasted unsweetened
   shredded dry coconut
1½ cups short-grain
   pudding rice
1 tsp. melted butter
2 mandarin oranges, peeled
   and pith removed

1 carambola or star
   fruit, sliced
⅓ cup finely diced
   preserved ginger
1¼ cups sweet white wine
superfine sugar, to taste

Preheat the oven to 325˚F. Using a sharp knife, split the vanilla pod in half lengthwise, scrape out the seeds from the pods, and place both the pod and seeds in a large, heavy casserole dish. Pour in the coconut milk, low-fat milk, and heavy cream, and stir in the sugar, star anise, and 4 tablespoons of the toasted coconut. Bring to a boil, then simmer for 10 minutes, stirring occasionally. Remove the vanilla pod and star anise.

Wash the rice and add to the milk. Simmer gently for 25–30 minutes until the rice is tender, stirring frequently. Stir in the melted butter.

Divide the mandarins into segments, and place in a saucepan with the sliced carambola or star fruit and preserved ginger. Pour in the wine and 1¼ cups water, bring to a boil, then reduce the heat, and simmer for 20 minutes or until the liquid has reduced and the fruits softened. Add sugar to taste.

Serve the rice topped with the stewed fruits and the remaining toasted coconut.

Chocolate Pear Pudding

SERVES 6

½ cup plus 1 tbsp. butter,
   softened
2 tbsp. firmly packed
   brown sugar
14 oz. canned pear halves,
   drained and juice set aside

¼ cup walnut halves
½ cup unrefined
   superfine sugar
2 large eggs, beaten
¾ cup self-rising
   flour, sifted

½ cup unsweetened cocoa
1 tsp. baking powder
prepared chocolate custard,
   to serve

Preheat the oven to 375°F. Butter an 8-inch round pan with 1 tablespoon of the butter and sprinkle the bottom with the brown sugar. Arrange the drained pear halves on top of the sugar, cut-side down. Fill the spaces between the pears with the walnut halves, flat-side up.

Cream the remaining butter with the superfine sugar, then gradually beat in the beaten eggs, adding 1 tablespoon of the flour after each addition. When all the eggs have been added, stir in the remaining flour.

Sift the unsweetened cocoa and baking powder together, then stir into the creamed mixture with 1–2 tablespoons of the pear juice to give a smooth dropping consistency.

Spoon the mixture over the pear halves, smoothing the surface. Bake in the preheated oven for 20–25 minutes until well risen and the surface springs back when lightly pressed.

Remove from the oven and let cool for 5 minutes. Using a palate knife, loosen the sides and invert onto a serving plate. Serve with the chocolate custard.

HELPFUL HINT

To soften butter, cut into small pieces and leave in a warmed bowl at room temperature for a short time. Do not use the microwave, as this makes the fat oily and affects the cake's texture.

Maple Pears with Pistachios & Simple Chocolate Sauce

SERVES 4

2 tbsp. unsalted butter
½ cup unsalted pistachios
4 medium-ripe firm pears, peeled, quartered, and cored
2 tsp. lemon juice

pinch ground ginger (optional)
6 tbsp. maple syrup

For the chocolate sauce:
½ cup heavy cream

2 tbsp. milk
½ tsp. vanilla extract
5 oz. unsweetened chocolate, broken into pieces and coarsely chopped

Melt the butter in a wok over a medium heat until sizzling. Turn down the heat a little, add the pistachios, and stir-fry for 30 seconds.

Add the pears to the wok and continue cooking for about 2 minutes, turning frequently and carefully, until the nuts are beginning to brown and the pears are tender.

Add the lemon juice, ground ginger if using, and maple syrup. Cook for 3–4 minutes until the syrup has reduced slightly. Spoon the pears and the syrup into a serving dish and let cool for 1–2 minutes while making the chocolate sauce.

Pour the cream and milk into the wok. Add the vanilla extract and heat just to boiling point. Remove the wok from the heat.

Add the chocolate to the wok and leave for 1 minute to melt, then stir until the chocolate is evenly mixed with the cream. Pour into a pitcher and serve with the pears while still warm.

Coffee & Peach Creams

SERVES 4

4 peaches
¼ cup superfine sugar
2 tbsp. coffee extract
7-oz. carton Greek-style
    yogurt

11 oz. canned ready-made
    custard

To decorate:
peach slices
fresh mint sprigs
crème fraîche

Cut the peaches in half and remove the pits. Place the peaches in a large bowl, cover with boiling water, and leave for 2–3 minutes.

Drain the peaches, then carefully remove the skin. Using a sharp knife, halve the peaches.

Place the sugar in a saucepan and add ¼ cup of water.

Bring the sugar mixture to a boil, stirring occasionally until the sugar has dissolved. Boil rapidly for about 2 minutes.

Add the peaches and coffee extract to the saucepan. Remove from the heat and let the peach mixture cool.

Meanwhile, mix together the yogurt and custard until well combined.

Divide the peach halves evenly among four individual glass dishes.

Spoon over the custard mixture, then top with the remaining peach mixture.

Chill in the refrigerator for 30 minutes and then serve decorated with peach slices, mint sprigs, and some crème fraîche.

Fudgy Mocha Pie with Espresso Custard Sauce

CUTS INTO 10 SLICES

4 oz. unsweetened
  chocolate, chopped
½ cup (1 stick) butter, diced
1 tbsp. instant
  espresso powder
4 extra-large eggs
1 tbsp. light corn syrup
½ cup sugar
1 tsp. ground cinnamon

3 tbsp. milk
confectioners' sugar
  for dusting
fresh strawberries, to serve

**For the espresso
  custard sauce:**
2–3 tbsp. instant espresso
  powder, or to taste

1 cup prepared
  custard
1 cup light cream
2 tbsp. coffee-flavored
  liqueur (optional)

Preheat the oven to 350°F. Line with foil or lightly grease a deep 9-inch pie plate. Melt the chocolate and butter in a small saucepan over a low heat and stir until smooth, then set aside. Dissolve the instant espresso powder in 1–2 tablespoons of hot water, and set aside.

Beat the eggs with the corn syrup, sugar, dissolved espresso powder, cinnamon, and milk until blended. Add the melted chocolate mixture and beat until blended. Pour into the pie plate.

Bake the pie in the preheated oven for about 20–25 minutes or until the edge has set but the center is still very soft. Let cool, remove from the plate, then dust lightly with confectioners' sugar.

To make the custard sauce, dissolve the instant espresso powder with 2–3 tablespoons of hot water, then beat into the prepared custard. Slowly add the light cream, beating constantly, then stir in the coffee-flavored liqueur, if desired. Serve slices of the pie in a pool of espresso custard with strawberries.

Chocolate Mousse

SERVES 6

6 oz. milk or semisweet
   dark chocolate
1 lb. canned custard
2 cups heavy cream

12 Cape gooseberries,
   to decorate
cookies, to serve

Break the chocolate into segments and place in a bowl set over a saucepan of simmering water. Leave until melted, stirring occasionally. Remove the bowl in the saucepan from the heat, and allow the melted chocolate to cool slightly.

Place the custard in a bowl, and using a metal spoon or rubber spatula, fold the melted chocolate into it. Stir well until completely combined.

Pour the cream into a small bowl and beat until the cream forms soft peaks.

Using a metal spoon or rubber spatula, fold in most of the whipped cream into the chocolate mixture.

Spoon into 6 tall glasses and carefully top with the remaining cream.

Leave the desserts to chill in the refrigerator for at least 1 hour or preferably overnight.

Decorate the chocolate desserts with a few Cape gooseberries and serve with some cookies.

FOOD FACT

Cape gooseberries are also known as physalis and can be found in specialty produce markets. They have a sweet flavor with a slight acidity, and taste similar to yogurt.

Chocolate Fudge Sundae

SERVES 2

For the chocolate fudge sauce:
3 oz. unsweetened chocolate, broken into pieces
2 cups heavy cream
¾ cup unrefined superfine sugar

¼ cup all-purpose flour
pinch salt
1 tbsp. unsalted butter
1 tsp. vanilla extract

For the sundae:
1 cup raspberries, fresh or thawed if frozen

3 scoops vanilla ice cream
3 scoops chocolate ice cream
2 tbsp. toasted, slivered almonds
wafers, to serve

To make the chocolate fudge sauce, place the chocolate and cream in a heavy saucepan and heat gently until the chocolate has melted into the cream. Stir until smooth. Mix the sugar with the flour and salt, then stir in sufficient chocolate mixture to make a smooth paste.

Gradually blend the remaining melted chocolate mixture into the paste, then pour into a clean saucepan. Cook over a low heat, stirring frequently until smooth and thick. Remove from the heat and add the butter and vanilla extract. Stir until smooth, then cool slightly.

To make the sundae, crush the raspberries lightly with a fork and set aside. Spoon a little of the chocolate sauce into the bottom of two sundae glasses. Add a layer of crushed raspberries, then a scoop each of vanilla and chocolate ice cream.

Top each one with a scoop of the vanilla ice cream. Pour over the sauce, sprinkle over the almonds, and serve with a wafer.

HELPFUL HINT

Store any remaining fudge sauce in the refrigerator for 1–2 weeks, warming it just before serving.

Chocolate Marshmallow Pie

SERVES 6

1¾ cups (about 18) graham crackers
6 tbsp. butter, melted

6 oz. semisweet dark chocolate
20 marshmallows

1 large egg, separated
1 cup heavy cream

Place the crackers in a plastic container, and crush finely with a rolling pin. Alternatively, place in a food processor and blend until fine crumbs are formed.

Melt the butter in a medium-sized saucepan, add the crumbs and mix together. Press into the bottom of the prepared pan and let cool in the refrigerator.

Melt 4 oz. of the chocolate with the marshmallows and 2 tablespoons of water in a saucepan over a gentle heat, stirring constantly. Let cool slightly, then stir in the egg yolk, beat well, then return to the refrigerator until cool.

Beat the egg white until stiff and standing in peaks, then fold into the chocolate mixture.

Lightly whip the cream and fold three-quarters of the cream into the chocolate mixture. Set the remainder aside. Spoon the chocolate cream into the flan shell and chill in the refrigerator until set.

When ready to serve, spoon the remaining cream over the chocolate pie, swirling in a decorative pattern. Grate the remaining unsweetened chocolate and sprinkle over the cream, then serve.

TASTY TIP

Replace the graham crackers with an equal amount of chocolate-covered cookies to make a quick change to this recipe.

Fruit & Nut
Refrigerator Fingers

MAKES 12

14 pink and
    white marshmallows
½ cup luxury dried
    mixed fruit
3 tbsp. candied orange
    peel, chopped

3 tbsp. candied
    cherries, quartered
¾ cup chopped walnuts
1 tbsp. brandy
2¼ cups graham
    cracker crumbs

8 oz. semisweet dark
    chocolate
½ cup (1 stick) unsalted butter
1 tbsp. confectioners' sugar,
    for dusting (optional)

Lightly grease and line the base of a 7-inch pan with nonstick baking parchment. Using greased kitchen scissors, snip each marshmallow into 4 or 5 pieces over a bowl. Add the dried mixed fruit, orange peel, cherries, and walnuts to the bowl. Sprinkle with the brandy and stir together. Add the crumbs and stir until mixed.

Break the chocolate into small pieces and put in a heatproof bowl with the butter set over a saucepan of almost-boiling water. Stir occasionally until melted, then remove from the heat. Pour the chocolate over the dry ingredients and mix well. Spoon into the prepared pan, pressing down firmly.

Chill in the refrigerator for 15 minutes, then mark into 12 fingers using a sharp knife. Chill in the refrigerator for an additional hour or until set. Turn out of the pan, remove the lining paper, and cut into fingers. Dust with confectioners' sugar before serving, if desired.

Almond Cake

CUTS INTO 8 SLICES

1 cup (2 sticks) butter
  or margarine
1 cup superfine sugar
3 extra-large eggs

1 tsp. vanilla extract
1 tsp. almond extract
1 cup self-rising flour
1½ cups ground almonds

⅓ cup blanched
  whole almonds
1 oz. semisweet
  dark chocolate

Preheat the oven to 300°F. Lightly grease and line the base of an 8-inch round cake pan with waxed paper or baking parchment.

Cream together the butter or margarine and sugar with a wooden spoon until light and fluffy.

Beat the eggs and extracts together in a small bowl. Gradually add to the sugar and butter mixture, and mix well between each addition.

Sift the flour, and mix with the ground almonds. Beat into the egg mixture until mixed well and smooth. Pour into the prepared cake pan.

Roughly chop the whole almonds, and sprinkle over the cake before baking.

Bake in the preheated oven for 45 minutes or until golden and risen, and a skewer inserted into the center of the cake comes out clean.

Remove from the pan and let cool on a wire rack. Melt the chocolate in a small bowl placed over a saucepan of gently simmering water, stirring until smooth and free of lumps.

Drizzle the melted chocolate over the cooled cake, and serve once the chocolate has set.

Honey Cake

4 tbsp. butter
2 tbsp. superfine sugar
⅓ cup honey
1½ cups all-purpose flour

½ tsp. baking soda
½ tsp. pumpkin pie spice
1 large egg
2 tbsp. milk

¼ cup slivered almonds
1 tbsp. honey, to drizzle

Preheat the oven to 350°F. Lightly grease and line the base of a 7-inch round cake pan with lightly greased baking parchment.

In a saucepan, gently heat the butter, sugar, and honey until the butter has just melted.

Sift the flour, baking soda, and pumpkin pie spice together into a bowl.

Beat the egg and the milk until mixed thoroughly.

Make a well in the center of the sifted flour and pour in the melted butter and honey.

Using a wooden spoon, beat well, gradually drawing in the flour from the sides of the bowl.

When all the flour has been beaten in, add the egg mixture, and mix thoroughly. Pour into the prepared pan and sprinkle with the slivered almonds.

Bake in the preheated oven for 30–35 minutes until well risen and golden brown, and a skewer inserted into the center of the cake comes out clean.

Remove from the oven, cool for a few minutes in the pan, turn out, and allow to cool on a wire rack. Drizzle with the remaining tablespoon of honey, and serve.

Fruitcake

CUTS INTO 10 SLICES

1 cup (2 sticks) butter or margarine
scant 1 cup packed brown sugar
finely grated zest of 1 orange
1 tbsp. molasses

3 extra-large eggs, beaten
2½ cups all-purpose flour
¼ tsp. ground cinnamon
½ tsp. pumpkin pie spice
pinch freshly grated nutmeg
¼ tsp. baking soda

½ cup mixed candied peel
¼ cup candied cherries
⅔ cup raisins
⅔ cup golden raisins
⅔ cup chopped dried apricots

Preheat the oven to 300°F. Lightly grease and line a 9-inch round cake pan with a double thickness of waxed paper.

In a large bowl, cream together the butter or margarine, sugar, and orange zest until light and fluffy, then beat in the molasses.

Beat in the eggs, a little at a time, beating well between each addition.

Set aside 1 tablespoon of the flour. Sift the remaining flour, the spices, and baking soda into the mixture. Mix all the fruits and the remaining flour together, then stir into the cake mixture.

Turn into the prepared pan and smooth the top, making a small hollow in the center of the cake mixture.

Bake in the preheated oven for 1 hour, then reduce the heat to 275°F.

Bake for an additional 1½ hours or until cooked and a skewer inserted into the center comes out clean. Let cool in the pan, then turn the cake out, and serve. Otherwise, when cool, store in an airtight container.

Carrot Cake

1¾ cups all-purpose flour
½ tsp. ground cinnamon
½ tsp. freshly
    grated nutmeg
1 tsp. baking powder
1 tsp. baking soda
⅔ cup brown sugar

scant 1 cup vegetable oil
3 large eggs
½ lb. carrots, peeled and
    roughly grated
½ cup chopped walnuts

For the frosting:
¾ cup cream cheese
finely grated zest of
    1 orange
1 tbsp. orange juice
1 tsp. vanilla extract
1 cup confectioners' sugar

Preheat the oven to 300°F. Lightly grease and line the base of a 6-inch square cake pan with waxed paper or baking parchment.

Sift the flour, spices, baking powder, and baking soda together into a large bowl. Stir in the brown sugar and mix together. Lightly beat the oil and eggs together, then gradually stir into the flour and sugar mixture. Stir well.

Add the carrots and walnuts. Mix thoroughly, then pour into the prepared cake pan. Bake in the preheated oven for 1¼ hours or until light and springy to the touch and a skewer inserted into the center of the cake comes out clean.

Remove from the oven and allow to cool for 5 minutes before turning out onto a wire rack. Set aside until cool.

To make the frosting, beat together the cream cheese, orange zest, orange juice, and vanilla extract. Sift the confectioners' sugar and stir into the cream cheese mixture.

When cool, discard the lining paper, spread the cream cheese frosting over the top, and serve cut into squares.

Banana Cake

CUTS IN 8 SLICES

3 medium-sized,
  ripe bananas
1 tsp. lemon juice
⅔ cup brown sugar
6 tbsp. butter or margarine

2¼ cups self-rising flour
1 tsp. ground cinnamon
3 large eggs
½ cup chopped walnuts

1 tsp. each ground
  cinnamon and superfine
  sugar, to decorate
heavy cream, to serve

Preheat the oven to 375°F. Lightly grease and line the base of a 7-inch round cake pan with waxed paper or baking parchment.

Mash two of the bananas in a small bowl, sprinkle with the lemon juice and a heaping tablespoon of the sugar. Mix together lightly, and set aside.

Gently heat the remaining sugar and butter or margarine in a small saucepan until the butter has just melted. Pour into a small bowl, then allow to cool slightly. Sift the flour and cinnamon into a large bowl and make a well in the center.

Beat the eggs into the cooled sugar mixture, pour into the well of flour, and mix thoroughly.

Gently stir in the mashed banana mixture. Pour half of the mixture into the prepared pan. Thinly slice the remaining banana, and arrange over the cake mixture.

Sprinkle over the chopped walnuts, then cover with the remaining cake mixture. Bake in the preheated oven for 50–55 minutes until well risen and golden brown. Allow to cool in the pan, turn out, and sprinkle with the cinnamon and superfine sugar. Serve hot or cold with a pitcher of heavy cream for pouring

HELPFUL HINT

The riper the bananas used in this recipe, the better! Look out for reductions in supermarkets and fruit shops, as ripe bananas are often sold very cheaply.

Cappuccino Cakes

MAKES 6

½ cup (1 stick) butter or margarine
½ cup superfine sugar
2 large eggs

1 tbsp. strong black coffee
1¼ cups self-rising flour
¼ lb. mascarpone cheese
1 tbsp. confectioners'

sugar, sifted
1 tsp. vanilla extract
sifted unsweetened cocoa, to dust

Preheat the oven to 375°F. Place six large paper baking cups in a muffin pan, or place them on a cookie sheet.

Cream the butter or margarine and sugar together until light and fluffy. Break the eggs into a small bowl, and beat lightly with a fork. Using a wooden spoon, beat the eggs into the butter and sugar mixture, a little at a time, until they are all incorporated.

If the mixture looks curdled, beat in a spoonful of the flour to return the mixture to a smooth consistency. Finally, beat in the black coffee.

Sift the flour into the mixture, then with a metal spoon or rubber spatula, gently fold in the flour. Place spoonfuls of the mixture in the baking cups.

Bake in the preheated oven for 20–25 minutes until risen and springy to the touch. Cool on a wire rack.

In a small bowl, beat together the mascarpone cheese, confectioners' sugar, and vanilla extract.

When the cakes are cool, spoon the vanilla mascarpone on top. Dust with cocoa and serve. Eat within 24 hours and store in the refrigerator.

TASTY TIP

Make sure that you use a good-quality coffee in this recipe. Colombian coffee is generally good, and, at its best, possesses a smooth, rounded flavor.

Coffee & Pecan Cake

CUTS INTO 8 SLICES

1⅓ cups self-rising flour
½ cup (1 stick) butter
   or margarine
¾ cup brown sugar
1 tbsp. instant coffee
2 extra-large eggs

½ cup roughly
   chopped pecans

For the frosting:
1 tsp. instant coffee
1 tsp. unsweetened cocoa

6 tbsp. unsalted
   butter, softened
1½ cups sifted
   confectioners' sugar
whole pecans, to decorate

Preheat the oven to 375˚F. Lightly grease and line the bases of two 7-inch layer-cake pans with waxed paper or baking parchment. Sift the flour and set aside.

Beat the butter or margarine and sugar together until light and creamy. Dissolve the coffee in 2 tablespoons of hot water and allow to cool.

Lightly mix the eggs with the coffee liquid. Gradually beat into the creamed butter and sugar, adding a little of the sifted flour with each addition.

Fold in the pecans, then divide the mixture between the prepared pans, and bake in the preheated oven for 20–25 minutes until well risen and firm to the touch.

Leave in the pans for 5 minutes before turning out and cooling on a wire rack.

To make the frosting, blend the coffee and cocoa with enough boiling water to make a stiff paste. Beat into the butter and confectioners' sugar.

Sandwich the two cakes together using half of the frosting. Spread the remaining frosting over the top of the cake and decorate with the whole pecans to serve. Store in an airtight container.

Index